Accelerated Spanish

Accelerated Spanish

Learn fluent Spanish with a proven accelerated learning system

CREATED BY TIMOTHY MOSER
with Josiah Moser and Samuel Moser

Kamel Press, LLC

Visit SpanishIn1Month.com for an abundance of materials that accompany this book, including video, audio, and quizzes, as well as further volumes in the series.

Published by Kamel Press.

Library of Congress 2016950770

ISBN: 978-1-62487-060-6

Book design and cover design by Timothy Moser.

PRINTED IN THE UNITED STATES OF AMERICA

Contents

Acknowledgments

This book would never have been created if I hadn't annoyed thousands of people in the process.

First of all, Tamara Mathov: You have my eternal gratitude for your immense help in creating the Accelerated Spanish system, for correcting dozens and dozens of my dumb mistakes, and for enduring all kinds of ridiculous challenges from me and the many dozens of Spanish students that I've thrown at you.

My other instructors, Diana, Gaby, Alex, and Sofia: Thank you for putting up with insane student schedules and setting me straight day after day.

To our hundreds of Spanish coaching students: You're the reason this book exists. Thanks for being my guinea pigs for the last two years. I'm more proud of your Spanish fluency accomplishments than I can express.

To all my friends in Buenos Aires: Marcos, Vicky, Javier the engineer, Javier the conductor, Douglas, Jenny, and dozens of others who entertained me, did life with me, and winced at my bad Spanish for months: It was your friendship that brought the language to life for me.

Tim Ferriss: You laid the groundwork and have set the bar high. Here's to accelerated language learning methods that only get faster and better.

Azul, Jorge, and Kermit, thanks for your advice and encouragement throughout the process of editing and formatting this book. I couldn't have done it on my own.

Jim Halpert and Pam Beesly: Thanks for incentivizing me to finish each chapter when all else failed.

Samuel, my brother and top go-to concept artist: Your impossibly endless imagination has breathed meaning into Spanish verb conjugations in ways I couldn't have dreamed were possible.

Most importantly, my brother, best friend, and second-harshest critic, Josiah: Thanks for understanding me when nobody else does, for brainstorming some of the most ridiculous mnemonics in the course, and for always bringing me back to earth when I need it most.

Introduction:

Why You Haven't Learned Spanish

"Learning only results from what the student does and thinks. The teacher can advance learning only by influencing what the student does to learn."
- Herbert Simon

"There is no such thing as teaching, only learning."
- Timothy Moser

IF A STRIPED INSECT the size of a toaster flew into your house, sat on your kitchen stove, told you that it was from another planet, and demanded to be supplied with tea, you would remember that shocking incident for the rest of your life.

But if I presented you a chart of verb conjugations, or a list of Spanish adverbs, you'd be unlikely to remember that information an hour later.

This contrast of situations may sound silly, but it's actually very profound. In fact, it's the basis of the entire Accelerated Spanish book and course. Our brains aren't computers. We don't easily remember numbers and information. Instead, we remember experiences and impressions, especially the strangest ones.

This is why the typical classroom experience lets us down so much. If you're like the majority of US high school graduates, you've (1) taken Spanish at some point and (2) already forgotten most of it. There wasn't anything unique enough or unusual enough to tell your brain to hold on to it, so those hundreds of hours now seem like a total waste of time.

I became frustrated with this system myself, and that's why I developed a course that teaches effectively, the way that native speakers talk, using proven mnemonic techniques that you won't be able to forget once you've learned them.

I've used this system to coach hundreds of students, bringing dozens to fluency in a short period of time, sometimes as little as eight weeks.

This three-volume system has the potential to make you fully fluent in Spanish.

- The first volume will teach you to think like a Spanish speaker and give you the vocabulary that makes up 50% of the Spanish language.

- The second volume goes on to 80% of the vocabulary and allows you to converse comfortably on a variety of subjects.

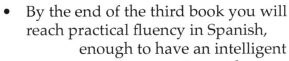

- By the end of the third book you will reach practical fluency in Spanish, enough to have an intelligent conversation with a native speaker on practically any subject.

A word of warning, though: Success will only come if you put time and effort into practice. My most successful students are always the ones that are the most diligent and consistent in getting focused practice with their native-speaking Spanish trainers.

Despite all the learning hacks and shortcuts you'll find in this book, there's no replacing conversation practice, with serious feedback and critique from Spanish speakers. In order to become fluent, that's something you need to make a top

priority. If you do, this course will give you everything else you need.

The concepts and stories that you discover on the pages of this book will seem very strange to you at first. As you find yourself engulfed in an imaginary world with a yellow sky, demented shopkeepers, and clumsy stuffed pandas, your mind and senses will be challenged at every moment. Don't let this discourage you; this is how it's meant to be. From the very first chapter, you will see for yourself that to get into the mindset of another language, your mind needs to experience a new world.

LESSON 1

Find Your Voice

A language is not vocabulary. It's a personality.

No matter how many new words you learn, you're not speaking Spanish if you're thinking in English. To be a true Spanish speaker, the first thing you need to do is lose your English-speaking personality and create your Spanish self.

In this first lesson, you'll need to forget everything you know about language learning. We're going to take a step back and find your Spanish voice from scratch.

Lesson 1 Theory:
Find Your Voice

"Learning another language is not only learning different words for the same things, but learning another way to think about things." - Flora Lewis

"I enjoy translating; it's like opening your mouth and hearing someone else's voice emerge." - Iris Murdoch

ONE OF MY earliest memories happened at a park when I was about five years old. Two women on a bench were speaking with each other in a foreign language. I was amazed: They seemed to be communicating, and yet to my young English-speaking ears, it sounded like complete gibberish.

In the car on the way home, I proposed a theory to my parents. Perhaps to those foreign women, English also sounds like complete gibberish, with the exact same sonic effect on their ears. If this were true, languages would be like radio stations, each one sounding like indefinite, neutral static to someone who is not tuned in.

But this isn't quite true. To Spanish speakers, English doesn't sound like Portuguese or German. It sounds like English. Rather than sounding like random nonsense, it actually has a voice of its own, even to people who don't understand it.

In fact, every language has its own distinct sound. For example, even if you don't know a word of Mandarin or Arabic, you can easily learn to tell the two apart just by the way they sound.

This Spanish "sound" is part of the foundation we'll be laying here at the beginning of Lesson 1.

But we won't be able to talk about the sound of the language without also covering the personality of the language.

I moved to Argentina a year after I started learning Spanish. While there, I made many new friends with whom I only spoke in Spanish. But during the first three months, I didn't feel like myself.

The version of me that my Argentinian friends knew was a brand-new creation. They saw a different side of me, a different voice and personality, that none of my friends at home had ever known. This was the Spanish-language version of me. It forced me to express myself very differently than I was used to doing.

When I speak Spanish, many of the quirky idiosyncrasies of my own personality are lost. Since I was raised speaking English, my personality is intertwined with the English language. But the Spanish rendition of myself is not a lot like my English-speaking personality. At first, it was like bad movie subtitles that don't really express the original meaning.

But at the same time, the Spanish language has its own idiosyncrasies. During my time in Argentina, I began to develop new stories, jokes, and personality traits in this language, all of which were all entirely separate from my English-speaking personality. I had opened up a new side of my mind that I never knew existed. By learning Spanish, I discovered a whole new amazing world that I could live in, entirely hidden from my native tongue.

It's time for you to start building that world. And speaking of your native tongue, the "tongue" is a good place to start.

Samuel
Sofía
Félix
Tamara
Leonardo
Victoria
José
Julieta
Nicolás
Sara

The Spanish Voice

It's tempting to think that Spanish speakers were born with a different variety of tongue or voice box. They make certain sounds that we never produce in English.

But it's simply not true. Spanish speakers' vocal and oral apparatuses are physically identical to those of English speakers.

The difference is in the language itself.

Let's do a quick exercise to demonstrate. Here I've listed a few names

that are quite common in Spanish-speaking countries and are also well-known to English speakers.

If you were to read these names off in an English voice, they would sound extremely different from the Spanish way of saying them.

But on the other hand, if you go to the effort to pronounce a Spanish speaker's name the correct way, the way he or she has said it and heard it his/her whole life, it's a big compliment to them. They'll be honored and will feel a much closer connection to you.

Bottom line: If you truly want to communicate on a personal level, it's much more than just saying the right words. *How* you say those words makes an enormous difference.

We'll work on that Spanish voice soon, but we have to go a little deeper. Before we can produce accurate Spanish sounds, we need to think about Spanish more deeply than that.

A new language doesn't just sound different. It *thinks* differently.

"Named Must Your Voice Be Before Brandish It You Can."

Look again at the names listed above. If you were to hear a bilingual person reading them over and over, first in a Spanish voice and then in an English voice, it would sound as if she were two different actors reading the same script.

In fact, the term "actor" is a good analogy for language learning. When you switch into a differ-ent language, it's not just your voice that should change. There are other aspects of communication that require a different mindset.

If you've worked on learning a language be-fore, you may be used to studying grammar, vo-cabulary, and idioms sep-arately. But what you're about to learn will turn them all into one entity.

Let's imagine for a sec-ond that you decide to talk like Yoda from Star Wars. Instead of say-ing "Your fear must be named before you can banish it," Yoda says, "Named must your fear be before banish it you can."

He mixes up the word or-der in a strange way. But hey, it's Yoda. It's part of his personality.

If you start imitating Yoda on purpose, you might find that you start to <u>think</u> differently as well. Your personality will change slightly based on what you're saying.

But for efficiency, we're going to go the opposite direction: We're going to change our personality first.

For the Star Wars fans, I'm afraid Yoda isn't quite going to do the job. We need to create a very unique personality, some-thing that really encom-passes everything about the Spanish language. It has to be a person sep-arate from yourself, but you have to be able to switch back and forth between your own per-sonality and that separate personality.

For the rest of this book, our Spanish personality is a bee named Joel.

Joel talks kind of like Yoda, but he follows his own strange rules about it.

Let's take an example from the Spanish verb for "liking" something. In these situations, the grammar is completely reverse that of English. The subject and the object are switched. There's no literal way to say "I like tea" in Spanish; instead, Joel always says *"me gus-ta el té"*, which literally means "to me is pleasing the tea".

This confuses a lot of English speakers. Even after they've learned the grammar and memorized loads of phrases, it can be all too easy to make a silly mistake with this verb.

But I make it simple. When I'm Timothy, my English self, I "like" things. It's something I do: It's my opinion of the tea, my own action.

However, when I'm Joel, my Spanish self, I don't "like" things. In my Joel personality, I'm too lazy to "like" things. Joel doesn't want to be the one doing the action; instead, he wants the thing itself to do the action. He wants the tea to do the work for him.

So instead of saying "I like tea", Joel says "The tea is pleasing to me." Notice how Joel makes it sound like the tea is the one that's doing the action.

This is automatic for me when I switch into my

Spanish personality. I don't have to think about it. It's a part of who I am, as Joel.

Now you have to become the bee.

You need to associate everything you learn about Spanish with Joel. Each time you come across a new Spanish word, idiom, or grammar rule, you can associate it with Joel, and it will become a part of your developing Spanish personality.

Let's begin by learning some more things about Joel.

Putting On Your Wings

When you get your Joel character on, you'll want to understand everything about Joel, including the world that he lives in. So before we can become the bee, we have to stop and get to know him really well. For the next few pages, pay close attention and try to remember every detail of his personality.

First of all, Joel is no mere human bee. He's not even from Earth.

He lives on a planet called "Yol". If you think about it, "Yol" sounds kind of like "Joel", and in fact Joel sometimes gets his own name confused with the name of the planet he lives on because they sound kind of similar.

Joel is a mischievous bee. While he tries to appear attractive and charming, he really just uses his wealth for his own selfish purposes, and he tries to get everyone else to do work for him because he's extremely lazy.

It's important to note that Joel's tastes are pretty strange: He loves drinking tea, and he'll do almost anything to get a nice hot cup. But he has a strong distaste for all mammals (that is, animals with fur such as dogs, horses, bears, and giraffes); in fact he's generally frightened of all such animals.

However, his best friend is a lizard. He has no problem with him, be- cause he's a reptile, not a mammal. As you'll see in future stories, this lizard has no name, can't talk, and likes to spend time in dark caves.

Joel also hangs out with a group of stuffed pan- das. They're OK because they aren't real pandas; they're living stuffed animals, which is not a problem by Joel's strange standards. Since the pandas are clumsy and simple-minded, Joel loves causing mischief to these stuffed pandas. He thinks it's funny when they get dizzy or blown around by wind, which happens pretty often.

Also be aware that Joel has a tendency to get into a strange sort of mood and to talk with an old-fashioned, almost formal British mode of speech. This especially happens when he's about to do something mischie- vous, so be on the look- out for that. If he starts speaking in a pompous voice, it usually means that he's up to no good.

Another funny thing about the way that Joel talks is that he can be extremely redundant. He'll say the same thing more than once in a sentence, sometimes even to the point of bad logic, such as double negatives, like "I didn't see nothing".

We absolutely must imitate this kind of thing if we want to speak like Joel authentically. It may be uncomfortable or feel wrong, but just remember that you aren't the one saying "I didn't see nothing"; it's just Joel, and it makes perfect sense for him.

Pronunciation: Get Them Moves Like Joel

Of course, in order to develop a voice like Joel's, one of the first things that we want to think about is the accent that he uses when he speaks. This isn't just about "pronunciation". It's about physical movement.

Joel is a bee, and he has a long tongue. So instead of "D", his "D"s are not formed against the roof

of his mouth, but rather against his teeth because his tongue goes so far forward in his mouth, so it's more like "thee". And then T is similar: It's like a cross between "tee" and "thee".

Now at the same time, his R kind of replaces the letters D and T. So his D and T are in the front of his mouth, but his R sounds a lot like our D or T when spoken really quickly. Unlike our "Rrr-rrr", which can go on for a long time, it's normally pronounced as a single-moment event.

To practice this, let's use Joel's favorite drink: Say "pot of tea" really quickly, over and over. If you say it fast enough, the T at the end of "pot" will probably be pronounced exactly like a Spanish R.

Say "pot of..." again,

and then using the same sound, say "Et-ah". That's the sound of *"era"*, a Spanish word with R in the middle, though it doesn't sound to English speakers like an R; it sounds to us almost like a T.

Alternate between "pot of" and "et-ah", hopping back and forth quickly from one to the other. Let your tongue dance like Joel's tongue. This exercise is your portal between your English voice and your Joel voice.

You want to be able to imitate these sounds as soon as possible if you really want to sound like a native Spanish speaker. Every time you're in Spanish mode, try to speak the way that Joel does, because again, he represents all native speakers for us in standard

Spanish pronunciation.

Another letter that's different for Joel: The letter for "J" actually sounds like "H"; imagine that the letter J is hanging down in front of Joel's mouth, and he's trying to blow it away: "H".

(Incidentally, this is why Joel likes to call himself "yol" sometimes, spelling it with a Y instead of a J. When he tells his friends that his name is Joel, if he were to write it out J-O-E-L, they would end up calling him "Hoel", which he doesn't like very much. He thinks "Yol" sounds better.)

Now, Joel is a bee, and the letter B for him buzzes a little bit, just like the letter V in English. In fact, for Joel, the letters V and B sound identical. The sound is half-way in between the two. A safe bet for English speakers is to pronounce both letters as B, but with a little bit of a buzz. Just remember that Joel is a buzzing bee, and that should help with both of those letters.

Other than the T, D, R, V/B, and J, Joel's consonants are very much like English consonants, except that Joel does not believe in the letter 'H'. It looks too much like prison bars, which is some-

thing he is always trying to avoid. So H never, ever makes the "H" sound for Joel, and it's basically always silent.

Now for the vowels. Since Joel talks very quickly and directly, his vowel sounds are extremely short. If you put a silent "H" after the letters A, E, and O, you basically get the sound that Joel always uses for these letters. It never changes: A is always "ah" (as in "lot"), E is always "eh" (as in "get"), and O is always "oh".

Those are approximate sounds, because the Spanish vowels don't sound exactly like any English vowels. Some would argue that E almost sounds like "ay" as in "stay", and A is actually half-way between the vowel sounds from "dog" and "cat". To imitate these sounds properly, you really need to hear Joel's voice pronouncing them. But for now, just remember that it's pretty simple: A is "ah", E is "eh", and O is "oh".

I and U are a little different. If you think of an I and imagine that the little

dot is Joel flying above the I, imagine that the tiny Joel makes an "eeee" sound as he's flying. That's the sound that the letter I makes in Spanish. So whenever he sees the letter I, he sees the dot flying above it and says "ee" (as in "bee").

Meanwhile, the letter U is "oo" (as in "boot").

Of course, for all of these words, you'll need to hear them pronounced so you can imitate an authentic voice. To get immediate practice with this, you can find exercises with recordings at SpanishIn1Month.com.

Be the Bee

Going beyond pronunciation, there are also some interesting nuances to the ways that Joel talks and the ways that he structures his sentences. So you'll want to pay close attention to him whenever he says something and be able to imitate the way that he says those. You don't want to have to think about the rules all the time; instead, you want to put yourself in Joel's frame of mind so that you can say things the way that he does in general.

As some examples, he has a tendency to put his adjectives after his nouns instead of before his nouns about half the time. (NOT all the time, but in several situations that you'll pick up on soon.) Also, it's important to note that Joel does not like the word "like". He'll pretty much say anything else he can say instead of "like". So instead of saying "I like food", he might say "to me food is pleasing". Or instead of saying "I walk like he does", he would say "I walk as he does". Why is that? Simply because

Spanish doesn't have a word for "like". Instead there are words for being pleasing, for wanting something, or for acting "as" something else.

Also, for personal reasons, Joel avoids the ubiquitous English word "get". He's very greedy and always looking to get things, especially if he can get them for free and without working, but he doesn't want people to know that he's always out to get something. So he almost always finds other ways to say "get".

Now before we dive in and start learning some actual Spanish words, we need to set the scene by talking little bit about the planet of Yol, which is where Joel lives.

The planet of Yol is a very strange planet. Everyone here speaks Spanish, but since they think that it was invented here on the planet of Yol, they call it "EspanYOL", after their own planet's name. Yol is a warm but somewhat dim planet with a yellow sky. As you'll hear in upcoming stories, their currency is actually the Japanese Yen.

In Joel's own neighborhood, there's an amusement park where he likes to hang out, there's a countryside that Joel has to travel through to get home from the amusement park, there's a plaza where fresh foods are sold, and there are also hundreds of shops lining the streets close to Joel's home.

Joel's own house is very large, and he is a very wealthy bee, so he has lots of stuff both outside (in his messy yard) and various things inside that are organized by room.

You'll get to know these environments a lot better as we progress through the lessons, but keep that

in mind: Everything that takes place in the lessons will occur in Joel's local neighborhood, at these distinctly different places that he likes to visit.

If you think it's strange to go to an imaginary planet and change your personality, remember one thing: It works. It has worked for hundreds of our students in the past, and it will work for you. If you want to be able to speak Spanish effectively, you need to be able to turn off your English personality when you turn on your Spanish personality.

It's not just my students and I who use this method. Language-learners

always eventually develop separate personalities for the two languages. And whenever I survey bilinguals, they state that this is how they switch back and forth, as two different personalities.

This brings up a crucial principle of accelerated learning: Discover what it is that other people do involuntarily, and then shortcut the process by doing that thing as soon as possible.

If your Spanish personality is going to emerge eventually, why not go ahead and create it now? Shed your English personality and enter Joel's world. Be the bee.

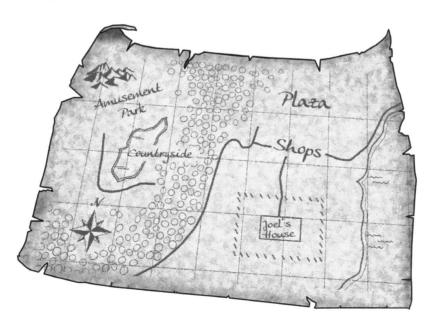

Lesson 1 Vocabulary:

Yol

(Joel's World)

W E'RE ABOUT TO learn our first Spanish words. But before we start dumping words in our heads, let's plan very carefully, starting with our goals in mind.

One of the essential rules of accelerated learning is that we never just start memorizing for the sake of memorizing. We always start by considering the specific results we're wanting to achieve.

And in the case of vocabulary, of course, we want to start thinking like a native speaker as quickly as possible.

In this lesson, we're going to learn only 15 words. But these 15 words will be extremely valuable for learning how the Spanish language works. This little handful of vocabulary will provide the most important anchors in our Spanish voice.

Don't skim over this section, even if you think you already know these words. We've worked with Spanish students of all levels, and even some of the most advanced speakers found

their biggest breakthroughs in this first lesson.

If you lay the foundation properly, you'll be set to start thinking in Spanish like a native speaker very soon.

Remember that we're not just learning words. We're building a Spanish universe. The 15 words you're about to learn will provide you with significant landmarks in Joel's world, scenes where later we'll be storing hundreds of words. So even if you already know the words, these stories about Joel are important to read before you continue to Lesson 2.

Our first scene is one of Joel's favorite hangout places: An amusement park.

"Eeh!" The Easiest Word

Check out this picture of the local park where Joel spends a lot of his time and money.

We'll start learning words here soon, but first, familiarize yourself with the area. As you can see, there's a roller

coaster, a carousel, and a ferris wheel. There's also a strange type of water slide on the right side, which we'll describe in detail later.

Imagine yourself walking between the different rides, using the paths. You'll notice that the main path runs along the whole length of the park from the roller coaster to the water slide, and the other paths meet that path in the middle. This forms a sideways K shape.

Travel along all these paths in your head, imagining that you visit each ride. Start with the roller coaster on the left side, briefly walk up to the carousel and ferris wheel, and stop in the water on the right side. Look down at the puddle that you're standing in. Your socks should feel wet in your imagination.

Now that you're familiar with the park, notice the power lines above you.

These power lines are suspended between the rides, and some neighborhood kids have thrown shoes over the lines. This causes the lines to hang down. Notice that this creates a Y-like shape.

Today, Joel has brought some new friends to the amusement park: The pandas, these stuffed toys. They've never been to an amusement park before.

Joel gives the pandas a quick tour of the park. He flies between the rides, listing them one by one.

But Joel is afraid of shoes. See, Joel is a bee, and bees can be squashed by shoes. So he gets scared whenever he encounters a pair of shoes, and he yells "eeh!" when he has to fly past them.

So he names off the rides, but between each ride, he yells "eeh!"

It sounds like this:

"Roller coaster (eeh!), carousel (eeh!), ferris wheel (eeh!), water slide."

Notice again the Y shape created by the power lines and the shoes. The letter Y, by itself, is actually a Spanish word. It means "and", and it's pronounced as "eeh".

It's like Joel is listing the rides, with the word "and" between them, but

the word "and" is replaced by a little scream: "Roller coaster *y* carousel *y* ferris wheel *y* water slide."

So if you ever want to use the word "and" between items that you're listing, just remember Joel flying around the park listing rides and yelling "eeh!" between them.

After a few uses, of course, you'll get used to the fact that Joel says the word "and" by saying *y*, and you won't have to use this ridiculous story anymore. It will quickly become second nature, an integral part of your "Joel voice".

Make careful note of what we've just done.

The word *y* is now stored in a place: The power lines between rides.

It also has a meaning attached to it: It's the word "and".

This is one of the simplest, easiest words in the Spanish language. It means the exact same thing that the English word "and" means. (Most Spanish words don't have direct equivalents in English, but this is a convenient exception.)

"Eeeeh!"

The Rides
(Prepositions)

Now that we've covered *y*, our first word, let's start exploring the park more deeply by visiting the rides themselves.

Joel is done listing the rides, so next the pandas ask him to demonstrate each of the rides one by one. Joel agrees to ride everything except for the roller coaster, because the roller coaster takes too long. So he begins with the carousel.

But there's a problem. Joel doesn't particularly like the carousel. It doesn't have any interior lights, and Joel doesn't like spending time in a dark place with a bunch of representations of horses. Remember that Joel dislikes mammals. These horses aren't real, but they are covered with real horse hair, which bothers Joel.

In the end, Joel finally agrees to show

the pandas what it's like to ride the carousel. But during the entire ride, he wishes he was out in the beautiful bright daylight again. While he sits there, all he can think about is the daylight.

A stranger on the carousel asks him, "Where are you from?" and Joel blurts out, "Day!"

This is actually half true. Notice that Joel is yellow, just like the color of the sky in Yol. Joel considers himself "from" the daylight, or perhaps "of" the daylight. And, of course, he just now came from the daylight before entering this dark carousel.

In the paragraph above, I used the words "from" and "of". The word *de* means both of these, roughly speaking. This is an example of a word that doesn't have an exact one-to-one translation in English. But that's OK.

To learn this word, we'll listen to the way that Joel uses it, and we'll just use it the way he does. An easy example is to say where someone is from: Joel is *de* the daylight.

After the ride is (finally) over, Joel has a new problem. He's gotten stuck on the steep back of his horse. This is humiliating. Not only does Joel hate being on the carousel, he's now being embarrassed in front of his friends.

Look closely at the horse's back, and notice the tight angle between the horse's neck and the carousel pole. This creates a sharp angle, and it resembles the letter N.

This letter is important to Joel. When he calls for help, he wants to say that he's stuck "in" this angle, or "on" the horse. Both of these words would work, so he just yells out, "I'm stuck *en* the carousel!"

The word *en* means "at". It's kind of like a cross between the words "in" and "on", and it can mean either one. But the best translation is the word "at".

So when you want to say that someone is at, in, or on something, remember the N where Joel is stuck. We'll learn some specific uses in the next section

when we get into sentence examples.

Joel finally gets free, but he's still uncomfortable. Some of the fake hair from the horse got stuck in his joints, and he wants to wash himself. Even though the pandas want him to demonstrate the ferris wheel, Joel skips it and flies straight to the water slide.

When Joel flies over the water from the slide, he thinks about how relieving it will be to be in that water. As he approaches the ride, he says "aahh", anticipating the beautiful feeling of water.

Since Joel is going "to" the slide while saying "aahh", you should be able to remember that the word for "to" is *a*, pronounced as "ah".

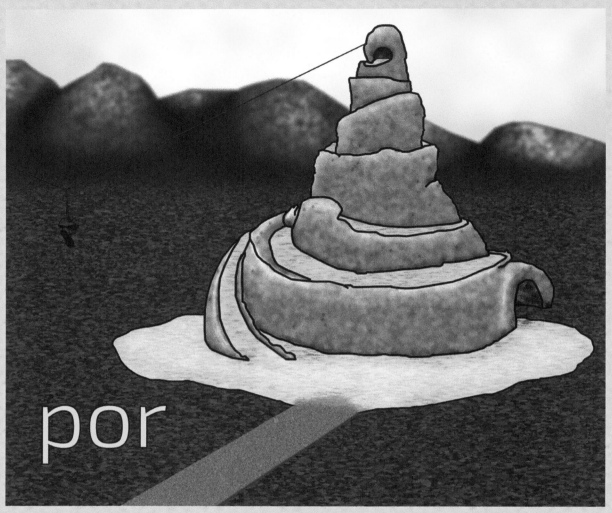

por

This word can be used when someone goes "to" a place. Joel is going a the water slide.

Speaking of the water slide, this is an area that causes a lot of problems for English speakers. The next word that we learn here is very difficult, because it has so many applications.

Why am I making you do something so hard in the very first lesson? Because it pays off. Remember, some of the hardest words are also the most common. If we get used to them now,

we can leverage that later and learn the rest of our vocabulary very easily.

The water slide is one of the strangest rides in the amusement park. It's made of stone, and the water is actually produced by the stone itself, pouring the water from an opening at the top. But look carefully: Since the slide itself is made of rock, the water doesn't just leave the rock; it flows down along the rock and then goes around it in circles until it reaches the bottom.

The word *por* literally means "by". But

you have to extend the meaning of the word "by" to include lots of different meanings, such as "along", "near", "around", and "in place of someone else". And those are just a few of the meanings of this very strange word.

Clearly we can't simply translate this word into English. It's a very nuanced word, just like the water slide is very nuanced. Let's look at a few examples of how *por* is used, but we'll refer to them in relation to the water slide. In every single case, it's crucial to understand that the water is "*por* the stone."

Use #1: A book can be "by" an author, or *por* an author. Note that the water is poured out by the stone, or "*por* the stone."

Use #2: Someone can walk "by" a house, or *por* a house. Look at how the water runs by the stone, or "*por* the stone."

Use #3: Something can happen for a long time, or *por* a long time. If you think of the stone as "a long time", the water is running "*por* the stone", or "*por* a long time."

Use #4: We might say that someone is from "around here", which would be "*por* here" in Spanish. See how the water on the ground sits close around the stone, or "*por* the stone."

There are many other uses of this word, but we'll encounter them later. For now, just remember the word *por* to mean something roughly equivalent to "by", and remember to think of how the water relates to the stone of the slide. We'll get used to the nuances of this word later.

Before we go on to our last word in the amusement park, make sure you can remember the four words that we just learned. Two were at the carousel and two were at the water slide. See if you can review them in your head.

"K, let's move on."

Our last word in the amusement park is the number one most common word in the Spanish language.

Joel goes to the path between rides to join his friends, the pandas. Often,

when he's here, he has trouble deciding which ride he wants to go to next. He has a habit of thinking a long time, and then finally saying, "K…" (as in "okay") before he says where he wants to go.

Today, he tells the pandas, "I've decided… K… we're going to ride the ferris wheel."

Now that word, "K", is a connecting word that means "that". It's actually spelled *que*, but its pronunciation is similar to the English letter K.

This word is used to join all kinds of phrasings together. Joel said "I've decided *que* we're going to ride the ferris wheel", but you can also use it in other situations, such as "I hope *que* we get there soon."

Again, it roughly equates to "that" as a connector. Be very careful, though: It's not a noun, such as "I want that". There's a different word

for that, which we'll learn in Lesson 3. Remember to use it strictly as a connector. You'll see examples in the next section.

The word *que* also means "than" when you're comparing two things. For example, if Joel and the pandas are trying to pick a tall ride, Joel might point out that the ferris wheel is taller than the carousel (because he doesn't want to ride the carousel). He tells the pandas, "The ferris wheel is taller *que* the carousel."

As you can see, Joel uses the word *que* a lot when he's deciding between rides. There's a reason for that. Look at the path under his feet. That path branches out in different directions, and it looks like a sideways letter K.

So the word *que* is stored on the path between rides. You'll notice that every single word has a place: *y*, *de*, *en*, *a*, *por*, and *que*.

Now that we've placed these words throughout the amusement park, test this memory technique out for yourself. If you have to list more than one item, you can remember the *y* between items in the amusement park. If you're connecting whole phrases with "that", or comparing things with "than…", you use the word *que*. When you want to say that you're "at" something, just think of Joel sitting in the carousel and you can remember *en*. To describe where you or someone else is from, remember the word *de*, as in "Joel is *de* the daylight". If you're going "to" something, think about Joel saying "ahh!" as he goes to the water slide: *a*. And if something is "by", "near", "against", or "along" something, you can think of the water "pouring" down the water slide (*por*).

"Oh Stella, your choice of words…"

We've learned a few essential connecting words. That was fun, but let's face it: We only learned six words. How much progress is that?

Actually, we've already made a lot more headway than you might think.

Even though there are thousands and thousands of words in the Spanish language, some words are more important than others. For example, you only have to learn about 1000 words in Spanish to understand 85% of everything spoken or written. Those 1000 words, chosen correctly, can make you functionally fluent if you know how to use them well.

However, to get from there to 95%, it would take about 20,000 more words. So in this book, focusing exclusively on those first 1000 words is our priority.

Now, along the same lines, you've just now learned six words, but those six words, in and of themselves, comprise more than 12% of the Spanish language.

By the time you've finished Lesson 1, you'll be at 25% percent, which is exciting. That means that if you take a page of Spanish text and mark out all the words you don't know, 25% of the words will still be showing.

More importantly, you've learned words that represent how Joel thinks. Always remember that we're trying to adopt Joel's voice. If you've truly learned these six words, you're already beginning to think like Joel.

Take a deep breath, and let's move on to nine more essential words.

Sheep

The six words that we learned in the amusement park were what I call "connecting words". Technically, these words function as conjunctions and prepositions, but don't worry about those terms for now. Just remember that they're little words that connect phrases together, and we're keeping all of them in the amusement park.

The words we're about to learn won't

be in the amusement park, because they don't belong there. Think about your own kitchen: You can keep all kinds of dishes in a kitchen cabinet, but you probably won't find your socks there. Socks belong in a different place in the house.

So let's go to a different part of Joel's world, where there are new types of words to learn.

When Joel leaves the amusement park, he always has to make a long trip through the open country before he gets back to town. Joel rarely enjoys this trip, because the countryside is full of hairy animals, especially sheep.

The first scene he encounters isn't too bad, because the sheep are behind fences. Later he'll run into some other scenes that aren't so friendly. For now, all he needs to do is walk along the path between sheep pastures.

As Joel braces himself to pass by the sheep, the shepherd says, "Hi! Who are you?"

Joel is distracted, and his knee-jerk response is to say, "Yo!", as if to say, "Hey, what's up!" He's trying to seem cool and unphased by the presence of large wooly animals.

The shepherd finds it interesting that Joel's name is "Yo." Of course, that's not Joel's real name. But now that he said it, he decides to stick with it: Whenever he's with the shepherd, Joel refers to himself as *yo*.

In fact, this is Joel's word for "I", as in "I am a bee" ("*yo* am a bee"). This word is pronounced just about as you would expect it to be pronounced in

English, but some Spanish speakers (especially in Argentina and Uruguay) pronounce the "y" as a "zjh", almost like the letter J. This makes *yo* sound almost like "Joel".

As Joel looks around, he notices that the sheep are separated into two categories. The sheep on the left are all female, and the sheep on the right are all male. In each case, there's a sheep who is doing something interesting: One of the female sheep is singing, "Laa!", and one of the male sheep is drinking ale.

The shepherd is proud of his talented sheep. He tells Joel, "Look! Look at the sheep!"

But the shepherd wasn't specific: Which sheep is "the" sheep? Does he mean the female sheep or the male sheep?

yo

Joel is annoyed at this ambiguity. He really wants to get out of here, but the shepherd keeps insisting: "Look at the sheep!" Joel doesn't know how to obey, because he doesn't know which sheep he's supposed to look at: The male sheep or the female sheep?

Finally, Joel decides to do something about it. He pulls some spray paint out of his pocket, goes to a fence post on the left side, and draws some music notes on the fence post. Then he goes to the right side and draws a glass of ale.

The shepherd is shocked that Joel would deface his property, but Joel tells him, "I'm helping you communicate. You need to speak clearly. Do you want me to look at *la* sheep, or do you want me to look at *el* sheep?"

Joel wants him to specify whether he means "the female sheep" or "the male sheep". The word *la* means "the", but specifically for feminine nouns, such as a female sheep who is singing "laaa!" The word *el* means "the" for masculine nouns, for example a guy who's drinking ale.

Spanish doesn't have a simple word for "the". For Joel, every thing in the world is either feminine or masculine.

It's important to take note of the fact that the female sheep are on the left and the male sheep are on the right. This is going to be a theme throughout this book: You apply *la* to things on the left, and you apply *el* to things on the right.

The shepherd objects: "But you're still vandalizing my property!"

"No," argues Joel, "This isn't vandalism. It's art!"

After Joel puts his spray paint back away, he looks around. Even though he doesn't like sheep, he knows that they're pretty expensive in Yol, and the shepherd seems to have a lot of them. Joel is suddenly curious to know how wealthy the shepherd is.

"How much is one sheep worth?" he asks.

The shepherd tells Joel, "It depends. Do you mean a special, talented sheep? Or just any old sheep?"

Joel doesn't care about the talented sheep. Since he wants to calculate the shepherd's wealth, he's interested to know what the normal sheep are.

"Not *el* sheep or *la* sheep," he says. "Just any old sheep. —Hey, what are you doing?"

The shepherd suddenly takes Joel's

30

spray paint away and begins doing his own art on the right-side fence. He tells Joel that "*Un* sheep is worth 50 yens."

The word *un* means "a", as in "a (male) sheep". It sounds kind of like the English word "one", but imagine Joel's voice saying this: It sounds like the "oon" from "spoon". "*Un* sheep." This is how Joel talks, and you want to be able to imitate it. As another example, "a man" would be "*un* man."

But the shepherd doesn't stop there. He also goes to the left side and sprays the word *una* on the fence of the female sheep. This word is like *un*, but now it has the letter A at the end.

The shepherd explains: "*Un* sheep is worth 50 yen, but *una* sheep is worth 70 yen, because they can be taught how to sing."

According to the shepherd, the "ah!"

sound at the end of *una* is to indicate that these sheep are female, and therefore they can be taught how to sing. Apparently, the male sheep are less talented, so they're not worth as much.

We now have two words that mean "the": *la* and *el*. And we have two words that mean "a": *un* and *una*. Remember that the big, important ones in the front mean "the sheep", specifically, while *un* and *una* further

back simply refer to "a sheep" or "any old sheep".

Also make sure you can remember which words are on the left and which words are on the right, keeping feminine things on the left and masculine things on the right. For example, "a woman" is "*una* woman", while "a man" is "*un* man". "The man" is "*el* man", and "the woman" is "*la* woman".

Should you be stressed?

Before we move on, there's something important that I have to point out. You may have noticed that the word *una* has two syllables. That means that it has two different parts: "un" and "a". Most Spanish words have two or more syllables, but here's the important rule: ALL Spanish words have one stressed syllable.

A stressed syllable is the part of the word that you emphasize. For example, my name, Timothy, has three syllables. But the stress is on "Tim", so it sounds like this: "TIM-o-thy".

As another example, the English word "believe" has a stress on the second syllable: "Be-LIEVE."

This is critically important. Throughout this book, I'll refer to a word's "stressed syllable" as the most important part of the word. In fact, pretty much all of our funny stories will be based on the stressed syllable of a word. For example (warning: spoiler for Lesson 11), the Spanish word for "president" is *presidente*, but when Joel says it, the stressed syllable is "dent". To emphasize this, we put a big "dent" in the president's funny wig so that you know to emphasize "dent": "Pres-i-DENT-e".

In other words, when you're speaking in Joel's voice, you HAVE to emphasize the stressed syllable, which will be the part of the word that's emphasized in our funny story, like "dent".

In the case of *una*, the stressed syllable is "oon" (as in "spoon"), which is Joel's pronunciation of the word "one". So *una* is pronounced "OON-ah". Make sure to exaggerate this. Joel usually does.

Consider yourself warned: I'm going to talk about stressed syllables a lot in this book. Keep watching for me to say "stressed syllable", and get used to exaggerating that part of any word.

Direct Objects: A Hymn Scene

After talking with the shepherd, Joel walks past the sheep pastures as quickly as he can. By the time he's beyond them, he is tired.

Joel rests on the top of a hill. He leans against a large tree, trying to gather energy for the long journey home.

This is an extremely important place in Joel's world, and there are a few things to notice here. First of all, Joel is leaning against a tree on the top of a hill while a storm is about to start. In my opinion, that's a pretty bad idea, unless you want to be the victim of a direct lightning strike.

But Joel doesn't always think through

these things. And when he gets hurt, he usually victimizes himself; if he were to be directly struck by lightning, he would blame the storm, making himself the "direct object", or the "victim", of the strike.

This entire scene on the top of the hill is called the direct object scene. Unfortunately, this is a place that confuses English speakers pretty horribly. That's because we're talking about a type of pronoun that works very differently in Spanish than it does in English.

The best example is the word "him". In English, we say "I see him." But Joel never says that. Instead, he says something more like "Him I see."

Joel will show you how this works in a second. As long as you remember to imitate Joel, using his voice, you'll probably get this right.

The shepherd walks up the hill to the tree. It's the shepherd's break, and he wants to spend it drinking tea and singing quietly. The shepherd is a pious man and usually sings hymns on his off-time.

One of the shepherd's most interesting possessions is a self-heating tea pot, which the shepherd sets down on the right side of the picture. Meanwhile he sets his staff down on the left side and sits quietly, humming a hymn tune as the tea heats up. He doesn't realize how dangerous it is to heat up tea near Joel.

The steam from the tea enters Joel's nostrils, and in a moment's transformation, Joel is suddenly in his mischievous and mysterious mode.

Joel says gravely, "Lo and behold, I smell something."

The shepherd stops singing, surprised. He has seen Joel around, but he never expected Joel to use such quaint language as "lo and behold". These words seem more suited to an old hymn than to a rude bee who spray paints fences.

"What do you smell?" asks the shepherd.

Joel continues, "Lo, I smell… The tea I smell… *Lo* I covet. *Lo* I smell."

When Joel says "*Lo* I smell", he's referring to the tea. The word *lo* is a direct object. It's kind of like the word "him" in English: "I smell him."

You might think it would be more accurate for Joel to say "I smell *it*," since the tea is an "it", not a "him". However, the Spanish language doesn't have a proper word for "it". When you smell something (or see something, or hear something), it's always a "him" or a "her".

So when Joel says "*Lo* I smell," he means "I smell it" or "I smell him". He's referring to the tea. And as you might have noticed, the word *lo* is at the beginning of the sentence instead of at the end. It's a Joel thing; he always says "him" this way. For example, let's imagine that yesterday you met somebody for the first time. In English, you would say "I met him yesterday." But Joel would say, "*Lo* I met yesterday."

The shepherd is surprised. For a moment, he thought that Joel might be a very nice guy, because he was using the quaint type of "lo and behold" language that you find in a hymn book. But suddenly, Joel is talking about coveting something! How evil!

"What am I hearing?" asks the shepherd in disbelief.

Joel is blunt: "*Me* you're hearing."

The word *me* means "me", but remember to pronounce it with Joel's voice. It sounds sort of like "meh" or "may". Also, it happens at the beginnings of phrases, just like the word *lo*. So to say "You found me," Joel would say "*Me* you found."

You might be wondering why we have two different words for Joel. Didn't we call Joel *yo* when we were at the sheep pastures?

Yes, but that was a different version of the word. *Yo* means "I", as in "I am a bee." But *me* means "me", as in "he sees me." Just like the English words "I" and "me", each Spanish pronoun is used in its own particular situation. You'll learn more about this later as we study phrases. For now, just remember that *yo* refers to Joel in the sheep pasture scene, but *me* refers to Joel here under the tree.

We have one more word to learn here on the hill. The shepherd wants to begin singing hymns again, but he's forgotten what key he was singing in. He presses a button on his staff, and the staff produces a pitch that sounds like someone singing: "Laa…"

"Ah yes, A Major," says the shepherd, and he begins singing his hymn again.

Joel is amazed. "Wait a second. Your staff can sing? I hear it! That's bizarre."

To say "I hear it," Joel says "*La* I hear."

The word *la* is just like the word *lo*, except that it's used for feminine objects. It literally means "her", as in "I hear her."

Don't be confused: We've already learned the word *la* in the sheep pasture, where

35

it means "the". But that's a different word! In that scene it means "the", as in "the house" (*la* house). Here, it means "her", as in "I hear her" (*la* I hear).

Even though these two words are spelled and pronounced identically, they mean two completely different things. Whenever you use them, you're always going to know which one you're using: *La* meaning "the" vs. *la* meaning "her".

To review this scene, look at the picture that labels all three of our new words: *la*, *me*, and *lo*. Quickly practice using all three words using the following sentence:

"You found me/her/him."

There are three versions of this sentence: "*Me* you found", "*La* you found", and "*Lo* you found." Each one means something different, but as you can see, the three sentences are structured the same way, with the Spanish pronoun at the beginning of the sentence.

What...

Joel and the shepherd continue through the country and encounter a swamp.

The shepherd is startled to see a robe floating in the swamp. This robe, which looks very similar to the robe that he himself wears, belongs to the shepherd's wife.

The shepherd is worried. Did his wife sink in the swamp?

Joel notices the robe and says, "What's that?"

The shepherd yells out his wife's name in despairing fear: "Kay!"

Selfish Joel doesn't really care what the shepherd is worried about, but he is curious to know what that robe is. He asks the shepherd again, "What is that?"

But since the shepherd yelled, "Kay!", what Joel says is, "*Qué* is that?"

The word *qué*, pronounced kind of like "Kay", basically means "what" in a question. But don't get confused: We already learned a *que*

in the amusement park. This word is completely different.

One way you can remember the difference is that this version of *qué* has an accent mark over the letter E. This mark serves to point out that this new word is stronger than the other version of *que*. This sometimes happens when there are two versions of a word, one with an accent mark and one without. The stronger word is the one that has an accent mark.

So the *que* that we learned in the amusement park was just a connector, but this word, *qué*, is emphasized in questions. It's also sometimes used

37

in exclamations, as you'll learn in the next section when we learn phrases. For now, just remember that since it has an accent "mark", it's used along with question marks and exclamation marks.

Not No

We're ready for our last word.

Joel is bored of the shepherd's company, so he flies toward home as quickly as possible, leaving the shepherd alone at the swamp.

Before he can go home, he always has to go through a large plaza that serves as a marketplace. Every time he passes through, he is asked by the farmers, bakers, and butchers if he wants to buy anything.

Today, Joel is in a hurry to get home, so he has a simple answer: *No*.

As he flies past the last stand, a vegetable merchant asks him, "Please won't you buy something today?"

Joel responds, "No, I will *no* buy something today."

The word *no* means "not". Many English speakers are mis-taught to think of it as the word "no", but that's not exactly true, because the English word "no" can actually mean a few different things, as you'll learn in Lesson 9.

But Joel's *no* is used in two simple situations: When he wants to say "not" and when he's answering a question with "no".

As you'll see in the next section when we learn phrases, it's most common to use *no* to mean "not".

But before proceeding to there, go ahead and flip back through this section. Make sure you can remember all the words, how they're pronounced, where they are, and what they mean.

Once you're pretty familiar with all the words from Lesson 1, you're ready to learn about Spanish phrases.

Lesson 1 Application:
Essential Phrases

I HAVE A four-year-old niece who has gotten into a funny habit. She often uses perfectly phrased sentences in very illogical contexts.

For example, if I've spent an afternoon visiting her, I might start gathering my things so that I can leave. If she's holding my phone, I have to ask her to hand it to me, saying "Do you know why I need my phone back?" This question makes her realize that I'm leaving, and she blurts out the first response she thinks of: "Because I don't want you to go away!"

As she gets older, she'll have to be taught to think more logically about her "why-because" reasoning.

But there's one thing she won't have to be taught: The way she phrases these sentences.

Nobody taught her how to put together the sentence "I don't want you to go away." Nobody had to tell her that "don't" is a contraction of "do not", and nobody had to explain to her that she has to use the infinitive form of "to go" after the word "you" when expressing intention for a second person's actions. Those grammar rules sound really advanced, and yet a four-year-old is doing it all naturally.

That's because she's a native English speaker. She learned everything through phrases. Sure, words are the building blocks of phrases, but words are only valuable if you put them together in an understandable way.

In order to be proficient with the 15 Spanish words that we've learned, it's essential to know how to USE these words like a native speaker.

Most Spanish students make a huge mistake here, and that's because of a fundamental misunderstanding of how language works.

Think about the way my niece first learned to talk. She isn't thinking one word at a time. Like all young children, she's using entire phrases that she's familiar with.

Phrases like "Where'd he go?" and "I want you to do it" are constructs that fit together organically. When children learn these sentences, they aren't thinking about the individual words. They don't even know what "words" are! They're imitating entire phrases, and for that reason, they end up being understood perfectly.

In fact, let's look quickly at my niece's sentence:

English: "I don't want you to go away."

Spanish: "*No* I want *que* you leave."

As you can see, this sentence does not translate word-for-word. The Spanish version is more like "Not I want that you leave."

Children in English-speaking families begin speaking in a way entirely different from children in Spanish-speaking families. They're even <u>thinking</u> in a different way, because the people around them are expressing sentence structures entirely different from English sentence structures.

As another example, "Where'd he go?" in Spanish would be something more like "To where he went?"

Is this intimidating? It doesn't have to be. Going from English to Spanish like this is awkward, but it will pay off soon. If we go ahead and make ourselves comfortable with Spanish sentence structures now, we won't have to make that strange transition as much.

The easiest way to do this is to learn a few essential phrases.

Of course, this is no radically new tactic. 200 years ago, Giuseppe Caspar Mezzofanti was famous for speaking more than 30 languages fluently. When Mezzofanti tackled a new language, he would start by studying a translation of the Lord's Prayer. Although that would be less than 10 sentences, learning them would give him a strong understanding of how the language works.

For us, instead of using the Lord's Prayer, we're selecting several Spanish sentences that give good examples of this lesson's vocabulary. Below are about 20 sentences, and I recommend learning all of them by heart.

Maybe this memorization isn't the easiest or most fun aspect of the course, but it's a very effective way to shortcut your learning. Instead of slowly picking up thousands of random phrases like my niece, you'll be focusing on the most important sentence structures for developing your Spanish voice.

Warning: These sentences are going to look like a fusion between two languages, because we're using English words for parts of the sentence that we haven't learned yet.

However, although this may seem like a contradiction, they are indeed Spanish sentences! The structure and character of each phrase isn't at all how an English speaker would come up with it. In other words, this is definitely "Joel" talking, though he's borrowing some English words.

After presenting these sentences, I'll give you some suggestions for studying them effectively.

Conjunctions

I know that they were.	I know *que* they were.
Valentina is that way, and with her everything is like that.	Valentina is that way, *y* with her everything is like that.
He's taller than I.	He's taller *que yo.*

Prepositions

He was around there.	He was *por* there.
It has been this way for a while.	It has been this way *por un* while.

The following example demonstrates why *de* is one of the most-used words in Spanish: It's used to indicate possession. Instead of "his" or "hers", Spanish speakers often say "*de* him" or "*de* her".

The house was his.	*La* house was *de* him.
The child was from another world.	*El* child was *de* another world.
I'm going to your house too.	*Yo* also am going *a* your house.

In the next sentence example, we use the word "no" to negate the sentence. You can use the word *no* in any sentence to make it negative, but it's a little tricky. In English, the word "not" goes after the verb ("I should not"), but in Spanish, the word "not" has to go before the verb ("*no* I should"). If that's confusing, just use this sentence as a model, and you'll get used to it eventually.

I shouldn't get worried by those things.	*No* I should get worried *por* those things.

Take another look at that example. We've translated the word *por* as "by", indicating that what follows is the source, cause, or reason for something. In that case, you could almost translate it as "because of" ("I shouldn't get worried *because of* those things"). In our next example, that's the best way to explain the way the word *por* is used.

| Because of this, she cannot be at his house. | *Por* this, she *no* can be *en* his house. |

Yo and Direct Objects

When you practice the following phrase, make sure you pretend that you're Joel. He never says "It's me"; he always says "It is I" ("it is *yo*").

It is I.	It is *yo.*
I don't have her.	*No la* I have.
My brother called me.	My brother *me* called.
Our father doesn't know it.	Our father *no lo* knows.

"What Luck!"

Before we study examples of *qué*, there are a few things to explain.

We've already learned that it means "what?" in a question; for example, "What can I do?" would be "*Qué* can I do?"

But consider this sentence: "What luck!" In Spanish, this would be "*Qué* luck!"

As you can see, the word *qué* is being used not in a question, but in an exclamation.

To take this a little further, how about this sentence: "*Qué* lucky!" In English, we would say "how lucky", but in Spanish, the exclamation is literally "what lucky".

Phrases like "*Qué* lucky!" and "*Qué* nice!" may seem awkward because they don't translate as "what". But this is one of the reasons that *qué* is such a common word: It's used both in questions and in exclamations.

What can I do on behalf of Isabella?	¿*Qué* can I do *por* Isabella?
What luck!	¡*Qué* luck!
How nice!	¡*Qué* nice!
How good that it's you!	¡*Qué* good *que* it's you!

One more thing to know about *qué*: It's used in the very common question *"por qué?"* Although this is literally translated as "by what?", the meaning is the question "why?"

Spanish doesn't even have a word for "why". When Joel wants to ask this question, he always uses *"Por qué?"*

Why did she leave?	*¿Por qué* did she leave?

Special Use of Articles

We've learned that the words that Joel spray-painted on the fence posts, *el* and *la*, mean "the". But for Joel, they mean a little bit more than this.

He put a lot of work into his artwork, so he puts a lot of significance into these words. Sometimes he even uses them by themselves, without a noun.

For example, if we're talking about sheep, I might say "I want the sheep that's singing." Joel would just say "I want *la* that's singing."

As you can see, in Joel's mind, the word *la* might mean "the sheep". Similarly, "the sheep that's drinking" could be *"el* that's drinking."

To be fair, we do this in English too. Instead of "the sheep", I can say "the one" if I'm being lazy. I've left out the noun, "sheep", and replaced it with the lazier word "one". What Joel does is similar, but he doesn't even bother to say "one".

So the English phrase "the one that…" is translated into Spanish as *el que* or *la que*, depending on whether the noun (which Joel left out because he's lazy) is masculine or feminine.

Check out this example:

Papa is the one that always gets worried.	Papa is *el que* always gets worried.

So when Joel says *el que* or *la que*, what he generally means is "the one that…" He chooses *la que* if the omitted noun is feminine or *el que* if it's masculine. Imagine Joel pointing at one of the sheep, masculine or feminine, and saying "the one that is singing" or "the one that is drinking".

Dialogue:
Phrases in Context

Congratulations! We've finally come to the point where we get to see how your vocabulary is used in real life.

Let's recap what we've done in Lesson 1:

- We've learned enough vocabulary to account for 25% of the Spanish language.

- We've internalized how these words are used in phrasal context.

In a few pages, we will talk about how to practice using all of this in your own Spanish conversations. But first, let's look at an authentic Spanish dialogue that uses all of today's words and some of the phrases we just learned.

This simple dialogue is a tool that we'll continue to use throughout the next several lessons. By the end of lesson 12, you'll have complete comprehension of not only this dialogue, but a couple of others as well, and you'll know Spanish well enough to carry advanced conversations.

As you look through this dialogue, study the way that your vocabulary is used by the characters. You'll notice that many of the phrases in this dialogue appeared in the examples we've already seen.

You should also listen to a native speaker reading the dialogue so that you can train your ears to identify these words in spoken context. You'll find a recording in the Lesson 1 materials at SpanishIn1Month.com.

The dialogue is between two friends, Santiago and Matías. Here are a few background facts that will be useful to know as you go through the comics:

(1) Santiago's sister, Isabella, has been staying with a mysterious man named Sebastián, but he disappeared unexpectedly. Now Isabella has no place to stay. This is why Santiago calls Matías, a wealthy family friend, to see if he can help.

(2) Valentina used to be a close friend of Isabella, but she doesn't approve of Isabella's life choices and would probably cause drama if she were to interfere.

(3) It's summer and many people are traveling on vacation. Matías himself has just come in from out of town. He's staying at his summer house, and he decides to offer it to Isabella since he is here.

- Hello, I'm Matías.
  Who is this?

- Hi Matías, it's me,
  Santiago.

- Santiago, all this
  time, ¿right?

- Yes I know! ¿How
  are you?

- Fine thanks,
  and you? ¿How is
  Isabella?

- Not so well, you
  know, she left her
  house.

- What! This isn't
  good at all.

- No, this time she doesn't have a place to be. You have to do her a favor, on my behalf.

- Yes, I want to be with her now. What can I do for Isabella or for you?

- You're very nice! I have her things at my house, as it should be, but…

- ¿Can I do something?

- I think so, it's a big deal.

- ¿But, why did she leave?

- She left, that's all... right, so, now we're going to do something when Valentina isn't around.

- ¿Valentina? But... why? If those two are like one, as you know, a...

- I know that they were, but now they aren't.

- Valentina is that way, and with her everything's like that, that's Valentina... And Sofía? She can...

- No, not Sofía, she isn't around.

- I am here, you are there... we're all here, the time is now.

- Maybe so, us both, with her. This time I don't know what to do.

- She can be at my house all the time. I can do you that favor, because I only want her to be well, and you to be well.

- That which was, is not anymore... now, everything's this way!

- Give it time. She's around, and her things at your house, at least it's something. And that gentleman?

- ¿Sebastián?

- I don't know, that man that was around with her at the house.

- Ah, yes, Sebastián, he isn't around anymore, and because of this she can't be at Mr. Sebastián's house.

- ¿He isn't? ¿What do you mean he isn't around? ¿Really? That can't be, but if the house was his!

- He left from the house, that's the truth. This has been this way for a while now. I know that she's doing badly.

- All right, well then, Isabella has been unwell for a while. Now we have to do something for her, I want to do something for her, both of us.

- Yes, I want... I'm leaving now, I'll go with Isabella.

- All right, I also will go to your house, I want to be with her.

As you can tell, this is a simplistic dialogue; it only uses 100 unique words. And yet these two birds were able to have a meaningful conversation even with a small selection of verbs and almost no nouns.

Spanish speakers are great at communicating not because of their vocabulary, but because of how effectively they use it. Before moving on to further lessons and learning more words, you need to make sure that you've genuinely mastered the 15 words that we learned in Lesson 1.

Focused Practice

I'm going to be honest with you. If you are pursuing Spanish fluency, there's no way you're going to attain it without serious, focused conversation practice.

The best practice is with native speakers who are dedicated to your success.

Ideally, your time with native speakers should be focused on the exact concepts that you've just learned. A good teacher will drill your abilities and help you sharpen your skills, without pushing you beyond your current objectives. Your efforts will be squandered if you try to practice words or concepts that go beyond the materials covered in Lesson 1. These are truly the essentials, and you shouldn't engage in any distractions until the content of Lesson 1 is second nature.

My own coaching students are required to participate in extremely focused, one-on-one practice multiple times per week. During this practice time, the coach pushes them hard to ensure that they've mastered the words and phrases well enough to use them in real-time conversation as a native speaker would use them.

If you don't have a coach to practice with, you can still simulate some of this practice using free tools. Simple flashcards of this lesson's phrases, with the English on one side and the Spanish on the other, provide a very effective drilling system. By presenting yourself with the English side and testing yourself on how quickly you can voice the equivalent Spanish phrase, you're practicing producing Spanish sentences in your mind. (This is an exercise that I require even my coaching students to do; it's a nice supplement to real practice.)

As you work with flash cards, it's not enough to produce these words and phrases in your mind; you should say them out loud as well, imitating the way that Spanish speakers pronounce them. It's essential that you listen to native speakers saying every Spanish word that you learn, and you should mimic the exact sounds that you hear.

Fortunately you can simulate this by listening to the lessons and dialogue recordings at SpanishIn1Month.com, where you can also find electronic flashcards and other resources that accompany the entire course, all available for free.

LESSON 2

Learn in Phrases

It's time to begin expressing ideas with words.

But words are worthless without phrases. Just as a single letter has no definite meaning until it's surrounded by other letters to create a word, a single word has no meaning until it's given phrasal context.

From this moment on, every word that you learn in Spanish will no longer be an isolated entity. Each one will be a piece of a genuine Spanish phrase, allowing you to speak your thoughts effectively.

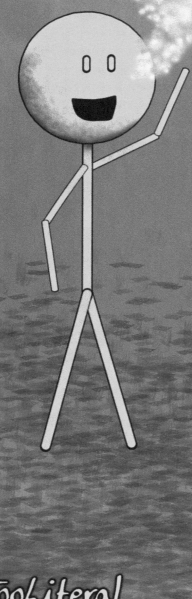

Lesson 2 Theory:

Learn in Phrases

"Imitation is not just the sincerest form of flattery; it's the sincerest form of learning."

- George Bernard Shaw

"Translation is the art of failure."

- Umberto Eco

WE'VE NOW learned 15 of the most-used words in Spanish. These words help to shape the structures of sentences.

But we left one word out. If you do a Google search for the most frequently used words in Spanish, you'll see a conspicuous stranger on the list: The 7th most commonly used word in Spanish is *es*.

There's a reason we've put this word off. It's impossible to discuss this word without opening a Pandora's box of confusing information about Spanish verbs. *Es* is complicated, because it's just one of the many manifestations of a bigger, more intimidating word: *Ser*.

Let's tackle this project head-on and discuss Spanish verbs. These are the words that give us the ability to speak entire sentences. And as you may have guessed, Spanish sentences don't work the same way that English sentences do.

In Spanish, verbs are a bigger deal than they are in English. A single verb, by itself, can be an entire thought. Some sentences are just one word, and that word will be a verb.

"Verb, you're so intense."

Verbs don't translate between English and Spanish.

For example, the Spanish word *es* can mean multiple things. It could simply mean "is", which works in these cases:

- He *es* a tall man.

- She *es* a strange woman.

- It *es* a beautiful day.

But frequently, this word translates to "it is", or "he is", or "she is", without needing the extra word at the beginning at all.

- *Es* a tall man.

- *Es* a strange woman.

- *Es* a beautiful day.

In fact, it's much more common not to include "he", "she", or "it".

This drives English speakers almost as crazy as it drives Spanish teachers, because it's very hard to explain. How do you know whether to include the subject pronoun or not? What's the rule?

It's very difficult to come up with rules for this. Instead, here's the guiding rule that will work in all situations:

Learn in phrases.

In fact, this is an essential skill that will apply to every aspect of your language learning. It's never enough to learn words and conjugations. You should learn all your vocabulary within Spanish phrasal constructs.

That's because Spanish words don't directly translate into English, and English words don't translate directly into Spanish.

This is why translation tools don't really work unless they're exceptionally sophisticated. If you take an English sentence and translate it word-by-word into another

language, it won't be correct and might not even make any sense. In order to translate it properly into Spanish, it has to be completely re-worked into a Spanish sentence structure.

Mr. Sentence Head

Constructing a sentence is like putting together a "Mr. Potato Head" face.

If you've ever played with a Potato Head toy, you know about the

changing parts, such as the hair, eyes, nose, and mouth. You can replace the hair with a hat, you can trade the open eyes for closed eyes or angry eyes, or you can switch the normal mouth for a stuck-out tongue.

Of course, you're not really supposed to put eyes where the mouth goes (unless you're a cubist). The face has a structure you're expected to follow: Hair on top, then eyes, then nose, then mouth.

Sentences are the same way. If you know what you can trade around, it's fun to replace the different parts.

As an example, let's use this simple English sentence:

"This is a sentence."

There are four words. I've illustrated them as four parts of a face ("this" is the hair, "is" is the eyes, "a" is the nose, and "sentence" is the mouth).

Let's start customizing this sentence. Suppose we replace the first word, "this", with a new word: "that".

Since those two words are grammatically equivalent, it works perfectly. "That is a sentence."

Let's get more creative. If "this" can be replaced with "that", what can the word "is" be replaced by? We can change it out for "was", "will be", or any other verb. To demonstrate, I've chosen the word "changed".

We can also replace "a" with "the" since they're equivalent. So now our sentence is "That changed the sentence."

As you can see, it's still the exact same sentence structure! But it's been

modified significantly to create a new meaning, kind of like switching out Potato Head parts to create our own face.

Now we'll go even further. Let's trade "that" for an interesting noun: "Dolphins."

Let's also replace our verb "changed" with "broke".

And our final noun will change from "sentence" to an entire phrase that operates as a noun: "local traffic laws".

"Dolphins broke local traffic laws." This is still the same sentence structure that we started out with: "This is a sentence." We just changed every word for something

grammatically equivalent.

Basic Phrase Units

Unfortunately, translating from English to Spanish is as awkward as moving pieces from a Potato Head face to a bee's face. Joel doesn't have any place to put the nose, and what are you supposed to do with the antennae? The structures simply aren't the same. Spanish phrases work differently from English phrases.

Instead of translating word-by-word (which frequently leads to disaster), let's learn how Spanish phrase structures work from scratch.

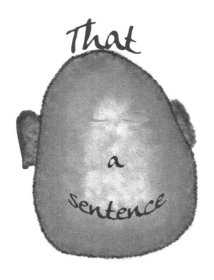
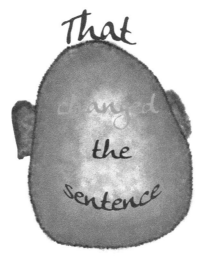

Fortunately, there aren't too many structures to learn. By the end of Lesson 6, you will have learned nearly all of the sentence structures used in Spanish.

Check out this example of a complete Spanish sentence that's only two words: "*Es* tall."

This sentence could mean "he is tall", "she is tall", or "it is tall" (depending on the context). It's a phrasal unit that can be used in many situations, and it's a complete sentence. Grammatically, there's no need for any more information.

But sometimes we need to clarify the context. Suppose we're in the presence of both a boy and a girl, and we want to talk about one of them specifically. The solution is simply to add a noun to the beginning: "The girl *es* tall."

In that case, we included a subject in the sentence. But a lot of the time, Spanish doesn't even need the subject to be named. "*Es* tall" is com-plete all by itself. "The girl" is extra information that can be added to the beginning.

If you learn the phrase "*es* tall", then you can use it in various ways. By itself, you can refer to any person you want. Or if you want to be specific, you can simply name the person at the beginning: "[person] *es* tall." Either way, you're using the same basic two-word phrase.

Now let's go a step fur-ther: Suppose we don't want to say "he is tall". What if we want to say "I am tall"?

You'll still use the basic sentence structure: "*es* tall." But you'll change the verb from "he is" to "I am", and you'll end up with "*soy* tall." (*Soy* means "I am", as you'll learn in part B of the lesson.)

These two phrases, "*es* tall" and "*soy* tall", are the same, but with one word changed. We didn't invent a whole new sen-tence. We just modified one word from our basic phrase unit.

To speak perfect Spanish, you'll never make up sen-tences from scratch. In re-ality, you've never made up a sentence in English either. You've been using variations on the same few sentences your entire life. Every sentence you speak imitates a phrase structure that you've heard before. You're just changing some of the words to create your own meaning.

Spanish (and every other language) works the same way: You always use the phrase structures that you learned in your formative days, but when you speak or write, you creatively switch out cer-tain words to create your own meaning, just like switching out the parts of a Potato Head face.

Two Sentences

As we learn vocabulary for this lesson, we'll introduce each word in the context of one of two basic phrase structures. Let's get introduced to each one.

(1) Es tall.

This sentence means "*He/she/it is* tall". It has two parts: The verb and the information after the verb.

This basic structure will be modified in a couple of ways. First, we could modify the verb:

- *They are* tall.

- *We were* tall.

- *He will be* tall.

Or we could change the information after the verb:

- *Es* a tall person.

- *Es* sarcastic.

As you can see, these are all directly based on the basic sentence structure "*Es* tall," with either "*Es*" or "tall" replaced by something else.

(2) I hope que he be tall.

This sentence is more complicated, but it's an extremely important Spanish structure.

First of all, notice the *que* in the middle of the sentence. This divides two separate phrases: "I hope" and "he be tall".

You'll learn the significance of this sentence structure soon. For now, rehearse it a little bit: "I hope *que* he be tall." Keep this exact wording in mind.

Once you're comfortable with both of these essential sentences, you're ready to begin learning this lesson's vocabulary.

Afterwards, in part C of the lesson, we'll dive much deeper into the construction of Spanish phrases.

Lesson 2 Vocabulary:

Ser
(the Apple Shop)

SER IS A VERY well-known (but not very well-liked) woman in Joel's neighborhood in Yol. Her actual name is Sarah, but her nickname is "Ser", which is what we'll continue to call her. She is the owner of several shops in Yol, but her favorite shop is an apple store, which she's named after herself: Ser.

As you can see, the name "Ser" is written on the front of the apple shop, but it's inscribed on a sign made out of a fish's fin. For some reason, this is how they always do it in Yol. A store's name is always on a fin on the front of the store. Any time that we refer to "Ser" in general, we are using the name of the store, the form of the word written on the fin.

What does *ser* mean? Well, the nearest translation is "to be", but that doesn't work in all situations. In English, we use "to be" to mean all kinds of things.

For example, we could say, "Joel is happy *to be* a bee," which refers to *what* he is. But we can also say "He likes *to be* at home, which refers to *where* he is. He could even say that he wants *to be* leaving soon, which has nothing to with what he is or where he is! These are all completely different meanings in Spanish, so how do you know when to use Ser?

To answer this question, let's talk about the owner of the store. Ser is very eccentric, and she only allows people to shop in her apple shop if they meet certain height requirements. As you can see, she's a grumpy-looking lady, and she's very discriminative. Trying to go to her store is kind of like getting in line for an amusement ride. You're required "to be" the right height; you have "to be a tall person" in order to shop at Ser.

Pay careful attention to that phrase: You have "<u>to be</u> a tall person".

So Ser doesn't care what you're doing or where you've been. She discriminates strictly based on what you are as a person. So think of *ser* as meaning "to be", in the sense of *what something is*. Keep in mind the image of Sarah measuring people before letting them buy apples. Ser doesn't care about where or how you are; she cares about <u>what</u> you are.

For this lesson, you won't have to give much thought to that. Every time we learn a Ser word, it will be a part of a phrase. Although there will be several words to learn, you'll know how to use all of them in the sentence that I provide with each one.

You might wonder why we have "several words to learn" if we're only focused on one word, *ser*. Well, Ser's store is a very complicated place. It

has many different areas, and each area has several words. But all these words, throughout the entire store, are considered different forms of the basic word *ser*.

To see how this works, let's begin by following Joel into the entrance of the store.

Cheating the Apple System

Joel lives very close to Ser, but he's never successfully shopped here, because he's much too short. In fact, none of Joel's friends would be tall enough to pass the height requirement. This has always bugged Joel, because he wants to buy some of Ser's famous apple tea.

But today, Joel has a plan. Calling the lizard and the pandas together, he tells them, "We're going apple shopping today! All we have to do is convince Ser that we're actually tall people. We just need to cheat the system."

After Joel whispers the details to each of his friends, they all go to Ser to try to gain admittance. Each one of them is using a particular strategy to look taller than they actually are.

The five friends burst into the store all at once. This takes Ser by surprise, and she quickly ducks behind the checkout counter somewhat suspiciously. Joel senses something strange about this, but he ignores it for the moment: He's focused on proving that he is tall.

In order to meet the height requirements, Joel has decided that since he can fly, all he really has to do is have something dangling down from him to look like long legs. Then, with his head up in the air (since he's flying), and the things hanging down, it should look like he's a very tall person.

What Joel has done is he's tied a bunch of soy beans together. Hanging these from his legs, he almost looks convincingly tall. Joel announces loudly: "I'm a tall person!"

But accidentally, Joel uses the word "soy", because he's thinking about the soy beans. So what he says is, "*Soy* a tall person."

In using the word soy, Joel means "I am". Thanks to this mistake that he's made, Joel decides that he'll always say *soy* to mean "I am" when he's talking about what he is as a person. Of course, that's what *soy* means in Spanish.

Joel's plot works. Ser seems to believe Joel's story, so he's in!

But what about the lizard? Ser demands, "Your friend there doesn't look tall enough."

Joel looks down at the lizard, and on cue, the lizard stands up on its tail in order to appear tall enough. Lizards have a hard time with this, so its whole body is hunched over in the shape of the letter S.

The lizard is unable to speak, but as you'll see throughout this book, that's not a big problem; Joel is more than capable of speaking on the lizard's behalf. So Joel says to Ser, "The lizard is a tall person."

But since Joel is looking at the lizard and thinking of the letter S, it comes out a bit differently: "*Es* a tall person."

The word *es* basically means "is". But actually, this word can be interpreted as "he is", "she is", or "it is". This is because the lizard doesn't really seem to have a very specific gender. For Joel, the word *es* (which is pronounced as if you were to say "S") can mean any of these. When Joel says "*Es* a tall person", this can be interpreted as "He's a tall person", "She's a tall person", or "It's a tall person."

Practice saying this phrase a few times: "Es a tall person." When you say this, you can be referring to any kind of person: A boy, a girl, or a lizard.

Next item on the agenda: The pandas.

While Ser has been busy examining Joel and the lizard, the pandas are following their part of the plan. Running over to the window, they climb up on top of a few jugs of apple juice. Now their heads are partially blocking the sun streaming through the window, and with the light behind them, they all look like shadows or silhouettes.

Ser looks at the pandas, and the sun is in her eyes, so she can't see them very well. But from her perspective, they now look like tall people.

To attest to this, Joel declares, "They're tall people!" But instead of "they are", he is thinking of the sun. So here's what he says: "*Son* tall people."

Let's pause for a second here. These are the three phrases we've learned so far:

> *Soy* a tall person.
>
> *Es* a tall person.
>
> *Son* tall people.

If you can remember all three of these phrases, while thinking of the different people, you're ready to learn two more words in this scene.

Now that Joel, the lizard, and the pandas are all in the store, they're in luck! They can go ahead and buy whatever they want.

However, there's something nagging at Joel. When they first walked into the store, Ser ducked behind the counter in a hasty, almost panicked rush. Not only that, but there's a strange image lingering in the air: Green streaks that look a lot like "air rays".

This needs a little explanation. In the planet of Yol, one of the most significant recent advancements is hovercraft technology. Hovercrafts use blowing air, but the air turns a bit green when the machine is moving quickly, creating the look of "air rays" going behind the craft.

Joel finds this situation very odd, because he thought that Ser was a tall, proud person. But when customers are around, she spends all day standing behind the counter. If she's actually using a hovercraft, maybe she's not as

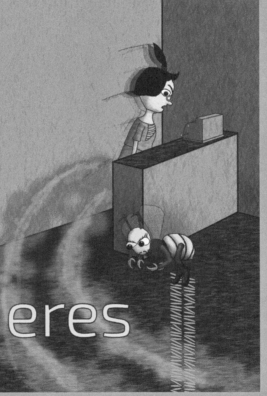

tall as she pretends to be!

In his doubt, Joel asks, "You ARE a tall person, aren't you?" But since he's thinking of the "air rays", it comes out like this: "*Eres* a tall person?"

The word eres means "you are". So "Eres a tall person" means "You are a tall person."

Important note: The word *eres* has two syllables. The stressed syllable is the first syllable, which sounds kind of like "air". So when you want to say "You are a tall person", remember that you're stressing the "air" syllable: "AIR-es a tall person."

Before Ser can respond, there's a loud noise: *SPLAT*

One of the apple jugs that the pandas were standing on has collapsed. The panda who was standing on it falls down, landing in a puddle of sticky apple juice.

Ser is furious when she realizes that she's been tricked. These cheaters are disobeying the height requirement! "What are you doing in here?" she yells, looking around the room. "You aren't really tall enough. You're just tricking me!"

This makes Joel a bit upset: Why should she blame all of them for one panda's mistake? Don't the rest of them still look tall, or at least some of them?

So Joel retorts, "What are you talking about? We're tall people!"

But since he's privately thinking "some of us", it comes out like this: "*Somos* tall people!"

Before moving on, make sure you can remember the stories associated with each of these words, and practice saying the phrases:

Soy a tall person. (Joel)

Es a tall person. (the lizard)

Son tall people. (the pandas)

Eres a tall person. (Sarah)

Somos tall people. (Joel with his friends)

Who's Who?

Why did we use different people for each of these words? The lizard for "it is", the pandas for "they are", and so on?

This is a very carefully planned mnemonic strategy that we'll continue to use every time we learn new verb forms.

You've already seen that the word Ser is very complicated, with the several different versions we've learned. But believe it or not, we've just begun to scratch the surface of this complex verb. Although we've covered the present tense, we also need to go to the past tense, the future tense, and some other areas as well. That's a lot to learn!

But Joel never gets these different forms confused. He always knows what to use in any situation, because he knows who is who.

When he's talking about one other person (he/she/it), he always thinks of the lizard. When he's talking about multiple people (they), he thinks of the pandas. To talk to one person (you), he thinks of Sarah, and when talking about himself (I), of course, he thinks of himself. So these different words are never confusing for him.

As we learn more forms of Ser, we'll continue to use the lizard for "he/she/it", Sarah for "you", the pandas for "they", and so on.

When you want to think of the present tense, you've already learned it: It's here at the entrance of the store. All of the words that we've learned are in the present tense.

But if we move all these people to a different area, we can learn a different tense. For example, when we go to the checkout counter, we'll learn the past tense for each of these people.

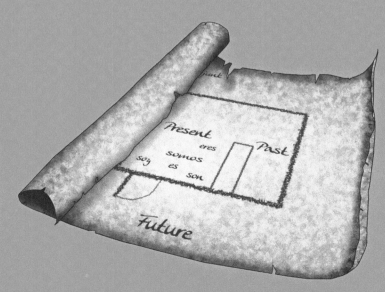

This is Joel's secret to never getting Ser's forms confused. Every time that he needs to say that someone "is" or "was" something, he first thinks of a particular place in Ser's store. For example, if it's something that's true right now, he thinks about the entrance of the store for the present tense.

Second, he thinks of the person he's referring to. Let's say it's the pandas, because he wants to say "they are". Based on what we've seen of the pandas, Joel is able to think of appropriate form of the verb: The word *son*, because the pandas are standing in the sun. "*Son* tall people."

But if he's thinking of a different person, maybe "you", he just thinks of our story about Sarah with the air rays: "*Eres* a tall person."

So our five words in the entrance of the store all work the same way: Each word means that someone "is" something. All we have to do is pick which word to use based on whom we're talking about: *soy* for "I am", *es* for "he/she/it is", *son* for "they are", *eres* for "you are", or *somos* for "we are".

Notice that we're following the same principle that we did in Lesson 1 when we were in the countryside. Remember the phrase "*lo* you found" to mean "I found him"? We were able to switch out the *lo* for other words in the same scene: "*me* you found" and "*la* you found". We know that *lo*, *la*, and *me* all work the same way, because we found them in the same area (on the hill under the tree). Just think of the correct person, and you can think of the appropriate word. But first, of course, you want to make sure you're in the right place.

So far, all of the Ser words that we've learned are in the entrance of the store, which means that they happen in the

present tense. But now it's time to go to other places in Ser's store, where we'll find the past tense, the future tense, and so on.

The Secret Behind the Counter

When Joel realizes that Ser is a fraud, he confronts her by going behind the counter. This is where we'll learn the past tense of Ser.

Joel confirms his suspicion: Ser is simply standing on a hovercraft! Although she pretends to be tall, only letting tall people into her store, she is in fact a very short person.

Ser stumbles and falls, and her hovercraft turns sideways, blowing air at Joel and his friends. The soy beans fall off of Joel's feet, and the lizard is knocked over.

When Ser sees this, she yells, "Neither of you is tall enough! Get out of here!"

Joel tries to defend himself: "Well, I WAS tall enough, until that air from your hovercraft blew at me!"

To say "I was", Joel accidentally uses the word *era*.

Era is a two-syllable word, but the stressed syllable sounds like "air". Joel is thinking about the air that blew the soy beans off of his legs. And the word *era* means "I was". So "*era* tall" means "I was tall".

It turns out that this word also applies to the lizard. Joel points at the lizard and says, "*Era* tall too."

To avoid confusion, sometimes Joel decides to be extra-clear and a little redundant: When he's talking about himself, he often adds the word *yo* to the sentence. So here are the phrases we've learned behind the counter:

Joel, "I was tall": *Yo era* tall.

Lizard, "He/she/it was tall": *Era* tall.

Remember that the word *era* has a stress on the syllable that sounds like "air".

Meanwhile, Ser is understandably very upset. Not only are these guests cheating against the height requirements, now she has suffered the embarrassment of being seen falling off of her hovercraft!

Ser tries to yell at Joel and the lizard, but nobody can hear her. The loud hissing noise from the hovercraft covers up everything she says.

Joel, who has very little sympathy for others, laughs at this situation. He taunts Ser: "You thought you were tall! Hahaha!"

But instead of "You were tall", Joel uses the word *eras*. This word is very similar to *era*, but it has the letter S at the end because of the hissing coming from Ser's direction.

Note that *era* and *eras* have the exact same stressed syllable: "air".

So what are the pandas doing this whole time? Well, they don't want to get involved at all. They're not looking for trouble, and they definitely don't like the rushing air, because strong wind causes their light stuffed bodies to lose control and blow around. So they jump off of their apple jugs and run away.

Ser sees this and her anger grows. She screams audibly, "Even they aren't tall enough!"

Joel mutters, "Well, they WERE tall before they ran away."

To say "They were tall," he says "*Eran* tall."

As you can see, the word *eran* looks like it has the word "ran" in it, as in "ran away". But it's very important to emphasize the first syllable, as in "AIR-an". Just like the other words, this one has the stressed syllable of "air".

One more word behind the counter. Joel continues to argue that it's all Ser's fault. "If it weren't for your hovercraft, we'd all be buying apples right now. Well, most of us. Most of us were still tall."

Once again, he's thrown off by the fact that one of the pandas fell down earlier; not all of them were "tall", but most of them were, until Ser's hovercraft fell over.

So to say "We were tall", Joel says "*Éramos* tall." This word has the stress on "air", but there's also an extra syllable at the end that sounds kind of like "most", as in "most of us were tall".

Practice the past tense of Ser using the sentences below. In each case, emphasize the first syllable, "air".

I was tall: *Era* tall.

He/she/it was tall: *Era* tall.

You were tall: *Eras* tall.

They were tall: *Eran* tall.

We were tall: *Éramos* tall.

Before moving on, take a moment to review. We've learned about ten different words already, but you should be able to tell them apart. For the present tense, use the entrance of the store, with *soy* for Joel, *son* for the pandas, and so on. For the past tense, go behind the counter, which has a stressed syllable of "air" for everybody: *era*, *eras*, *eran*, and *éramos*.

Future

When Ser recovers herself, she throws Joel and his friends out of the store. But Joel is not one to give up easily. He is determined to find a way to get apples.

Of course, it's probably impossible for them to go back inside the store right now. But Joel has a new idea. Somebody told him that reptiles grow quickly. Maybe there's a chance that the lizard will soon be tall enough to get apples for them.

Joel asks the lizard, "How tall do you think you'll be next week?"

In response, the lizard stands on its tail again, rears its head, and says, "Rah!"

Unfortunately, the syllable "rah" is the entirety of the lizard's vocabulary. It can't say anything else. Joel is somewhat disappoint-ed, but he is still hope-ful: Even if the lizard did just say "rah", maybe it will be tall enough some time soon.

Joel tells himself, "I'm sure the lizard will be tall soon." But since Joel is thinking of the phrase "say rah", this is how he says it: "The lizard *será* tall."

The word *será* means "it will be", "he will be", or "she will be". Note that

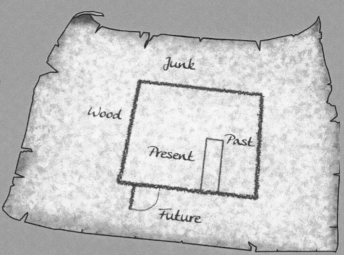

since the stressed syllable is "rah", it's pronounced like this: "seh-RAH".

This is the future tense word for the lizard. And actually, that's the only future tense word we're going to learn for now. There are a few more, but *será* is the most common by far, so we'll leave it at that.

So far, we've learned the present tense in the entrance of the store, the past tense behind the counter, and the future tense here in front of the store. We have a couple of more areas to learn, so go ahead and familiar-ize yourself with the map shown.

Make sure you can remember vividly what happened in the entrance (present), behind the counter (past), and in front of the store (future). Also note that there's a junk pile of apples behind the store, plus a woodpile next to the store. We're about to visit those areas.

Junk Mood

You might be wondering how we can possibly have more tenses than the present, the past, and the future. Isn't that all the time there is?

Well, the tenses that we've learned so far are very handy for indicating that something definitely is or isn't true. For example, "He is a tall person" would be "*Es* a tall person." Or "He wasn't tall" would be "*No era* tall."

But there are times when you're not trying to say something is or isn't the case. Instead, you're expressing a desire or intention that something *be* true.

For example, "I recommend that you be tall." When I say "you be", I'm not telling you whether it's true or not; I'm just expressing an intention. Maybe

you're already tall, and maybe you aren't, but either way, I'm recommending *that you be* tall.

In Ser, we have a scene that's specially reserved for this sort of situation. It's in the back yard, where the junk from the store is thrown, including old apples and empty juice jugs.

Joel isn't particularly interested in junk, but he does have a suspicion: Maybe Ser sources some of her apples from a tree in this back yard.

What Joel finds is a small tree that's completely covered in green leaves. He doesn't see any apples on the tree, but Joel assumes there are probably apples deep within the tree, hidden by these green leaves. His logic is that it MUST be an apple tree since it's here in the back yard of an apple shop. (It only makes sense, right?)

But in order to find apples in the tree, Joel will need to move the leaves around. He doesn't want to go to all that work (he is a very lazy bee), so he tells the lizard, "How about you climb up the tree and try to open it up. Maybe it will say 'Aaahhh' and reveal lots of apples for us."

But the lizard is having trouble climbing the slippery tree. So instead, it props itself up on its tail and tries to inch its way up the trunk, trying hard to reach the branches of the tree.

Joel says quietly to himself, "I hope that the lizard is tall enough!"

But since he's thinking about the phrase "say ah", this is what he says: "I hope *que sea* tall."

The word *sea* is pronounced like "SAY-ah", with a stressed syllable "say". This word means "he be", so it's like Joel's saying "I hope that <u>he be</u> tall."

If you're a nerd like me, that phrase might sound familiar to you. This is something that used to be more common in English than it is now.

Imagine an old person with a quaint-sounding accent saying, "I hope that *he be* tall!" They might instead say something like, "I hope that *he should be* tall," or maybe "I hope that *he may be* tall."

Each of those is something like the word *sea*. This is called the subjunctive mood. If the word "subjunctive" sounds intimidating, just remember that it's back here in the "junk" pile; subjunctive has the stressed syllable of "junk": sub-JUNK-tiv.

> *que sea*: "that he be…"
>
> *que sea*: "that he should be…"
>
> *que sea*: "that he may be…"

The point is that the subjunctive mood used to be common in English, but not anymore. One way or another, it refers to a hypothetical situation: Joel always uses a word like this when he's expressing intention toward a fact that may or may not be true. For example, "I recommend that he be tall" would be "I recommend *que sea* tall."

But don't worry about learning all the different uses of the subjunctive mood. Remember that we're learning in specific phrases. So for now, rehearse only this one phrase: "I hope that he be tall" is "I hope *que sea* tall."

Try to make this phrase sound natural. It's important, because Joel would NEVER hope that someone "is" tall ("*que es*"). He always hopes "that he be tall", or "*que sea* tall".

We have just one more subjunctive word to learn here in the junk yard.

Joel's hope for apples is interrupted when Ser suddenly bursts out the back door. Seeing Joel and the lizard trespassing, she explodes in anger, shouting at them to get off of her property and leave her junk pile alone.

But since the hovercraft is still malfunctioning in the background, Ser's scolding is impossible for Joel to hear. The hissing sound ("ssssss") covers up everything she says.

Joel has no idea what she's saying. Maybe she's sharing ideas for how to get apples out of the tree.

As she continues her futile screaming, Joel looks at her thoughtfully. If she were a bit taller, she would be able to reach up and pick apples for them straight out of the tree.

Joel says, "I know you are a fake, but at a time like this, I really want you to be tall."

To say, "I want you to be tall," he actually changes his wording a bit: "I want *that you be* tall."

And to say this, he uses a word that sounds a lot like *sea*, but this time with an S at the end (because of the hissing of the hovercraft):

"I want *que seas* tall."

Once again, this doesn't sound like modern English. But this is how Spanish works. Whenever Joel wants someone to be something, he wants "that they be" something.

For now, just remember these two phrases and associate them with the back yard:

"I hope that he be tall": "I hope *que sea* tall."

"I want that you be tall": "I want *que seas* tall."

With practice, you'll learn how to use these subjunctive words on your own.

There are other subjunctive words, but we can't learn them now. The pandas have run away, so we can't use them in our story anymore. But that's not a problem, because those subjunctive forms aren't very common, so we'll skip them for now. All we need at the moment are *sea* and *seas*.

Wood Mood

Sarah chases Joel and the lizard out of the back yard, and they hide beside the wood pile next to the store to plot their next idea for getting apples.

Looking at the wood pile reminds Joel of the far-off mountain of Ría.

Mount Ría is a very important place on Yol, but it's strange and mysterious. In fact, Joel has actually never been there. It's a dark mountain, covered by thick forest. The legends say that it's full of wonderful, magical things, but this is mostly hypothesis.

In fact, almost everything that Joel thinks about Mount Ría is a complete hypothesis with no grounds in truth. But Joel likes to imagine amazing things about Mount Ría.

Right now, Joel is considering the fact that the trees in Ría are extremely tall. This gives him an idea: Maybe the dark forests of Mount Ría are hiding

mysterious fruits with magical growing powers. The trees are growing very tall, but if animals and people ate those fruits, maybe they would grow to be very tall as well!

Of course, Joel is completely inventing this idea, but it's an interesting thought. Joel says to himself, "I bet that if the lizard went to Ría and ate the magical fruit, he would be tall."

But to say "He would be tall," Joel says "*Sería* tall."

The word *sería* has the stress on "Ría", and this word means "he would be", "she would be", or "it would be".

In other words, when we put "Ría" at the end of the word *ser*, we end up adding "would". Remember that Joel and the lizard are thinking about this while they're sitting at a wood pile, thinking about a thickly wooded mountain.

Sería can also refer to Joel, as in "I would be". Joel says to himself, "If I went to Ría and ate the fruit, *yo sería* tall as well."

This conjugation is much easier for English speakers than the subjunctive mood. It's simple: If you would use "would be" in English, you'll use *sería* in Spanish. Just think of the wood and the mountain of Ría.

Off the Ground: Fins, Bells, and Whistles

If you think we've learned enough conjugations of Ser, you're right.

Joel is ready to leave Ser. He's been in the entrance, behind the counter, out the front door, in the backyard junk pile, and beside the store at the wood pile. What else could possibly be left?

Before leaving, Joel examines the Ser sign. Remember that it's written on a fin, which is the normal way to put up a shop sign in Yol.

We've learned how to use many forms of Ser, including the past, the present, the future, the subjunctive, and the "would" version. But what do you call *ser* itself?

This version of the word is the basic form, written on the fin. We call it the infinitive (in-FIN-i-tiv).

But it's not like the other forms; it's special. *Ser* is an idea, the whole concept of "being" something. Instead of a verb, *ser* itself is treated kind of like a noun.

For example, sometimes Joel says, "I like <u>tea</u>." The "tea" is a noun.

Joel can also say, "I like <u>to be a bee</u>." When he does this, he's using the idea of *being a bee* as a noun. So he uses *ser* for that: "I like <u>*ser* a bee.</u>"

And Joel does like being a bee, because it means he can fly. Here he is, floating far above the ground, examining the sign. "Being a bee" is fun; "*Ser* a bee" is fun.

Note that *ser* can be translated as either "to be" or "being". Either way, it's being treated as a noun in a sentence instead of a verb.

Also note that this version of the verb doesn't change based on which person it refers to. It's the name of the store, so there's no reason for it ever to change.

This means *ser* is very different from the forms of the verb that we learned on the ground. For example, in the entrance of the store, we had five different words for the different people (*soy*, *es*, *eres*, *son*, and *somos*). Even outside there are different versions of each verb; for example, *sería* can change to *serías*, *serían*, and so on (but don't worry about those for now, because they're not common).

siendo

However, Joel has left the ground now, so we're above that. We're done learning the versions of Ser that change based on who is who. *Ser* is an example of an "unconjugated" form, something that has only one version: *ser*.

Still, there are a couple more versions of today's verb to learn. They are "unconjugated", like *ser*: They don't change based on which person they refer to. So they'll be found above the ground too.

There's a weird tradition in Yol that when you leave someone's house after a nice visit, you're supposed to ring a bell on the outside. Instead of a doorbell (which you ring when you arrive), this bell indicates "the end", meaning that you're going away. It's a way of saying goodbye; the pleasant visit is over. "The end! Have a nice day!"

Joel sees that Ser actually has one of

these bells on the store, even though presumably nobody rings it. A visit to Ser's store is never pleasant.

But Joel decides to be sarcastic. He flies up to the corner of the store and rings the bell, as if to say, "The end!"

Ser yells back from inside, "Now you're being sarcastic!"

But to say this, she says, "Now you're *siendo* sarcastic!"

The word *siendo*, with a stressed syllable that sounds like "end", basically means "being". It refers to what someone is being at a particular moment; for example, "You're *siendo* mean" or "You're *siendo* a baby." For now, just remember the phrase "You're *siendo* sarcastic."

This form of Ser isn't very common. But since a lot of the stores in Yol have bells, you'll see that many other verbs have a "bell form", similar to *siendo*, in future lessons.

Our last word is on the roof of Ser's store.

Joel goes up on the roof to look around; he wants to find out if he can see Mount Ría in the distance. But suddenly, he hears a whistling sound, and a shower of seeds fly out of the chimney of Ser's roof, pelting Joel with apple seeds.

Apparently, Joel triggered some sort of alarm, and the automatic response is to fire apple seeds from the chimney.

At this point, Joel is completely fed up with Ser's apple shop. Things have gone too far. Now he's done with the whole idea of being tall and trying to get apples.

Joel says, "I have been tall, but I'm done with all this nonsense. I'm ready to be myself and leave the apple shop alone."

But when he says "I have been tall", he's thinking of the apple seeds, and he says "I have *sido* tall."

The word *sido*, with the stressed syllable "seed", is one of my favorite forms of Ser. It's used to put things in the past; for example, "they have been tall" or "we have been tall".

But note that it's on the roof, which is above the ground. Just like *ser*, the word *sido* doesn't change based on whom it refers to!

So if you want to use the past tense of Ser, you have two options. You can do it the normal way and go behind the counter and choose between *era*, *eras*, *eran*, and *éramos*.

Or you can cheat and just use *sido*. This puts us in the past, but it can refer to anyone, without having to change forms. Here are some examples:

I have been tall: I have *sido* tall.

She has been tall: She has *sido* tall.

You have been tall: You have *sido* tall.

They have been tall: They have *sido* tall.

We have been tall: We have *sido* tall.

Meanwhile, Joel is now done with Ser, and he's probably never going to visit this shop again.

Before going on to the next section to learn phrases, make sure of two things. First, be sure you can remember ALL the words from this lesson and where they are. Second, make sure you can use them properly in the phrases that you found them in.

Then you'll be ready to learn more phrases and learn how to use Ser in a wide variety of ways.

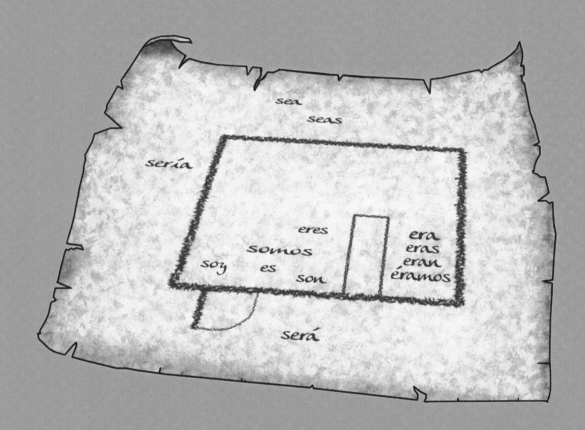

Lesson 2 Application:
Modifying Phrases

IN THE APPLICATION section of Lesson 1, we learned approximately 20 phrases that used your new vocabulary the way that native Spanish speakers do. For this lesson, we have 16 phrases. But instead of just learning them as they are, we're going to practice the "potato head" game by switching out different parts of the sentences to change the meanings.

So far we've learned all our vocabulary in the context of two basic sentence structures:

1. *Es* tall.

2. I hope *que sea* tall.

The first phrase is extremely flexible. We can easily modify "*Es* tall" into any of the following sentences:

- *Soy* tall.

- *Eran* tall.

- *Sería* tall.

As you can see, we're exchanging the verb form *es* for different forms that we know are grammatically equivalent. But this has to be done carefully; you can't use just any form of Ser in these sentences. I didn't use *sea* or *sido* in these examples.

What do those words (*somos*, *soy*, *eran*, and *sería*) have in common? Think about where they are in Ser's shop:

1. They're all on the ground (not above the ground like the fin, bell, and roof).

2. They aren't in the back yard (subjunctive).

We'll study the subjunctive words (*sea* and *seas*) as well as the unconjugated forms (*ser*, *siendo*, and *sido*) at the end of this section. First, let's see how much we can do with the rest of Ser's forms.

Note: Any sentence that's highlighted in red is considered essential material; we require our coaching students to memorize these sentences. All the other sentences in this section are simply variations on them.

Ser: Eight Simple Uses

Below is a sentence from one of our dialogues: "*Eres* very nice." As you're about to see, you can take this sentence and then use your creativity to make some modifications by switching *eres* for a different form of Ser:

You are very nice.	*Eres* very nice.
They are very nice.	*Son* very nice.
She was very nice.	*Era* very nice.

We can keep modifying this sentence by continuing to use the same structure with even more modifications. All we're doing is switching between different forms of Ser that are conjugated (on the ground) and that aren't subjunctive (they're not in the back yard). At the same time, we can change the second half of the sentence from "very nice" to "very mean" or any other descriptive adjective.

We are very mean.	*Somos* very mean.
He is very friendly.	*Es* very friendly.
It would be very unusual.	*Sería* very unusual.
It will be very fun.	*Será* very fun.

So let's keep practicing with some more examples. Here's our second sentence to learn, with a couple of modifications. In this case, you'll see that there's an added noun at the beginning of the sentence. We could just say "*es* all", but we've decided to be specific: *That* *es* all.

That is all.	That *es* all.
This was all.	This *era* all.
She would be all.	She *sería* all.

Before we go any further, make sure you're really comfortable with the sentences "*eres* very nice" and "that *es* all". In our coaching course, we make our students memorize these phrases, because they're so essential. Focus on memorizing them as they are, but also practice modifying them as demonstrated.

This next example is similar, but instead of a noun after the Ser conjugation, we have "that way". This often comes after Ser.

Valentina is that way.	Valentina *es* that way.
Everything was that way.	Everything *era* that way.
The time is now.	The time *es* now.
Matías will be tall.	Matías *será* tall.

In the next two examples, we don't have a noun or adjective after the verb. Instead, we have a *de* phrase. This frequently happens after a Ser word. The best way to internalize this is to learn the basic sentence, "*La* house *era de* him," and then practice modifying it.

The house was his.	*La* house *era de* him.
The house was hers.	*La* house *es de* her.
The car would be my friends'.	*El* car *sería de* my friends.
The child was from another world.	*El* child *era de* another world.

The next one is even more complicated, but it's similar. If you have trouble modifying it, just practice saying the original version and don't worry about switching out parts.

Papa is the one that always gets worried.	Papa *es el que* always gets worried.
Mom is the one that made dinner.	Mom *es la que* made dinner.
I was the one that caused trouble.	*Yo era el que* caused trouble.

Next, we have a common question: "Who is it?" It's important to point out that when we're asking a question in English, we change our word order by putting put "is" before "it" ("who <u>is it</u>" instead of "who <u>it is</u>"). But in Spanish, since they're just one word, *es*, the word order doesn't change when it's a question.

Who is it?	¿Who *es*?
Who will it be?	¿Who *será*?
Who were they?	¿Who *eran*?

Next, let's learn how Joel says "It's me!" Instead of "It's me", he's so egotistical that he names himself twice: "I am I", or "*Soy yo.*" Actually he does that with anyone. For example, instead of "It's them," he says "They are them."

It's me!	*¡Soy yo!*
It's him!	¡*Es* him!
It's them!	¡*Son* them!

As you can see, Joel creates his sentences in some funny ways. I recommend reviewing the eight sentences above before we go over an even stranger phrase structure.

"I'm on the right track, baby, I was born it!"

Joel's logic and attitude go beyond the understanding of an English-speaking personality. But we have to live with it and love it, because that's just Joel's nature.

We're about to learn one of the phrases that are particularly alien to English speakers: Sometimes when Joel wants to say "that way" or "this way", he actually just uses *lo* (from the hilltop in the countryside).

This is just because Joel really likes the word *lo*, especially when it has no definite meaning. The best way to understand this is with a few examples.

First of all, let's imagine that that Joel says, "Did you comb your hair? I did."

He actually never phrases it that way. Instead, he adds "it" to the latter sentence:

"Did you comb your hair? *Yo lo* did."

"Did you take the train? *Yo lo* did."

Next, let's say that Joel is comparing himself to someone else. A normal person would say, "Are you beautiful? I am!"

This is how Joel would say that: "Are you beautiful? *Yo lo soy.*"

As you can tell, the phrase *yo lo soy* literally means "I am it." But the "it" there doesn't represent a thing. It represents a way that someone is. It's like saying "I am that way."

So Joel throws an extra *lo* in a lot of the time. How do you know when *lo* should be added?

Generally it's when you emphasize the subject: "*I* am", "*She* did", "*They* do." Each of these sentences gets that extra "lo":

"You aren't? Well *I* am."

"He's not a lawyer? Well *she* is."

"You're not smart? Well *yo lo soy.*"

It's important to get used to this type of phrase, because Joel uses it all the time. First of all, practice the *"Yo lo soy"* sentence quite a bit. Then, once you think you're ready, try this more complicated sentence on for size:

I know that they were, but now they aren't.	I know *que lo eran,* but now *no lo son.*
I'm not tall, but she is.	*Yo no soy* tall, but she *lo es.*
They're beautiful, but he isn't.	*Son* beautiful, but he *no lo es.*

Eventually this will become second nature in such phrases. For now, just get comfortable with *yo lo soy* and *yo no lo soy*, and we'll learn more applications of this structure in future lessons.

Subjunctive Uses

When we learned the "junk" (subjunctive) words *sea* and *seas*, we learned them in this structure: "I hope that he be tall".

I hope that he be tall.	I hope *que sea* tall.
I hope that you be nice.	I hope *que seas* nice.
I hope that he not be mean.	I hope *que no sea* mean.

Technically, we have two verbs in the sentence. The verb before the *que* is "I hope", and the phrase after the *que* is subjunctive. When Joel hopes something, he always uses a subjunctive.

But there are other situations that trigger the use of these strange words in Ser's back yard. One is when Joel expresses emotion about a fact. Instead of saying "How nice that it's you!", Joel says "How nice that <u>you be</u> you!"

How nice that it's you!	*¡Qué* nice *que seas* you!
How nice that it's her!	*¡Qué* nice *que sea* her!
How nice that it's me!	*¡Qué* nice *que sea yo*!

In this case, Joel isn't expressing intention. He's expressing emotion. But as you can see, the *sea* or *seas* still happens right after the connecting word *que*.

There are a few cases in which a subjunctive word doesn't have *que* before it. One is when Joel says "maybe".

| Maybe it be very late. | Maybe *sea* very late. |
| Maybe it be a mouse. | Maybe *sea* a mouse. |

Don't worry too much about the theory behind subjunctives. Just learn these four sentences, and practice modifying them a little, and then you'll be ready to move on to phrases using the forms of Ser that are not found on the ground.

Using Unconjugated Forms

Before we look at our examples of *ser*, *siendo*, and *sido*, it's important to clear something up. Students get *ser* and *siendo* confused a lot.

That's because they think that *siendo* translates directly to the English word "being". However, it turns out that the English word "being" is often translated as *ser*. Why is that?

Remember that the infinitive, *ser*, can be equivalent to a noun. Here's an example:

English: I love being a student.

Spanish: I love *ser* a student.

Why is this *ser* instead of *siendo*? Let's try the "noun test". Can we replace it with a noun, such as "food"?

I love *being a student*.

I love *food*.

As you can see, the phrase "I love" is followed by a noun. When I say "I love food", the word "food" is clearly a noun. It's the same thing when we talk about "being" something. If I love "being (something)", the phrase is exchangeable with a noun.

One more example:

Being a doctor is enjoyable.

Food is enjoyable.

Every time "food" works, it has to be *ser*, not *siendo*.

As always, don't stress about the theory too much. For now, focus on the sentence examples and get comfortable with them. Eventually this should become second nature.

A knight wanted to be king.	*Un* knight wanted *ser* king.
A knight wanted food.	*Un* knight wanted food.
I wanted to be a pilot.	I wanted *ser* a pilot.
My sister enjoys food.	My sister enjoys food.
My sister enjoys being a student.	My sister enjoys *ser* a student.
He likes food.	He likes food.
He likes being the boss.	He likes *ser* the boss.

We'll practice using the word *siendo* in only one context: Someone is "being" a certain way. This is often used in insults ("you're being a baby", "he's being a jerk", "they're being difficult", etc.).

You are being mean.	You are *siendo* mean.
He is being a baby.	He is *siendo* a baby.

You might notice that in that example, we have the word "are", which seems like a form of "to be". But that's not Ser. There's a different verb that we use before *siendo*, as we'll learn in Lesson 4.

As mentioned in the lesson, the word *sido* can be used to put Ser in the past for any person. We'll learn more about how this works in Lesson 6, but for now practice it in this sentence construct.

It's been very helpful.	It's *sido* very helpful.
I've been a good boy.	I've *sido* un good boy.
We've been good friends.	We've *sido* good friends.

Practice the Phrases

Between Lesson 1 and Lesson 2, you've learned about 30 sentences and phrases. It may seem like an intimidating list:

FROM LESSON 1	
He's taller than I.	He's taller *que yo.*
He was around there.	He was *por* there.
It has been this way for a while.	It has been this way *por un* while.
I'm going to your house too.	*Yo* also am going *a* your house.
I shouldn't get worried by those things.	*No* I should get worried *por* those things.
Because of this, she cannot be at his house.	*Por* this, she *no* can be *en* his house.
I don't have her.	*No la* I have.
My brother called me.	My brother *me* called.
Our father doesn't know it.	Our father *no lo* knows.
What can I do on behalf of Isabella?	*¿Qué* can I do *por* Isabella?
What luck!	*¡Qué* luck!
Why did she leave?	*¿Por qué* did she leave?

FROM LESSON 2	
You are very nice.	*Eres* very nice.
That is all.	That *es* all.
Valentina is that way.	Valentina *es* that way.
The house was his.	*La* house *era de* him.
The child was from another world.	*El* child *era de* another world.
Papa is the one that always gets worried.	Papa *es el que* always gets worried.
Who is it?	¿Who *es*?
It's me!	*¡Soy yo!*
I know that they were, but now they aren't.	I know *que lo eran,* but now *no lo son.*
I hope that he be tall.	I hope *que sea* tall.
How nice that it's you!	*¡Qué* nice *que seas* you!
Maybe it be very late.	Maybe *sea* very late.
A knight wanted to be king.	*Un* knight wanted *ser* king.
You are being mean.	You are *siendo* mean.
It's been very helpful.	It's *sido* very helpful.

But this isn't a textbook. I'm not going to make you sit and study a list.

Instead, after you've said these sentences a couple of times, you should practice using them in context.

Many of the phrases listed above can be found in the dialogue that we're studying. On the next five pages, you'll see the same dialogue that we used in Lesson 1, but this time you'll be able to understand the Ser conjugations.

To practice quizzing on the essential sentences and phrases, as well as explore Ser's shop to make sure it's in your long-term retention, go to SpanishIn1Month.com for the free materials that accompany this lesson.

- Hello, I'm Matías. Who is this?

- Hi Matías, it's me, Santiago.

- Santiago, all this time, ¿right?

- Yes I know! ¿How are you?

- Fine thanks, and you? ¿How is Isabella?

- Not so well, you know, she left her house.

- What! This isn't good at all.

- No, this time she doesn't have a place to be. You have to do her a favor, on my behalf.

- Yes, I want to be with her now. What can I do for Isabella or for you?

- You're very nice! I have her things at my house, as it should be, but…

- ¿Can I do something?

- I think so, it's a big deal.

- ¿But, why did she leave?

- She left, that's all... right, so, now we're going to do something when Valentina isn't around.

- ¿Valentina? But... why? If those two are like one, as you know, a...

- I know that they were, but now they aren't.

- Valentina is that way, and with her everything's like that, that's Valentina... And Sofía? She can...

- No, not Sofía, she isn't around.

- I am here, you are there... we're all here, the time is now.

- Maybe so, us both, with her. This time I don't know what to do.

- She can be at my house all the time. I can do you that favor, because I only want her to be well, and you to be well.

- That which was, is not anymore… now, everything's this way!

- Give it time. She's around, and her things at your house, at least it's something. And that gentleman?

That which **era**, **no es** anymore… now, everything **es** this way!

Give it time. She's around, **y** her things **en** your house, at least **es** something. ¿**Y** that gentleman?

- ¿Sebastián?

- I don't know, that man that was around with her at the house.

- Ah, yes, Sebastián, he isn't around anymore, and because of this she can't be at Mr. Sebastián's house.

¿Sebastián?

No lo I know, that man **que** was around with her **en la** house.

Ah, yes, Sebastián, he **no** is around anymore, **y por** this she **no** can be **en** Mr. Sebastián's house.

- ¿He isn't? ¿What do you mean he isn't around? ¿Really? That can't be, but if the house was his!

¿**No** he is? ¿What do you mean **no** he is around? ¿Really? **No** that can **ser**, but if **la** house **era de** him!

- He left from the house, that's the truth. This has been this way for a while now. I know that she's doing badly.

*He left **de la** house, that **es la** truth. This has been this way **por un** while now. I know **que no** she's doing well.*

- All right, well then, Isabella has been unwell for a while. Now we have to do something for her, I want to do something for her, both of us.

- Yes, I want... I'm leaving now, I'll go with Isabella.

All right, well then, **por un** while Isabella **no** has been well. Now we have to do something **por** her, **yo** want to do something **por** her, both of us.

Yes, I want... I'm leaving now, I'll go with Isabella.

- All right, I also will go to your house, I want to be with her.

All right, **yo** also will go **a** your house, I want to be with her.

LESSON 3

Focus on Location

Now that you're speaking sentences in genuine, perfect Spanish, you're ready to start loading up on vocabulary.

But there are dangers in learning words in bulk. How can you keep these words in permanent mental storage for a lifetime of use? And how will you remember where a word needs to be positioned in a phrase?

Lesson three will show you how you can always find the right word at the right moment.

THIS I YOU
THEM IT THIS
I YOU MY WHO
you're I'm you're
I'm you're you're
I'll you're I'll
you're I'm
serenading found let is are have rest miss getting is stop hate is tell parading
ballad National gallery sonnet top Nile mama Strauss Mahatma Gandhi Dante Durante balloon baby green
smile ditty rose time words wreck top bottom salary Napoleon Brandy least top Fred Astaire top tread salad Spain drama symphony color Tower of Pisa
light camembert cellophane dinner lout bar top bonnet chest feet Mickey Mouse melody flop Mona Lisa nose check coliseum top museum
Bendel toy Berlin Waldorf Louvre turkey derby summer Shakespeare O'Neill
Garbo's Inferno's Whistler's
if
so always how
instead just not
soon probably
as so not
lazy unexpressed pretty poetic total great pathetic fated
what a but till
ON OF ON OFF AT AT ABOUT ON OF FROM ON AT IN AT OF OF AT OF AT ON
the a the a the a the the a the a the the

Lesson 3 Theory:
Focus on Location

BETWEEN Lesson 1 and Lesson 2, you learned a total of 30 individual words.

In Lesson 3, we're picking up the pace. You'll be introduced to 25 new words, and several new grammatical concepts will crop up as well.

Meanwhile, you don't want your brain to become a junk heap of disorganized information. As you learn more and more Spanish, you must keep all the vocabulary and phrases clearly organized in your head.

There's a method to this, and you're about to learn it.

So before we learn any more words, I'm going to prove that even now, you do NOT have a horrible, disorganized memory. You actually have a phenomenally organized mind. You just have to

use it the way it wants to be used.

Let's see how amazing your brain is, and how you can use it to its fullest potential, not only for Spanish vocabulary, but for any information you want to learn.

The following story is not true. (I've endearingly titled it *Rolling in the Deep Kitchen Sink, or How to Lose Everything You Own*.)

Last Tuesday morning I woke up late, surprised to see the sun shining in my window. I panicked and looked at my phone. It wouldn't turn on. When I flipped open my computer to check the time, I saw that it was 8:30; I had slept in by over 3 hours. Apparently my phone had died during the night so the alarm never went off.

Oops.

My calendar told me that I had a meeting at 9:00 at a nearby coffee shop. I plugged in my phone, hoping it would charge quickly enough to give me time to request an Uber. Meanwhile I ran to the kitchen to prepare some breakfast.

I'm such an addict that I always have to have a cup of coffee, even before leaving the house to join a friend for more caffeine. (Otherwise I'm a complete zombie when I meet them.) So my mission was clear: I was about to see how quickly I could make coffee and fry eggs at the same time. What could possibly go wrong?

First I went to the kitchen sink and fished around for a coffee filter. I found one under a pile of spoons and forks, shook the dust off of it, and dropped it in the coffee maker.

Then I dug to the bottom of the sink and scooped out a handful of coffee beans with my left hand (scraping my finger slightly on a knife). I dropped the beans into the grinder and then ran to the bedroom to check on my phone.

It was just then booting up. After waiting a few seconds I sent out an Uber request, then rushed back to the kitchen to fry some eggs.

Fortunately, I had used the frying pan recently and found it near the top of the sink. A stick of butter happened to be just underneath it.

But eggs were a little harder to come by… at least, unbroken eggs were. Raw egg and shell pieces were scattered all throughout the sink, not really usable. Eventually I found three non-cracked specimens rolling around under an upside-down saucepan in a hard-to-reach corner.

I quickly fried them up, then wolfed down the result while clawing around in the sink for my hat. After hastily wash-ing the frying pan in the bathroom, I tossed it and everything else back into the kitchen sink on the way out the door.

As I stepped out I saw my Uber arriving. But unfortunately, when I turned around to lock the house, I realized that I'd forgotten something. I shouted to my driver that I'd be right back, then flew back inside to dig desperately around in the kitchen sink for my keys.

end of fictional story

Obviously, I don't really keep everything I own in the kitchen sink.

It turns out that cabinets, shelves, and drawers are a good idea. It's much easier to find things if we know where they are.

This demonstrates how powerful the human mind is. I bet that if I mention just about any household item to you, you'll know where it is normally kept in your house.

Spoons? In the silverware drawer, next to the forks.

Mugs? In the cabinet to the right of the kitchen sink.

Carrots? In a drawer in the refrigerator.

Scissors? In the bedroom, on the left side of the desk.

The notion of keeping everything we own in a single pile (or in the kitchen sink) is completely ridiculous.

But here's a serious question: Why do we do that with the things that we learn?

Why do we dump hundreds of facts, vocabulary words, and names into our heads, all in one pile… and then expect

to find the right piece of information when we need it?

Hmm. If only there was a way to organize your brain the way that your house is organized…

The Mental Matrix

Your mind is incredible. If it can store information about most of the locations in your house, it can do basically anything.

Try to imagine the different pieces of information in your house that you know. Assuming there are 10 rooms, and then each of those rooms has a few shelves and several

pieces of furniture, the math says that you have hundreds of locations already stored in your memory, and you can access them with your mind pretty quickly.

But this can apply to more houses as well. Think back to any other house you've lived in. If you lived in just one other house for a significant amount of time, that's already hundreds of more facts stored.

It doesn't end there. You also probably know your way around the houses of a few friends, as well as several dozen public buildings such as libraries, schools, and restaurants. Then there are larger outdoor areas such as parks (with details like benches and trees), streets you've driven down or walked along, and train stations. Not to mention fictional locations such as the workspace from The Office or Marty's house from Back to the Future.

If you can close your eyes

and imagine yourself walking around some of these places, it's clear that the universe in your head is incredibly vast.

It doesn't end there. I'm betting that you have some sort of memory attached to almost any of these locations, even down to some of the tiny details. When I think of the front left burner of my sister's stove, I remember that that's where I burned a pot of lentil soup. When I think of a particular platform in a subway station in Buenos Aires, I remember giving directions to someone who walked by.

These memories can be thought of as "facts". As you can see, we have millions of these facts stored in our heads. The steps for remembering them are simple: Just think of a particular location, and the memory comes back.

So you actually have an incredible memory! That's millions of pieces of information already in your brain, sorted and filed by location for easy access.

When you have trouble remembering something, it's often because you don't associate that thing with a unique location. If you have a location for something, you can remember it much more easily.

Maybe you lose your keys all the time. But that's not a problem with your memory; that's just because your keys don't have a consistent place where you can always find them. There are always dozens of places they could possibly be. But you never have trouble finding them if they're in the right pocket, in the proper drawer, or hanging on the hook where they belong.

Facts and memories are just like your keys. You'll lose them if you don't put them in a place that's easy to find.

Let's take this a step further. Maybe you think it's smart to leave your keys close to other things that you need when you go out of the house. You might hang them near your coat and hat, or perhaps you leave them on a table next to your wallet and cell phone.

That's a great habit. You're categorizing your keys with other items that you carry around. This is kind of like keeping your forks with the knives and spoons: You're categorizing them with the silverware.

You habitually know that it's good to have an organized system: Forks/knives/spoons the silverware drawer, keys/wallet/phone on the nightstand, clothing in the bedroom closet. Ultimately, hundreds of household items are sorted by category.

Let's go back to the subject of Spanish vocabulary.

Pretty soon we'll be learning hundreds of words. We can't afford to dump them all in the kitchen sink.

This whole book is designed as a manual to help you build a geographic world of vocabulary. A world where no word gets lost. A world so big that Joel can live in it and fly around it all day, picking different Spanish words based on what he needs at the time.

These words are intentionally placed in very specific locations for a carefully planned reason.

During this lesson, as well as the rest of the book, really try to immerse yourself. Make yourself truly at home in Joel's world. Get know it as well as you know your own house.

Lesson 3 Vocabulary:

Plaza
(the Neighborhood Marketplace)

ALL THROUGHOUT this lesson, we're going to revisit most of the locations that we used in Lesson 1, but we'll be adding more details to them.

Before we start, I strongly suggest that you do a little exercise. We need to ensure that you can remember your way around Joel's world just like you can remember your own house.

Look at the list of places that I've put below. For each one, close your eyes and mentally explore it. Make sure you can remember the words that belong to each area.

- amusement park: paths (1 word) and power lines (1 word)

- amusement park: carousel (2 words)

- amusement park: water slide (2 words)

- countryside: sheep pastures (5 words)

- countryside: tree scene (3 words)

- countryside: swamp (1 word)

- marketplace (1 word)

If you had trouble with that, you might want to review Lesson 1 really quickly. Flip through the Lesson 1 images and make sure each word is concretely stored in its location.

Meanwhile, for this lesson, make sure to focus and visualize everything even better than you did in Lesson 1. Immerse yourself in the environments until they feel almost as real as your own world.

Con Man (connectors)

When Joel returns to the amusement park today, he is resolved to have more fun than last time.

In Lesson 1, you might have noticed that Joel spent a lot of time between the rides, but he didn't seem to do much on the rides themselves. When gave the pandas a tour of the park,

between the rides, they occur at the rides themselves, usually when Joel is sitting on the rides. Grammatically speaking, these words are considered *prepositions*. These words happen at the rides, usually when you're sitting down, and "sit" sounds similar to the stressed syllable of the word *preposition*.

Today, Joel wants to spend more time sitting on the rides. We'll learn more prepositions today, especially on the longest, most exciting ride: The roller coaster.

But before Joel can go to the roller coaster, he has to drop the pandas off at the carousel. After leaving them there, he flies away from the carousel as quickly as he can.

Joel wants to go to the roller coaster, but his first priority is just to get away from the carousel as quickly as possible. He tells the pandas that he's "flying from the carousel" as fast as he can.

using the word *y* between each ride, he wasn't actually riding anything. It was the same with the word *que*. That was when he was between rides, choosing which one to go on.

The only ride that he actually rode on was the carousel, the one he doesn't like. There, he got stuck *en* (at) the ride, went away *de* (from) it as quickly as possible, flew *a* (to) the water slide, and cleaned the horse hair off his body by sitting in the water *por* (next to) the slide for a while.

The four words *en*, *de*, *a*, and *por* are in a special category. Instead of being

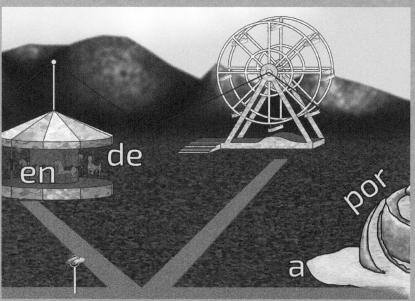

When Joel says "from the" carousel, you might think that he uses the words *de* (from) and perhaps *el* (the). But remember that Joel is in a hurry. He slurs his two words together, creating a new word: *del*.

The word *del* means "from the", and it sounds like *"de el"*. But it's a contraction; the two words are stuck together. In fact, Joel never, ever says *"de el"*. He always uses this word, *del*.

Joel is in such a hurry that he flies in the wrong direction. Before he knows it, he almost crashes into the water slide.

Joel realizes that he's made a mistake, and he says, "I didn't mean to go to the water slide!"

But when he says "to the water slide", he doesn't say *"a el* water slide", as you might expect. Instead, he says, "*al* water slide."

Once again, *al* is a result of Joel running his words together. It means "to the", or *"a el"*. But Joel never says *"a el"*. He always says *al*.

These new words are not entirely new; they're just slightly more complex versions of words that we already learned in Lesson 1. As you can see, we've stored *del* along with *de* at the carousel, and we've stored *al* along with *a* at the waterslide.

Even though Joel just flew *del* carousel *al* water slide, he really wants to go to the roller coaster. He flies over there and sneakily skips past the line.

As Joel enters, he notices a very interesting man sitting on the ride. This man's slicked-back hair, impeccable clothing, and suave mannerisms are attractive to Joel. He wants to get to know this guy.

Unfortunately, this man is actually

a con man who goes to the amusement park to find naïve victims. He grins as the wealthy bee scoots in next to him: Joel looks like an easy opportunity.

As you can see, Joel is riding the roller coaster "with" the con man. Joel's word for "with" is *con*.

As the ride starts, the con man asks Joel a question:

"You seem like a wealthy, respectable fellow. Do you ever play golf?"

Joel's ego is stroked by the flattery, so he feels like playing along: "Sure, I love golf! I'm really good at it, too."

The con man continues, "But you're not the best in the world, are you? Do you always make par?"

Joel hesitates. "Well, usually… not always." In reality, Joel rarely plays golf, and he's very bad at it.

The con man grins. "I have something that will make you so good at golf, you'll always make par. It's a special golf ball. No matter what course you visit, you'll make par every single time."

Joel is interested, but skeptical: "Has anyone else been able to prove this? How many other people have used this ball?"

"Oh, it's meant only for you!" says the con man. "Nobody else could ever use it. You're the person that this ball is intended for, and you're the only one who can use it to make par."

The con man convinces Joel that he's the only person who can make par using this ball, because it's intended for him. Since this golf ball is intended specifically for Joel, the word *para* is used. The stressed syllable sounds like "par", and the word mean "for" or "intended for". The ball is *para* Joel; it's not *para* anyone else.

Eventually, Joel is duped into spending most of his pocket money on this magical golf ball. The con man drops the ball into Joel's pocket and Joel walks away.

But when Joel pulls the "ball" out of his pocket, he discovers that it's just a pear!

Joel is infuriated, and he sputters: "But… but… it's just a pear!"

To say "but", Joel uses the word *pero*. The stressed syllable sounds like "pear".

But when Joel looks around, he doesn't see the con man anywhere. He mutters to himself, "I wish I could get my money back, *pero* it's too late."

Frustrated, Joel drops the pear on the ground. It rolls and hits a set of binoculars that are used to look around at the park.

These binoculars are an important feature of the park. They're near the middle of the connecting paths, and if you put a couple of coins in, you can use them to look around at the rides.

Joel wonders where the pandas are. He wants to leave and go home, but he needs to take the pandas with him. He left them at the carousel, but they might have gone to another ride by now.

Joel puts the last of his pocket change into the binoculars. He uses the binoculars to look around the park for the pandas.

These binoculars are often used in Joel's decision-making process, especially when the word "if" is involved. Thinking logically, Joel says to himself, "If I see the pandas at the carousel, I'll go there. But if I see them at the ferris wheel, I'll go there instead."

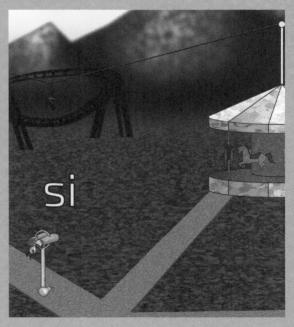

When he says "if", he uses the word *si*, which sounds like the English word "see". Since he doesn't like the carousel, he says to himself, "I'll only go to the carousel *si* I see the pandas there."

The word *si* means "if". It's used to connect phrases together logically.

In fact, since Joel is leaving the pear here at the binoculars, the word *pero* is stored here as well. Both *si* and *pero* are used in logical statements. For example, in the sentence "I'll be happy *si* you'll get here soon," you could grammatically exchange the word "if" for "but": "I'll be happy *pero* you'll get here soon."

It's important for you to notice that these words, *si* and *pero*, are not at the rides. Instead, they're between the rides. Joel uses them when he's trying to decide what he wants to do, just like the words *y* and *que*.

These words are called conjunctions. We'll be putting a lot more of them on the path between rides, or hanging them on the power lines. That will end up looking pretty messy, but unfortunately lots of people litter in this park, so the paths are sometimes referred to as "junk" paths. "Junk" is the stressed syllable of the word conjunction, just like "sit" is the stressed syllable of preposition.

For now, don't worry too much about the terms conjunction and preposition.

Instead, make sure you have a clear picture of the four words between rides (*pero*, *si*, *y*, and *que*,) and the eight words that are at the rides (*con*, *para*, *en*, *de*, *del*, *a*, *al*, and *por*). Remember where each word is and what it means. The location matters more than you might think.

Fence Art (articles)

Speaking of locations, Joel is so upset about being ripped off that he decides to leave the amusement park. As always, he has to walk through the countryside to get home.

Let's quickly recap what we've learned about the sheep pastures. Joel introduced himself as *yo* here, which means "I". Meanwhile, the words for "the" and "a" are artistically spray-painted on the fence posts.

These are two different categories of words. The words on the posts are called *articles* (stressed syllable: "art"), which means they're used before a noun, such as "*la* woman" or "*un* man".

But the word that Joel calls himself is a *subject pronoun*, which means that it's usually used all by itself as the subject of a sentence. In other words,

yo actually serves as another name for Joel. These other words are just labels or "articles", so they're painted on the fences.

Today we'll use the fence art to learn two more articles.

Joel sees that the female sheep are all lost. He tells the shepherd, "Hey, the sheep are gone!"

The shepherd is startled awake. He takes quick inventory of the male sheep, which is what he was doing before he fell asleep. When he sees that they are all there, he tells Joel, "What? I can see all those sheep," pointing at the male sheep. "What are you talking about?"

"No, no," says Joel, "I'm not talking about *los* sheep, I'm talking about *las* sheep."

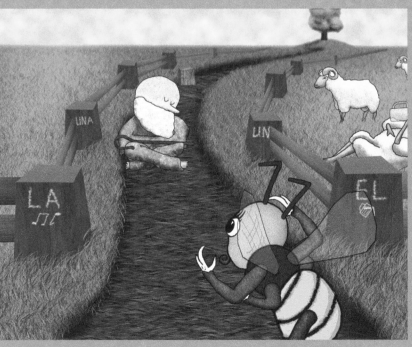

Looking at the left side, the shepherd sees that sure enough, all the female sheep escaped while he was occupied with counting the male sheep.

The word *las*, which sounds like "lost", means "the". But it's used when there are more than one. So "*la* sheep" means "the sheep" (singular), but "*las* sheep" means "the sheep" (plural). Joel is referring to all the female sheep.

Meanwhile, *los* means "the", but it's masculine. It sounds kind of like "those".

To represent this, Joel paints the words *las* and *los* on the fences. "*Las* sheep" are the female sheep, and "*los* sheep" are the male sheep.

Then Joel notices a short post sticking up in the middle of the path. He asks the shepherd, "What is that fence post for?"

The shepherd responds, "Oh yes, it's very inconvenient, sitting in the middle of the path like that."

Of course, this doesn't answer Joel's question. He demands, "But what is it? What's it for?"

"It's short and useless, and I trip over it all the time. And it's way too low to be useful as a fence."

Joel is frustrated. The shepherd has described it as inconvenient, short, useless, and "low", but he hasn't said what it is or what it does. Apparently this post doesn't do anything, and it isn't called anything.

Since Joel has his spray can out, he goes over to the post and sprays a word on it: "*Lo*".

Then he tells the shepherd, "I don't understand why you even have the inconvenient, the useless, the short, the 'low' at all."

112

When Joel says these phrases, he uses the word *lo*: "*Lo* inconvenient, *lo* useless, *lo* short."

The word *lo* here is used to mean "the", but as you can see, there's no noun in any of these phrases. All nouns in Spanish are either feminine or masculine. But this fence post is used when there's no noun at all.

This is actually pretty common in Spanish. For example, Joel might invite a friend over for dinner but realize that he has no food. English speakers might say "The difficult thing is that we have no food." Joel would simply say "The difficult is that we have no food."

So as you can see, *lo* is in two locations. We have it on the hill in the distance to mean "him" or "it", but here it means "the" when there's no noun. Just like *la* was in two locations

for two completely different meanings, *lo* is in two locations because it's basically two different words.

The shepherd now suggests that they go and sing a hymn, praying that the sheep will come back. They both go to the hilltop, which is the location where we learn <u>direct objects</u>.

Tea and Hymn (direct objects)

The shepherd starts to talk to Joel about the hymn they're about to sing, but Joel isn't listening. He has no interest in hymns or prayers.

But at the same time, the shepherd's tea kettle is heating up in the hot sun. When it begins boiling and starts to whistle, Joel gets excited and interrupts the shepherd:

"Do you hear that? It's tea!"

The shepherd pauses for a second. He is clearly disappointed in Joel. "Have you been listening to me?" he asks. "Do you even hear what I'm saying?"

"Of course," Joel lies to the shepherd, "*Te* I hear."

Joel meant to say "I hear you", but he accidentally said "*te* I hear." The word *te* means "you" as a direct object, and it sounds kind

of like "tea" (but it's pronounced more like "teh").

The word *te* is the only word we're learning in this direct object scene, but let's do a quick recap of how these words work. They're all similar to the word "him" in English. (Maybe it helps that this is where the shepherd always likes to sing "hymns").

In English, we say "they found him", but Joel says "*lo* they found." All four words in this scene work the same way: You can also say "*me* they found", "*la* they found", or "*te* they found" (they found you).

As you'll see soon, Joel will continue to call the shepherd *te* a lot of the time, even though that's not his name. He does it teasingly, because he thinks of the shepherd as his source of tea.

Meanwhile, the shepherd gives up on singing hymns. He tells Joel, "It's time to go look for the lost sheep."

As shepherd gets up to go, he almost forgets the kettle of tea. Joel picks it up, saying, "I think I'll carry this for you so you don't get tired." The two of them continue along the path.

Indirect Paths

The path that Joel and the shepherd are following gets confusing. When it ran past the tree on the hill, it was very direct: It just went straight. But as it continues through the countryside, it begins branching off in different directions.

Joel and the shepherd stop when they encounter a four-way crossing. The shepherd ponders: "Which way would the female sheep go?"

This scene is the location where we store <u>indirect objects</u>. You'll learn what that means soon.

As the shepherd wonders where to go, one of the lost sheep shows up and lies down on the left side. The shepherd is excited, and he asks the sheep, "Where are all of your friends?"

But the sheep is exhausted from running around, and it has fallen asleep.

The shepherd tells Joel, "She lay down. Quick, we need to wake her up. Give some tea to the sheep that lay down!"

Joel hasn't been paying attention. He's just been staring covetously at the tea pot in his hands this entire time. When he hears the shepherd make this demand, Joel snaps back: "No! I won't give the tea to her!"

To say "to her", he refers to the sheep as *le*: "*Le* I won't give the tea!"

He calls her *le* because she's the sheep that "lay down". The word *le* basically means "to her".

Suddenly, Joel's friend the lizard shows up, coming from the right side

Joel tells the shepherd, "*Le* I'll give the tea," pointing at the lizard. If Joel gives tea to his friend, maybe they can both steal it and take it back to Joel's house.

To say "to him", Joel uses the exact same word as "to her"; *le* can mean both of these things. So as you'll see, *le* is on both the left side (for the sheep) and on the right side (for the lizard).

The shepherd glares at Joel sternly. "Look, you bee," says the shepherd.

"If you obey me, just this once, I can give you so much tea that you'll never steal from me again."

This gets Joel's attention. Just how wealthy is this shepherd? An unlimited supply of tea sounds amazing!

"Okay," says Joel, finally agreeing. "*Te* I'll give the tea." And he gives the teapot back to the shepherd. "But only if you promise that *me* you'll give lots of tea."

The words *te* and *me* can mean "to you" and "to me".

You might find this confusing, because we already learned *te* and *me* on the hill (the direct object scene). But remember the importance of location. The words that you've learned here at the crossroads scene are different

words, with a different meaning, even though they're spelled and pronounced the same way.

The words under the tree are used when someone is directly affected. For example, "I see him" is "*lo* I see". All the other words in that scene can be used in the same way: "*la* I see", "*te* I see", and "*me* I see".

But the words here at the crossroads are used when someone is the recipient of something. For example, "I gave a book to her" is "*Le* I gave a book." As you can see, the word is still at the beginning of the sentence, before the verb, but it's different from *la* because it's a different kind of object pronoun.

If this seems to be getting technical, don't worry. We'll learn exactly how to use these words later.

For now, just make sure that you know which words go in which locations: On the hill, we have *lo*, *la*, *me*, and *te*. But at the indirect crossroads we have *le*, *le*, *me*, and *te*.

The shepherd can't get the sheep to respond, so he and Joel continue along one of the paths.

A Reflexive Stream

The path ends at an enchanted stream that runs through a meadow. When Joel and the shepherd look down at the water, but the stream magically alters some of the reflections.

First of all, Joel looks into the water, sees his own face, and says, "I see myself." To say this, Joel says "*Me* I see."

In this case, the word *me* means "myself". Even though it looks and sounds the same as the *me* on the hill and the *me* at the crossroads, this is a completely different word, because it's in a different location. Instead of meaning "me" or "to me", this word means "myself".

When Joel sees the shepherd's reflection, he laughs. Instead of the shepherd's face, the reflection in the stream displays the image of a large, brown tea bag.

"Do you see yourself? Your face looks like a tea bag!"

To say "You see yourself," Joel says "*Te* you see." The word *te*, in this case, means "yourself".

But the strangest thing of all is what has happened to the objects that they're holding. In the water, the shepherd's staff appears as a giant mouth. This mouth seems like it's trying to say something.

This makes Joel wonder if the staff is alive. After all, he did hear it singing "laa" earlier! Is it now trying to communicate some message, using its magical reflection?

Joel wonders, "Does it see itself in the water?"

He continues staring at the mouth that's trying to *say* something. To say "It sees itself," Joel says "*Se* it sees." The word *se* means "himself".

Meanwhile, Joel also looks at the reflection of the the teapot that he is holding. It also looks like a mouth that's trying to say something.

So we have three words here: *me* for "myself", *te* for "yourself", and *se*, which means "itself", "herself", or "himself".

These words are called *reflexive* pronouns, because they indicate that someone is doing something to himself. For example, "I hurt myself" is "*me* I hurt," and "he hurt himself" is "*se* he hurt."

Before proceeding, stop for a second. There are three or four words in each of the last three locations: The direct object scene (with the tree), the indirect object scene (with the crossroads), and the reflexive object scene (with the stream). Go back in your mind and make sure you know each word in its location.

Later we'll see many real-life examples of all of these pronouns. For now, Joel and the shepherd are bored of their reflections, so let's go on to the next scene.

118

Ace on the Lake ("this" and "that")

Joel and the shepherd follow the stream until it flows into a lake.

This is a very calm and tranquil scene, and Joel pauses to take it in. Even though he's a very mischievous and immoral bee, there's one good thing that can be said about him: He knows how to enjoy the beautiful things in life.

But on second glance, the lake isn't as perfect as it might be. There's something floating in the middle of the water, and it looks like a littered playing card.

This upsets Joel: "What is THAT?"

The shepherd responds, "It's an ace, of course." Sure enough, the thing floating on the water is a playing card, specifically the ace of spades.

When Joel says "What is that," he uses the word *eso*. Joel uses this word a lot when he's not sure what something is, and the stressed syllable sounds like "ace".

"¿Qué es eso?"

Interestingly, this is an entire sentence that is within your vocabulary. You'll see many more sentences like this in the near future.

Joel moves toward the lake to get a closer look, but he trips over something in the grass. It seems to be a nest of Easter eggs, which Joel finds strange.

"What is this?" he asks. To say this, he says *"¿Qué es esto?"*

The word *esto* sounds kind of like "Easter", and it means "this".

Joel examines the nest and picks up one of the eggs. It's shiny and magenta. Joel thinks it's beautiful, and he says, "I like this thing!"

But to say "this thing", he says *"esta* thing".

The word *esta* means "this", but it specifically refers to feminine nouns. As you can see, Joel is holding it in his left hand. So for example, if he is talking about a female sheep, he might say *"esta* sheep" ("this sheep").

Meanwhile, the words *esto* and *eso* don't have a gender. They're stuck in the middle, without an identity, and they're often used in questions such as "what is this?" or "what is that?"

These are the only three words we're learning here for today, but make sure to have them clear. To avoid confusing *esto* with *eso*, remember that *eso* refers to the "ace" further in the distance, so it means "that". But *esto* refers to the "Easter" nest closer up, so it means "this". You'll use *esto* for something that's close and *eso* for something that's further away.

Before we go on, there's yet another thing to make sure you remember about locations. We've already learned the word *que* to mean "that". This confuses a lot of English speakers. Why are there two words for "that"?

It's because English has one word for two completely different things. When we say "I hope *that* he's

120

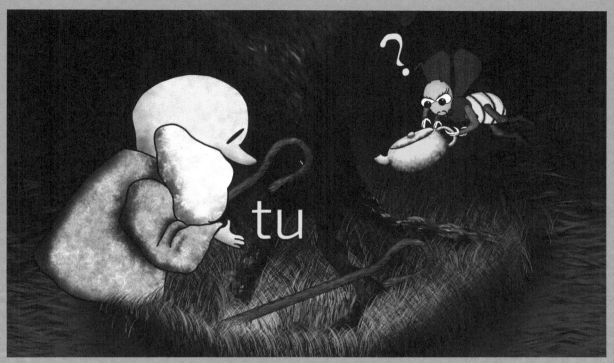

OK," we're using a connector. But when we say "I like that," we're using "that" to indicate an actual thing.

The word *que* was in the amusement park, and it's the connector: "I hope *que* he's OK."

But the word *eso* is here at the lake, and it serves as a noun: "I like *eso*."

Joel wants to get home now, so let's go to one more location that we haven't seen in the countryside: The woods.

Possessed in the Woods

Every time that Joel and the shepherd end up walking together, the woods is where they always have their final argument before parting ways.

Joel tells the shepherd, "All right, it's time to split. How about I take the tea and you take the staff, and it's fair. OK?"

But the shepherd isn't listening, because he's found something interesting: There's a stick lying on the ground, and it looks just like the one he's holding.

"Aha, here's my staff," says the shepherd.

This confuses Joel. How is that the shepherd's staff? Does the shepherd have two staffs?

"Wait, that's your staff?" he asks. But when he says this, he's thinking about the word "two", so he says, "That's *tu* staff?" The word *tu* means "your".

Then the shepherd says to Joel, "Can you give me back my tea now?"

Joel wants to keep the tea, so he says, "No, the tea is for ME! It's *my* tea!" But instead of "my tea", Joel says "*mi* tea".

The word *mi* sounds like the English word "me" (and rhymes with "tea"). It's a very selfish-sounding word that Joel uses all the time to talk about his things: "*mi* house", "*mi* stuff", "*mi* car", and so on.

"I'll give you tea later," promises the shepherd. "But I do need the kettle. I'll see you tomorrow. Right now, I have a lawsuit to resolve."

The shepherd spends a lot of his spare time suing other people in Yol. This is how the shepherd has gotten all of

his wealth: Although he refers to his possessions as his own (the sheep, the staff, and the teapot), they used to belong to other people. He's been finding creative ways to get other people's possessions by suing them.

Joel asks, "What are you hoping to get out of this case?"

The shepherd responds, "Actually, this tree right here. My neighbors own this tree, but I'd like to build a treehouse in it if I win this lawsuit."

Joel refers to the tree as "*su* tree". Currently it's not the shepherd's tree (*tu* tree) and it's not Joel's tree (*mi* tree). It's "their tree", which is "*su* tree".

The word *su* can actually mean "his", "her", or "their". It's used for basically anything that's owned by anyone

other than the shepherd or Joel.

With that, the shepherd takes the kettle back and walks away.

Joel looks around the woods a little before he proceeds to the marketplace. This location is where Joel and the shepherd emphasize what they own. "*Mi* tea" means "my tea", "*tu* tea" means "your tea", and "*su* tea" means "his tea", "her tea", or "their tea".

Before moving on to the marketplace, quickly revisit all of this lesson's countryside locations in your mind. Make sure you can remember the words in every scene.

Comb Like a Con Man (adverbs)

Joel often goes through the marketplace to get home. In Lesson 1, he was in a hurry, and the only thing we learned was the word *no* for "not".

But today, Joel has decided that he does want to look around and see what the vendors have to offer. So when they ask him, "Do you want to see what we have to sell?", Joel answers "yes".

To say "yes", Joel uses the word *sí*. This means something like "yes", but not exactly. It also means something like "indeed". Basically, it's

exchangeable with the word *no* ("not") to mean the opposite. For example:

"I *no* want to buy something." (I don't want to buy something.)

"I *sí* want to buy something." (I do want to buy something.)

"He *no* was happy." (He wasn't happy.)

"He *sí* was happy." (He was happy.)

There's no way to translate these sentences completely literally. Just remember that next time you use *no* in Spanish to mean "not", practice switching it out for *sí* to mean the opposite. You'll see more examples when we look at phrases.

Notice that Joel goes up to the top of the statue in the middle of the plaza. He's looking around to "see" what he indeed wants to buy (what he *sí*

wants to buy). Meanwhile, the word *no* is stored on the ground behind the statue, which is where Joel wants to be if he doesn't want to buy anything. In future lessons, we're going to keep using the statue for yes/no words.

But there are other places in the marketplace that we'll use for other things. When he looks around the plaza, the different types of food are sorted by category. There's the "Fresh Flesh" meat stand, where Joel buys one of his favorite foods: Steak. Next, "Grains Today Without Delay!" is where Joel tries to buy bread. "Foreign Fruits" sells an entire catalogue of fruits from many different locations around the planet. "Quality Vegetables", run by a gardening monkey, sells other kinds of produce.

Let's jump in and start with steak. (BTW, you're about to see one of my favorite mnemonics in the whole book.)

Joel is dubious of the quality of the steak. Something smells strange. So he asks the butcher, "How fresh is this steak?"

"Oh, it's VERY fresh," responds the butcher.

"How fresh?" asks Joel.

Suddenly, he hears a "Moooo!" sound coming from the steak. It sounds like a cow mooing.

Wow, the steak must be very fresh if it's mooing! The butcher emphasizes, "It's *muy* fresh."

The word *muy* means "very". I have to point out that many English speakers mispronounce this word, saying "moy" (like "boy"). This is an error that we make because the "oy" sound is so common in English. It's not as common in Spanish.

To avoid this mistake, always remember the "moo" sound, like a cow, to emphasize that something is "*muy* fresh".

As you might imagine, this is a <u>very</u> common adverb (a *muy* common adverb). You're likely to use it quite frequently. Fortunately, it's pretty easy to use, because it corresponds directly with the English word "very".

Before moving on from the steak stand, note that this is where we'll

learn adverbs related to <u>degree</u>. For example, a person can be "very tall" (*muy* tall), but they can also be "kinda tall", "less tall", "more tall", and so on. Anything that can be exchanged with "very" will be kept here.

Right now, we don't have any more words at "Fresh Flesh", so we'll move on to the bread stand. This place is interesting, because there's a very strange dynamic between Joel and the baker, based on two funny facts:

First, even though this stand is called "Grains Today Without Delay", the baker is actually reluctant to sell his bread. He's a complete hypocrite, and he always has some sort of excuse for not selling anything. In fact, Joel has never, ever seen him make a sale.

Second, Joel himself doesn't even like bread (or grains of any kind). But at the same time, he comes to this stand all the time with mischievous motives. It's a challenge: Will he succeed in convincing the baker to sell something today?

So the baker doesn't want to sell anything, and Joel doesn't like bread but tries to buy from him anyway. This makes for some interesting stories.

Today, Joel is not successful. As soon as he comes to the grains stand and asks if he can buy bread, the baker recognizes Joel and knows what he's up to.

"Oh, sorry, it's too late. The stand is now closed."

Joel says, "Already?"

"*Ya*," says the baker. The store is closed… *YA!*"

As he says "ya!", he slams down the sliding front of the stand.

He does this so hastily, he doesn't even think about the fact that he's left a knife in a piece of bread sticking off the front of the stand. As the cover comes down, it hits the knife, which cracks this wooden cover. The point of the knife is still sticking out the front of the stand.

The word *ya* is very confusing for English speakers, even though it's the most frequently used adverb related to time. In English, our favorite time-related adverb is "now", as in "now I'm at home" or "now the store is closed." But that word doesn't translate directly into Spanish.

The word *ya* basically means that something has just changed. Many people translate it as "already", but that doesn't usually work. *Ya* actually means something more like "anymore".

Let's stop being abstract and use an example. When the baker slammed the stand closed, he said that the store is "*ya* closed." That can mean "already closed". Most Spanish speakers would say "*Ya* the store is closed" to mean "now the store is closed" or "already the store is closed". As you can see, *ya* tends to happen at the beginning of a sentence.

They would also say "*Ya* the store isn't open", which means "The store isn't open anymore." Once again, it occurs at the beginning of the sentence, but in this case we'd translate it as "anymore" rather than "already".

Ya the store is closed: The store is closed "already".

Ya the store is closed: "Now" the store is closed.

Ya the store isn't open: The store isn't open "anymore".

126

So *ya* basically means "anymore", "already", or in some cases "now". It generally indicates that something recently changed, and it emphasizes the point at which the change occurred, kind of like the point of the knife that's sticking out of the baker's stand.

As another example, the baker might say, "I'm not selling bread anymore" with the phrase "*Ya no* I'm selling bread." And then he might say, "Now I'm going home": "*Ya* I'm going home." In both cases, it indicates that something has just recently changed.

We'll learn more nuanced uses of this word later. For now, just remember that it's our first adverb related to time, and it's here at the baker's stand.

Joel is a bit upset that the stand isn't open anymore, so he goes over to the next place in the plaza.

At "Foreign Fruits", Joel asks the merchant if they have any fruit from Mount Ría, one of the most mysterious foreign places on the planet of Yol.

"Yes, I think so," says the clumsy merchant. "Let me see, I think we keep it in a locked drawer, back… hmm, where's the key?"

Joel rolls his eyes and points to something that's sticking out of a fruit, right in front of the merchant's nose.

"What's that?" Joel asks.

"Oh, it's *aquí*!" says the merchant.

The word *aquí* sounds like "a key", and it means "here". So "it's *aquí*" means "it's here". We represent this word using a key sticking out of a fruit in the middle of this basket.

As you can see, the word *aquí* would answer the question, "Where is it?" The Foreign Fruit stand is the scene where we'll keep all adverbs related to location, such as "here", "there", "inside", "outside", and so on: Anything that answer a "where?" question.

127

context. You're very likely to hear this word along with **muy** if you ask someone how they're doing: ***"Muy bien."*** ("Very well.")

This word can also be used to describe how pretty much anything is happening. For example, "How is the vegetable business going?" "Oh, it's going **bien**."

We'll continue to use this stand to answer the question "how?"

Joel asks this question when he sees the gardener's hair. It looks really cool to Joel's eyes: parted in the middle and heavily greased (kind of like the con man's hair). Joel asks, "How can I get hair like that?"

Next Joel goes over to the "Quality Vegetable" stand. Since Joel is very money-minded, the first thing he notices is the can where the gardener receives cash. This gardener is proud of the fact that he accepts many kinds of currency; Joel notices the symbols for US dollars and British pounds. But what about Yen?

Joel asks, "It is OK for me to pay in Yen, right?"

The vendor says, "Oh yes! That would be **bien**."

Bien literally means "well". It can also mean "fine", depending on the

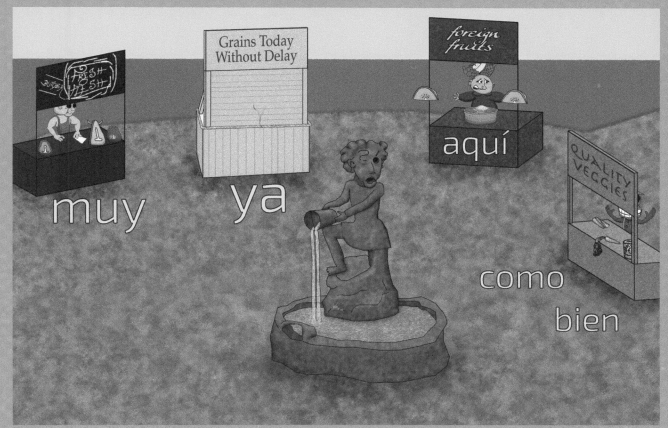

The gardener answers, "That's easy: Just comb it as I do!" And then he pulls out a comb and proceeds to comb the leaves of a carrot in the middle of the stand.

But here's how he says it: "Just comb it *como* I do."

The word *como* (with the stressed syllable "comb") basically means "as". But in English, we often change this word out for "how" or "like":

Comb it <u>as</u> I do.

Comb it <u>like</u> I do.

Comb it <u>how</u> I do.

In each of these cases, you could use the word *como*. For now, remember that it means "as", but remember that it can also be translated as "how" or "like".

Joel is discouraged. Personally, he doesn't have hair, so he has nothing to comb. Upset about this, he flies home without buying anything.

Before we follow Joel home, take a quick look around the marketplace at the different stands. See if you can remember how each of these adverbs is used.

Then close your eyes and walk around the plaza, recalling each location in your imagination. If you can remember each word, you're ready to move on and see Joel's house for the first time.

Home at Last

Take a look at the map of Yol found on the following page. Let's quickly review the major locations on the map.

When we first started exploring Joel's world, we began at the amusement park, up in the northwest, where we store connecting words. We also visited the countryside where we store pronouns, and by the time the lesson was over, we had just barely made it to the marketplace, where we store adverbs.

But today, we've finally come all the way

to Joel's home. Here we store two types of words we've never seen before: Adjectives in the yard and nouns inside the house. We'll look at just one of each.

On the driveway is a blue car. Joel loves his car, and he considers it to be the standard of all beauty, comparing anything else he sees to this car.

In fact, he idolizes this gorgeous car so much that he never even drives it! So it simply sits on his driveway, growing moss.

Every time Joel comes home, he sees that there's more moss on his car. His word for "more" is *más*.

Next we'll go inside. Joel's house is full of many strange things, and we'll explore a lot of them later in the book. For now, we'll go straight to his bedroom.

As you can see, Joel has many objects crowding all around his bed, which must make it hard to sleep. But the most distracting thing of all is probably the crowd of toads all over the floor. These toads almost completely cover the floor, making it nearly impossible to walk across the room without stepping on them.

The word *todo* (with the stressed syllable "toad") means "all". When Joel says "All the floor is covered with toads", he says "*Todo* the floor is covered with toads."

In future lessons, we'll be using Joel's bedroom to learn words related to amounts or parts of something. The most common of these nouns is "all".

Just like in English, this word is usually used before a noun that's preceded by the article "the", as in "all the things" or "all the people". We'll see this as we learn phrases in the next section.

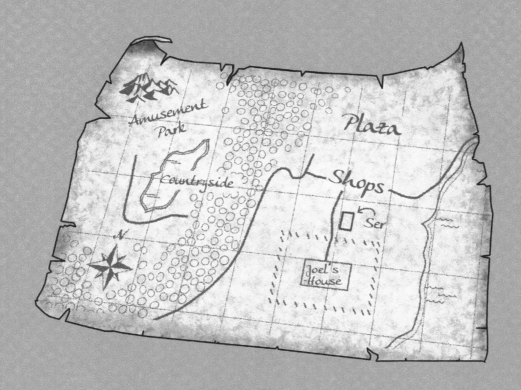

Lesson 3 Application:
Thinking in Spanish

IN LESSON 2, we started customizing sentences, switching out equivalent words as if playing with a "potato head" toy. We mostly did it with conjugations of Ser. But now we're going to practice changing all kinds of words to create our own sentences.

How do you know which words you can switch out? Simply use words from identical places in Joel's world. For example, check out this sentence:

I'll give him the name of the place.

Le I'll give *el* name *del* place.

Since the word *le* is being used, you know that this is an indirect object. So any word in the indirect object scene will work (the scene at the crossroads). So you can exchange *le* for *me* or *te*, and it will still make grammatical sense.

This goes for pretty much all the different areas of Yol. If the word *de* is used, you know that you can switch it out for *por* or *en*, which are other prepositions (at the amusement rides), and the sentence structure will still be grammatically correct.

Use the sentences below the highlighted sentences as examples for how to modify the originals. But for memorization purposes, make sure you always go back to the original highlighted sentence and practice that the most. These sentences will keep coming up in future lessons and in the dialogues that we study.

Conjunctions

If you tell me.	*Si me* you tell.
If you help me.	*Si me* you help.
But you tell me.	*Pero me* you tell.
And you help me.	*Y me* you help.

Remember that conjunctions are located between rides. These words can generally be used between entire sentence structures. Notice how the next examples use two different sentences, joined by a conjunction between them.

He is very confident, but I'm not.	*Es muy* confident, *pero yo no lo soy.*
He's not tall, but I am.	*No es* tall, *pero yo lo soy.*
He's very confident if I am.	*Es muy* confident *si yo lo soy.*

| It would be strange if I saw you around here. | *Sería* strange *si te* I saw *por aquí.* |
| It would be strange if you were around here. | *Sería* good *si* you were *por aquí.* |

Prepositions

Prepositions, located at the rides themselves, are used right before nouns. They can't be used to join sentences together, but they point directly to a person or a thing in the sentence. Notice that there's always a noun (or pronoun) after each preposition in these examples (right after *del*, *al*, and *para*).

I'll give him the name of the place.	*Le* I'll give *el* name *del* place.
I'll give you the man's book.	*Te* I'll give *el* book *del* man.
He'll give me the boy's apple.	*Me* he'll give *la* apple *del* boy.

I'm going to go to the place.	I'm going to go *al* place.
We're going to the hospital with Sofia.	We're going *al* hospital *con* Sofia.
We're going to the house with Camila.	We're going *a la* house *con* Camila.

| The hardest for me is not to worry. | *Lo más* difficult *para* me *es no* to worry. |
| The gift for me is beautiful. | *El* gift *para* me *es* beautiful. |

Remember that *ser* can be treated as a noun. So logically, we should be able to use a preposition right before it. In fact, it's common to do that, especially with the word *para*. When *para* is used before an infinitive (like *ser*), it means "in order" to do something.

I did it in order to be the first.	*Lo* I did *para ser* the first.
He did it in order to be the winner.	*Lo* he did *para ser* the winner.
She did it in order to be your favorite.	*Lo* she did *para ser* your favorite.

The next example is more complicated, and it uses *para que*, which needs even more explanation.

As you know, prepositions like *para* are normally followed by either a noun (e.g. *para* the boy) or an infinitive (e.g. *para ser* the first).

But sometimes it's possible for an entire phrase to be treated as a noun, IF the sentence is preceded by *que* ("that"). For example, "that you should be first" can be thought of as a noun. To understand this, try out these sentences:

Noun: I like <u>food.</u>

Infinitive: I like <u>being a bee.</u>

"That" phrase: I like <u>that you should be first.</u>

In the last case, we replaced "food" with "that you should be first". Here are those same sentences, but in Spanish:

Noun: I like <u>food.</u>

Infinitive: I like *<u>ser</u>* <u>a bee.</u>

Que phrase: I like *<u>que seas</u>* <u>first.</u>

Bear with me a little longer. If "food", "*ser* a bee", and *"que seas* first" can all be treated as nouns, we should be able to use any of these after a preposition like *para*. Try this out:

Noun: I did it *para* <u>food.</u>

Infinitive: I did it *para <u>ser</u>* <u>a bee.</u>

Que phrase: I did it *para <u>que seas</u>* <u>first.</u>

I know that about 10% of you are fascinated by this, and the other 90% are either confused or bored. So instead of beating this out any further, I'll ask that you practice this with one highlighted sentence:

I did it in order that you should be the first.	*Lo* I did *para que seas* the first.
He did it for his mother.	*Lo* he did *para* his mother.
He did it in order that he should be the first.	*Lo* he did *para que sea* the first.
You did it in order to be the first.	*Lo* you did *para ser* the first.

Now that we've spent lots of time on *para*, let's revisit the complicated word *por*.

Remember that *por* often indicates the source of something. For example, "The book is by an Argentinian author": "The book *es por un* Argentinian author."

But it can be translated more roughly to mean "because of". For example, I might say that I was late "because of" a delayed flight: "I was late *por un* delayed flight."

That's why *"¿por qué?"* means "why?"; you're essentially asking "because of what?"

Question: *"¿Por qué* were you delayed?"

Answer: *"Por* a delayed flight."

This is important for a very common idiom we're about to learn. When you combine *por* with *eso*, you get the phrase "because of that". This phrase is idiomatically equivalent to the English phrase "that's why…" at the beginning of a sentence.

For example:

English: "Our father still doesn't know, and that's why my brother is so worried."

Spanish: "Our father still doesn't know, *y por eso* my brother is so worried."

It's like saying, "and for that reason my brother is so worried." But of course in these cases we would more commonly say "that's why". In Spanish, they just use *por eso*.

But our father still doesn't know it, and that's why my brother is so worried.	*Pero* our father *no lo* knows still, *y por eso mi* brother is so worried.
But my mother still doesn't know it, and that's why I'm so worried.	*Pero mi* mother *no lo* knows still, *y por eso* I'm so worried.

Articles

Let's review the phrases *el que* and *la que*, which mean "the one that".

Papa is the one that always gets worried.	Papa *es el que* always gets worried.
Mom is the one that keeps calm.	Mom *es la que* keeps calm.
I'm the one that made dinner.	*Yo soy el que* made dinner.
You're the one that was there.	You *eres la que* was there.

In this lesson, we learned that *lo* is sometimes used as an article, kind of like *el* and *la*, when there's no noun. It turns out that one of the most common uses is in the phrase *lo que*.

Normally, the way to translate *lo que* is to mean "what". But it's not in a question (that would be *qué*). Instead, it's used to connect two parts of a sentence, just like *el que* and *la que*, without being specific.

Here's a simple example. If Joel is ordering food in a restaurant and he sees that the lizard got something really tasty, he might say, "I want what he has." This would be "I want *lo que* he has."

Of course, if Joel is more specific, he might say "I want the dish that he has", or "I want the tea that he has", or "I want *the one that* he has", in which case he would use *el que* or *la que*. But when you just use "what" in the middle of a sentence, you normally use *lo que*.

I am what I am.	*Soy lo que soy.*
It is what it is.	*Es lo que es.*
I want what he has.	I want *lo que* he has.
It's what I want.	*Es lo que* I want.

Direct objects

I'll help you.	*Te* I'll help.
I'll help him.	*Lo* I'll help.
She'll help me.	*Me* she'll help.
He'll help her.	*La* he'll help.

Indirect objects

Generally, indirect object pronouns such as *le* (words from the crossroads scene) are used when someone receives something.

You have to do her a favor.	*Le* you have to do *un* favor.
They did him a favor.	*Le* they did *un* favor.
They gave you a house.	*Te* they gave *una* house.
They'll give me this.	*Me* they'll give *esto*.

Sometimes the "thing" that someone receives is not a physical object. A common example is when someone says something to somebody. "I'll give him something" is "*Le* I'll give something", and "I'll tell him something" is "*Le* I'll tell something".

The next example begins with "I said to him", which is "*Le* I said". But you may find what he says confusing. We have an odd phrase, "*sea lo que sea*". This is impossible to translate; it sounds like "be what it be". This is how Spanish speakers say "whatever it is". Say it a few times to get used to it.

I said to him, "Whatever it is, I'll help you."	*Le* I said, "*Sea lo que sea, te* I'll help."
He said to me, "Whatever it is, I'll help you."	*Me* he said, "*Sea lo que sea, te* I'll help."
She said to you, "Whatever it is, I'll help you."	*Te* she said, "*Sea lo que sea, te* I'll help."

Reflexive objects

He finds himself with a girl.	*Se* he finds *con una* girl.
I find myself with too many problems.	*Me* I find *con* too many problems.
You'll find yourself with your friends.	*Te* you'll find *con* your friends.

As you learn new Spanish verbs in future lessons, you'll find that many verbs tend to be reflexive all the time. The verb for "sitting down" or "seating" is one of those verbs. In Joel's mind, people don't just "sit down"; they "seat themselves".

I'll seat myself in some cafe.	*Me* I'll seat *en* some café.
He'll seat himself at the restaurant.	*Se* he'll seat *en* the restaurant.
You're seating yourself alone?	¿*Te* you're seating alone?

Esto/Eso

"Eso" is an extremely common pronoun, despite the fact that it's neuter and doesn't have a noun assigned to it. If you think about it, that makes sense, because we use the word "that" all the time without having an actual specific noun that it refers to.

For example, if a friend and Joel are talking about meeting for tea some time at a cafeteria, Joel might say, "That would be great!" But what "that" is he referring to? The cafeteria (which would be feminine)? Or maybe the tea (which would be masculine)? But no, he's just using the general "that", so he doesn't give it a gender. He just says "*Eso* would be great!"

Our first official phrase using *eso* is similar. The speaker is saying "that is all", without being specific as to what "that" is. It's a general concept, something they've been talking about, not a specific noun.

That's all.	*Eso es todo.*
This was all.	*Esto era todo.*
That would be all.	*Eso sería todo.*

We use the word *esta* when referring to feminine nouns. We haven't learned any such nouns yet, but I'll spoil one for you: The word for "time" is femine in situations where you would say "this time" ("*esta* time").

This time I don't know what to do.	*Esta* time *no* I know *qué* to do.
This time he doesn't know what to say.	*Esta* time *no* he knows *qué* to say.
This time we do know what to eat.	*Esta* time *sí* we know *qué* to eat.

Possessives

They are at my house, as it should be.	They are *en mi* house, *como* it should *ser*.
They are at their house, as I said.	They are *en su* house, *como* I said.
They are at your house, as they hoped.	They are *en tu* house, *como* they hoped.

I'm going to your house.	I'm going *a tu* house.
They're coming to my house.	They're coming *a mi* house.
We're going to her house.	We're going *a su* house.

Adverbs

Ya is a complicated word. Generally, it means that something has changed at some point, as represented by the baker slamming closed the cover of his stand. In our first example, *ya* is translated as "already".

I already know that they were.	*Ya* I know *que lo eran.*
I already know that it is.	*Ya* I know *que lo es.*
I already know that I'm not.	*Ya* I know *que no lo soy.*

In this next example, *ya* means "anymore".

But they aren't anymore.	*Pero ya no lo son.*
But now it isn't.	*Pero ya no lo es.*
But now I am.	*Pero ya sí lo soy.*
But now he is.	*Pero ya sí lo es.*
But now we aren't.	*Pero ya no lo somos.*

Our next example of *ya* doesn't seem to make any sense. What does *ya que* mean? "Already that" or "anymore that"? This is very idiomatic and doesn't translate literally (which is frequently the case with the word *ya*).

Basically, *ya que* means "given that" or "since" (as a connector). It's followed by a complete sentence. Just practice this example, and you'll catch on eventually.

I'll help you with that, since we're brothers.	*Te* I'll help *con eso, ya que somos* brothers.
I called him, since we're friends.	*Lo* I called, *ya que somos* friends.
I'll help her with that, since she's my sister.	*La* I'll help *con eso, ya que es mi* sister.
She'll help me, since I'm her brother.	*Me* she'll help, *ya que soy su* brother.
I want it, since it's delicious.	*Lo* I want, *ya que es* delicious.

He was indeed here.	*Sí* he was *aquí.*
He wasn't here.	*No* he was *aquí.*
I was indeed here.	*Sí* I was *aquí.*
They weren't here.	*No* they were *aquí.*

The two of them are as one.	The two of them *son como* one.
The two of us are as enemies.	The two of us *somos como* enemies.
The two of them were as one.	The two of them *eran como* one.
He is as a maniac.	He *es como* a maniac.

Now I know that she's not very well.	*Ya* I know *que no* she is *muy bien.*
Now he knows that I'm not very well.	*Ya* he knows *que no* I am *muy bien.*
Now you know that we are very well.	*Ya* you know *que sí* we are *muy bien.*
Now they know that I'm not good at it.	*Ya* they know *que no* I'm good at it.
Now I know that you do it very well.	*Ya* I know *que sí lo* you do *muy bien.*

"Todo" and "Más"

And with her, everything is that way.	*Y con* her, *todo es* that way.
And with him, everything is strange.	*Y con* him, *todo es* strange.
And with us, everything is complicated.	*Y con* us, *todo es* complicated.

Time for something new. Let's think for a second about an English sentence: "It's the best!"

This is a great example of a situation where we say "the", but there's no noun. It's the best… what?

In Spanish, the word "the" in this situation is *lo* since there's no noun indicated. And sometimes, instead of saying "the best", Joel says "the more" or "the most": *lo más*.

It's the best!	*¡Es lo más!*
Their house is the best!	*¡Su* house *es lo más!*
Your art is the best!	*¡Tu* art *es lo más!*

Our last example uses the word *más* to mean "else". Spanish doesn't have a word for "else", so Joel always uses his word for "more". "Someone else" is "Someone *más.*"

And does anyone else in his family know about this?	*Y* does anyone *más en su* family know about *esto*?
Someone else in my family knows about that.	Someone *más en mi* family knows about *eso.*

Checkpoint: Start Thinking in Spanish

I know that I gave you a lot of sentences in this lesson, but I have a reality check for you: If you're not truly learning these sentences and phrases by now, you're going to fall behind or get lost.

Too many of our students run off the rails after lesson 3, because they don't begin doing something very important: **Starting to think in Spanish.**

We may not know very much vocabulary yet, but what we do know are most of the structures and a lot of the grammar. And that actually is a much bigger deal than you might think.

The most important thing that you can do for yourself right now, besides making sure you know all the words in the Joel's world up to this point, is to practice the highlighted phrases that I've provided until they're second-nature.

It's very difficult to catch up if you're behind on this, so take it seriously! But of course, don't just stare at them in the book. Good practice is more active than this, so here are two great ways to practice:

(1) Get recordings of these phrases (available for free at SpanishIn1Month.com) and practice speaking along with them whenever you can. You can do this while driving, doing household chores, or drinking tea, as long as you can give them your active attention.

(2) When you can sit down with a piece of paper, practice tweaking and modifying all of these sentences to customize them. If you're a SpanishIn1Month.com member, you can send your modifications of these sentences to me and my team, and we'll give you feedback on how well you're doing.

Try to make a part of your life. Once you've mastered the materials up to this point, you're truly well on your way to thinking in Spanish.

You'll notice that many of today's phrases show up in our comic about the birds, which is increasingly shifting from English to Spanish.

- Hello, I'm Matías. Who is this?

- Hi Matías, it's me, Santiago.

- Santiago, all this time, ¿right?

- Yes I know! ¿How are you?

- Fine thanks, and you? ¿How is Isabella?

- Not so well, you know, she left her house.

- What! This isn't good at all.

- No, this time she doesn't have a place to be. You have to do her a favor, on my behalf.

- Yes, I want to be with her now. What can I do for Isabella or for you?

- You're very nice! I have her things at my house, as it should be, but…

- ¿Can I do something?

- I think so, it's a big deal.

- ¿But, why did she leave?

- She left, that's all... right, so, now we're going to do something when Valentina isn't around.

- ¿Valentina? But... why? If those two are like one, as you know, a...

- I know that they were, but now they aren't.

- Valentina is that way, and with her everything's like that, that's Valentina... And Sofía? She can...

- No, not Sofía, she isn't around.

- I am here, you are there... we're all here, the time is now.

- Maybe so, us both, with her. This time I don't know what to do.

- She can be at my house all the time. I can do you that favor, because I only want her to be well, and you to be well.

- That which was, is not anymore... now, everything's this way!

- Give it time. She's around, and her things at your house, at least it's something. And that gentleman?

- ¿Sebastián?

- I don't know, that man that was around with her at the house.

- Ah, yes, Sebastián, he isn't around anymore, and because of this she can't be at Mr. Sebastián's house.

- ¿He isn't? ¿What do you mean he isn't around? ¿Really? That can't be, but if the house was his!

- He left from the house, that's the truth. This has been this way for a while now. Now I know that she's doing badly.

He left **de la** house, that **es la** truth. **Esto** has been this way **por un** while **ya**. **Ya** I know **que no** she's **muy bien**.

- All right, well then, Isabella has been unwell for a while. Now we have to do something for her, I want to do something for her, both of us.

- Yes, I want... I'm leaving now, I'll go with Isabella.

All right, well then, **por un** while Isabella **no** has been **bien**. Now we have to do something **por** her, **yo** want to do something **por** her, both of us.

Sí, I want... I'm leaving now, I'll go **con** Isabella.

- All right, I also will go to your house, I want to be with her.

All right, **yo** also will go **a tu** house, I want to be **con** her.

LESSON 4

Stick to the System

You learn most effectively when your capabilities are pushed to the limits.

In this lesson, you'll begin to discover the complexity of the language-learning protocol. Your dedication to the process is about to meet a serious challenge.

But you'll also learn the value of a step-by-step system that gets real results. If you internalize every detail of this lesson and make a resolution to stick to the system, your journey to fluency will be fully primed for success.

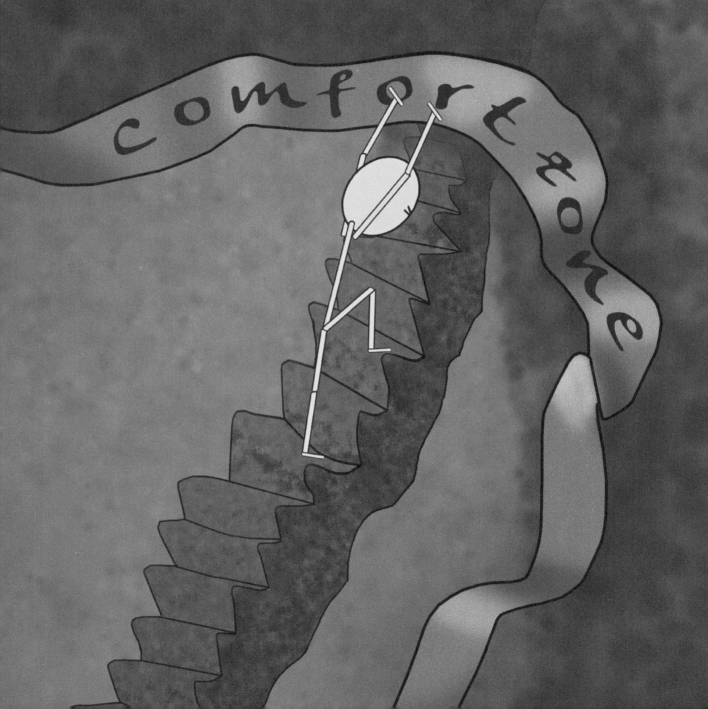

Lesson 4 Theory:
Stick to the System

"The more constraints one imposes, the more one frees one's self of the chains that shackle the spirit." -Igor Stravinsky

"Know thyself." - Apollo (attr.)

LEARNING a language is like climbing a staircase, without being able to see the top from the bottom.

At some point, every learner arrives at a crucial moment: The project suddenly seems much more daunting than first imagined. Metaphorically, you catch your first glimpse of the top of the staircase, and you're struck with the reality of how far you have to climb.

This can happen at any part of the process. In my case, I was struck with reality several times, including after I'd moved to Buenos Aires when I thought I was already fluent.

The Wrong Shop

Grocery shopping in Buenos Aires is an experience. It took me a while to figure out the ropes.

- *Rule 1:* Never pay with a card.

- *Rule 2:* Always try to have exact change.

- *Rule 3:* Expect to pay an extra peso for the grocery bag (which, of course, complicates Rule 2).

But for a while, the hardest rule was *Rule 0:* Make sure you're in the right grocery store in the first place.

General-purpose grocery stores in Buenos Aires come in two categories: "supermercados" (typical supermarkets) and "chinos". A "chino" is a smaller, cheaper, local corner store that's run, invariably, by a Chinese family.

If you're looking for cheap wine, dry beans, and fresh (dirty) eggs, go to the "chino". If you're looking for fresh vegetables, branded products, and longer lines, go to the "supermercado".

Theoretically, this rule was pretty simple. But I often still made the mistake of picking the wrong store when I was distracted or in a hurry. Why?

For the same reason that, under pressure, I often picked the wrong Spanish word. Although I "knew" which word was correct, I was in an environment outside my comfort zone. The various pressures and distractions often caused me to take a wrong turn. Even when it should have been obvious.

One time, about two weeks into my stay, I was shopping at a supermercado. I grabbed a box of English Breakfast tea off the shelf. At checkout, I was shocked to see that the grocery bill was about twice what I thought it should be. As it turned out, the English Breakfast by itself was responsible for 50% of the price. At 150 pesos ($12), it was *way* above my tight Argentinian grocery budget.

Surely the cashier would let me put it back on the shelf. As I struggled to explain the misunderstanding, I somehow used a conjugation of Ser instead of Estar to indicate where I had found the tea. Big oops.

The cashier figured out what I meant and cor-

rected me. In the end, we sorted out the issue, and I went home tealess.

I walked back to my apartment discouraged. Before this incident, I thought that my Spanish was near-perfect. Now I felt like I'd fallen down the stairs and had to start over again from near the bottom.

Hadn't I at least graduated from mistakes as elementary as choosing the wrong verb?

The Comfort Zone Myth

Fortunately, you have something that I didn't have when I learned Spanish: A step-by-step way to progress up the stairs. If you follow the Accelerated Spanish process, you'll always know which step you're on toward fluency, instead of repetitively leaping up and falling back down.

You may have heard that "magic happens" when you're outside your comfort zone. A popular illustration

shows "where the magic happens" as separate from "your comfort zone".

This is partly true. And like all partly-true myths, it's extremely dangerous and can lead to all kinds of trouble.

For example, at this moment, it's probably outside of your comfort zone to get on the phone with a native Spanish speaker and talk entirely in Spanish. If you do that right now, you're probably going to end up frustrated and disillusioned.

Even worse, if you switch to Spanish conversation too soon, you're actually not going to learn as quickly as you should.

Sadly, I've seen dozens of Spanish learners having to take enormous steps backwards, because they mis-learned and mis-practiced enormous parts of the Spanish language. By trying to go too far forward, they ended up only harming their own learning. In every case that I've seen, the students ended up having to spend months on unlearning.

To keep this from happening to you, follow the advice of the ancient Greeks: Know thyself.

Self-awareness is essential to progress. If you don't know where you are, how can you even take the next step? If you get a little too cocky and claim you've mastered the fundamentals before you're ready to move on, you're going to end up misstepping and falling backwards.

In the Accelerated Spanish system, self-awareness is built into the process, IF you take the time after each lesson to examine your actual level

of mastery.

By completely dominating each lesson, one at a time, you'll always be working where the magic truly happens: At the fringes of the comfort zone.

where the magic REALLY happens

comfort zone

You can only make step-by-step progress if you acknowledge where you are.

The Accelerated Spanish course is designed so that each lesson will feel like the hardest. Your mind will always be challenged in a new way.

For this to work effectively, you need to make sure

that you get comfortable with everything you encounter before moving on to the next step.

And yes, this applies to YOU, no matter how much Spanish you've learned before.

"But I already know soooo much Spanish!"

Some of our students have tried to skip lessons, because they'd studied Spanish in the past. Why relearn the basics, like *la*, *que*, *para*, *esto*, and *estar*?

This has always resulted in disaster, without exception.

One of my first students, Patricia, was already almost fluent in Spanish when she began the Accelerated Spanish course. In fact, she was already at a point where she was participating in business meetings that were conducted entirely in Spanish!

Still, she took my advice

when she joined, starting at Lesson 1 and progressing one step at a time from there.

Patricia discovered that she actually found the most benefit from the first five lessons. Sure, she was able to breeze through them quickly. But there were a few weaknesses in her Spanish that only the beginning of the course could patch up.

She didn't use the lessons just to learn vocabulary (she already knew all the words). Instead, she used them to become self-aware of her level of comfort with these fundamentals. As it turned out, she needed to get more comfortable with idioms like *lo que* and *el que*, and she needed to work on certain aspects of when to use Ser and when to use Estar.

By focusing exclusively on these essentials, instead of rushing into new vocabulary, she was able to build the momentum necessary to knock out all the other challenges she would face on her path to true fluency.

That's why I tell all my

students to start at the bottom of the stairs, even if they've already been spending years learning Spanish. It may turn out that you can climb the stairs more quickly than other students, but don't skip steps. Examine each aspect of the language one at a time, and master every step before moving on to the next one.

Depending on how well you already know Spanish, you may be able to run up the stairs instead of walking. But a self-aware learner will take every single step seriously.

Here's a summary of the steps we've taken so far:

- **Lesson 1:** Complete comfort with 15 essential words; deep

work on fundamental Spanish sentence structure with *que*, *de*, and direct objects (*lo*, *la*, and *me*); idioms that involve articles (*el que* and *la que*).

- **Lesson 2:** Fluid, comfortable use of essential conjugations of Ser; related grammar (including the subjunctive).

- **Lesson 3:** Comfort with 25 new words, including fluid use of several new idioms; indirect and reflexive objects.

If you've mastered the materials to this point, you're ready for our complex lesson on a new verb: Estar.

Before we learn Estar, let's look at a few of our future landmarks for the purpose of encouragement:

- **Lessons 5-6:** All essential Spanish grammar and 50% comprehension of the language.

- **Lessons 7-8:** Beginning conversation entirely in Spanish.

- **Lessons 9-10:** Verbs in bulk; 70% comprehension of Spanish.

- **Lessons 11-12:** Conversation on a variety of subjects.

- **Lessons 13-14:** Comfort with 80% of Spanish.

- **Lessons 15-16:** Easy conversation on familiar topics, with strong vocabulary and perfect grammar.

- **Lessons 17-18:** Understanding of 90% of Spanish; comfortable conversation on nearly any subject.

Your comfort zone will grow to meet each of those challenges as it comes.

For now, let's briefly revisit Ser.

"To be", or the other "to be"?

Hamlet's soliloquy opens with the question, *"¿Ser, or no ser?"*

In Spanish, the answer is usually *"no ser"*.

We learned in Lesson 2 that Ser means "to be", and we've learned all the forms of "to be" (as in "I am", "she was", "it will be", and so on).

As you learned that verb, you were taught to choose the correct word using this process:

1. Choose the appropriate scene based on tense or mood: Present tense? Future? Subjunctive?

2. Next, choose the person from that scene. That will give you the appropriate word.

But now we're going a step beyond that: Before choosing the right scene and the right person, you'll have to make sure you're in the correct shop in the first place.

Today we'll be focusing on a different verb, "Estar". But unfortunately this is a verb that really confuses English speakers, because this verb is also often translated as "to be". In fact, confusing Estar with Ser is one of the biggest and most frequent mistakes that English speakers make

when switching into Spanish.

Just for a little perspective on how different these verbs are, Estar isn't an apple shop. It's a magic shop that's run by Tara.

Now Tara goes by the nickname "Tar", like the black stuff that you put on a road. Unlike grumpy Ser, who is always frowning and disapproving of people, Tar is an energetic, hyper kind of person who is very interested in everyone, but she's also easily distracted, like a squirrel on caffeine.

She's also extremely gullible, which, naturally, is something Joel likes about her; he loves taking advantage of people.

Tar's magic shop is shaped like a giant top hat. Notice how it's cylindrical like a magician's hat. The theme of this magic shop is astronomy and magic. So if you go inside, it's all blue with yellow stars all over. Remember the name: "Estar", with a stress on the syllable "star".

For example, if you wanted to say "I want to be in

Tar's shop", you would say "I want *estar* in Tar's shop." So Estar means "to be" as it relates to a location, or where you want to be.

Another Myth

Unfortunately, I am going to have to spend the next few pages un-teaching anyone who's learned Estar in a certain way.

Some people are told that Estar has to do with "temporary" things, while Ser, the other verb for "to be", has to do with "permanent" things.

But unfortunately, that's a gross error.

Ser has to do with **what something is**, and estar has to do with most other "to be" situations.

For example, Tar "is" a woman, and she "is" outside of the store. In Spanish they consider those to be two completely different things.

When we say "Tar **is** a woman", that's something that she is. It an-

swers the question "What is she?" So you'd use Ser.

Also, If I was to say "Tar is short", that's considered a part of her identity, a part of **what she is**. So you'd use Ser in that case as well.

However, when we say "Tar **is** in the room", that's not what she is as a person. That's just where she happens to be. So this is an Estar case. Estar has to do with where or how you are, while Ser is what or who you are. And it has nothing to do with temporary or permanent!

As another example, I might say "Buenos Aires is in Argentina". That's not *what* Buenos Aires

is; it's where it is. So I would use Estar. On the other hand, if I say "Buenos Aires is the biggest city in Argentina", that is *what* it is, so I would use Ser.

Now let's imagine that Buenos Aires shrinks and another Argentinian city grows. Maybe, for some reason, everyone in Buenos Aires moves to Córdoba. Suddenly Buenos Aires is no longer the largest city in Argentina. In Spanish, to say "it isn't anymore", we would say *ya no es*. I used Ser, even though it's a temporary condition.

A more common example is when a person changes their identity somehow. For example, my brother Josiah is four inches taller than me (which really isn't fair, because he's four years younger than me). So I would say that he *es* my tallest brother, using Ser.

But if my younger brother Samuel grows a few inches, he'll be the tallest one, replacing Josiah. This changes Josiah's identity, so Josiah is not the tallest anymore, or "Josiah *ya no es* the tallest."

These are examples of Ser being used for something temporary. In both cases, there was an identity change. So Ser is not a permanent thing; it's just used to refer to <u>what something is.</u>

Another, more day-to-day example is something you might say when someone changes jobs. "She isn't a teacher anymore" is "*Ya no es* a teacher." Since it answers the question of "what is she?" or "who is she?", the verb Ser is used. It's identity.

Now let's look at a potent example of where Ser is not used. Suppose my grandfather is dead. Will I use Ser or Estar here? Does "dead" answer the question of "what is he"?

I would use Estar. It's not who he is as a person. I wouldn't answer the question "Who is your grandpa?" with the statement "He's dead"! Instead, if someone asked me that, I would probably say "Well, he *was* a truck driver, but now he's dead."

The first is what he is, and the second is how he is: "He *was (ser)* a truck driver, but now he *is (estar)* dead."

If you've been mis-taught that Ser is for permanent things and Estar is for temporary things, you're not alone. About

half of US high schoolers are taught this myth.

But it's time to get that idea completely out of your head. It's not true. Ser can easily refer to things that are temporary ("she isn't a teacher anymore"), and Estar often

refers to things that are permanent ("my grandpa is dead"). Even though it tends to be the other way around, it's not a rule you can depend on.

Instead, here's a rule you CAN depend on: Ser refers to **what something is**, as its identity. Estar is used in other situations.

It can still be very tricky. So I'll give you a few litmus tests that you can apply, and you can test yourself with some examples.

Litmus Test 1: Nouns

If the "to be" verb is immediately followed by a noun, it MUST be ser. For example, in the sentence "Colombia is a country", the word "is" has a noun right after it ("a country").

As a mnemonic to remember this, imagine that Joel likes to travel straight from the Ser shop to his own house, where nouns are stored. Ser is the closest shop in Yol to his own house, so it's very convenient for him. Ser goes with nouns.

The noun test is the most handy test that you can apply to your sentences. Almost any time you use Ser, it will be followed by a noun or something equivalent to a noun.

Test yourself with these examples to determine if they're Ser or Estar:

- "They **were** students."

- "She **is** a pilot."

- "We **are** friends."

- "We **are** at home."

- "It **is** going well."

- "They **are** sad."

- "It **is** what I found."

Answers: ser, ser, ser, estar, estar, estar, ser.

Litmus Test 2: Adverbs

If the "to be" verb is used to emphasize an adverb (words in the plaza), it's almost always Estar, with very few exceptions. For example, "They are *aquí*" and "He is *bien*" both emphasize adverbs.

As a mnemonic to remember this, Joel often goes from the Estar shop to the marketplace. In fact, they're very close to each other, as you can see on the map.

This rule is pretty easy to follow intuitively, so we'll move on.

Litmus Test 3: Prepositions

A preposition (at the amusement rides) often designates **where** something is, not **what** it is. For example, "They are *por* the neighborhood" or "He is *en* the house."

However, some of these little words are used for the identity of something. In particular, *por, para,* and *de* are often used after Ser.

Let's imagine that I buy a book written by Tolkien. I've decided to give it to my sister. There are several ways to think about what this book is:

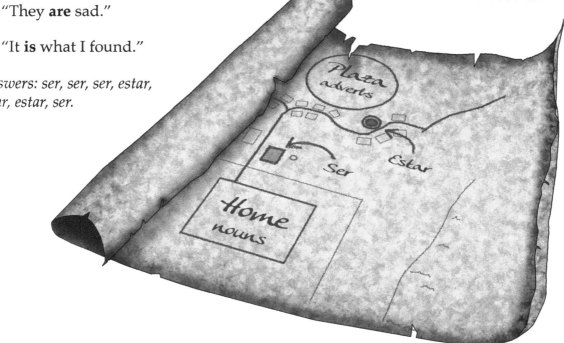

"The book is by *(por)* Tolkien." That's its identity, so we use Ser: "The book *es por* Tolkien."

The book is for *(para)* my sister. That's identity as well: "The book *es para* my sister."

The book is from (de) Argentina. Where something is from is identity: *"Es de* Argentina."

So if something is created *por* someone, intended *para* someone, or originating *de* somewhere, this is considered a part of its identity, so you use Ser before the preposition.

Test yourself with these examples:

- "She **was** around here."

- "You **are** from Spain?"

- "This puppy **is** for you."

- "This movie **is** by Christopher Nolan."

- "She **is** at home."

Answers: estar, ser, ser, ser, estar

Don't Sweat It

If all of this seems too complicated, don't worry too much. For now, simply focus on the fact that Ser is what something is. Estar is used in other situations.

There will be many more examples of both Ser and Estar as we go along, and you'll be able to get comfortable with the differences between them soon.

For now, let's go ahead and learn Estar and its many forms.

Lesson 4 Vocabulary:

Estar
(the Magic Shop)

JOEL'S ANTENNAE TINGLE with excitement when he hears that there's a magic shop in town.

Rumor has it that there are some very interesting magic wands sold at Estar. Supposedly, these wands actually perform real magic, and Joel is fascinated by the possibilities. Maybe he can turn his enemies into toads. (Especially his mammalian enemies.)

The store is only open at night, so Joel shows up at about 11pm. He has invited the lizard and the pandas to come with him. If there's any way to get free merchandise, Joel wants to take advantage to the maximum.

Since Joel always likes to fit in, he comes carrying a cardboard toy star, a leftover prop from a play. When Joel wants to manipulate people, he always tries to get on their good side first. This toy star is his impromptu strategy.

Meanwhile, the lizard is wearing sunglasses

to block out the astronomy-themed lighting from Estar's walls. Although the shop is dim, the lighting is a bit strange for a lizard who normally spends his nights in dark caves.

As Joel and his friends enter the store, the clumsy pandas accidentally stand on the lizard's tail. The dim room with small, bright lights on the walls confuses them.

Tar is very excited to see guests in her usually-empty store. She rattles off greetings and questions at nearly incomprehensible speed.

"I'm so glad to see you! You all look

amazing! How was your trip? Where are you coming from? Are any of you famous?"

Joel's antennae perk up at this last idea. If she thinks that one of them is famous, she'll probably give them free rein of the store.

Looking around, Joel realizes that the lizard's sunglasses look pretty cool. Hmm. Maybe Tar is gullible enough to believe that the lizard is a movie star.

Of course, Joel still wants to place emphasis on himself; perhaps he's the agent who manages the "star". He tries to say, "I'm here with a star!"

But then Joel realizes there's a problem with this declaration. If he says, "I'm here with a star", Tar might look at the

toy star in his hands. That really isn't very impressive at all. In his confusion, he ends up blurting this out:

"Estoy aquí con…"

Make sure to burn this image in your mind: Joel's holding a "toy", and his word is *estoy*.

Of course, he wants to correct himself quickly. So he changes his phrasing to "A star is here!"

"A star *está aquí!*"

The slight British accent is reflective of Joel's interest in fake formality, especially when he's trying to trick someone. Instead of "star", his reference to the lizard sounds like "stah".

Be sure to associate the word *estoy* with Joel and the word *está* with the lizard.

These words, *estoy* and *está*, are used to indicate location. *Estoy aquí* means "I am here", and *está aquí* means "he is here", "she is here", or "it is here".

Tar isn't quite sure what to think of this. Her mind is racing with thoughts: "What's a 'stah'? Is it a kind of houseplant? What's the bee doing here anyway? Do I like bees? I love most animals. Did I remember to feed my cat this morning? Do I even have a cat?"

In the flurry of thoughts, Tar tosses a couple of magic wands around in her hand.

Joel is distressed. Tar doesn't seem impressed that he's here with a "star", and now she's throwing wands around. She seems like a very clumsy person, and Joel has heard that these magic wands have strange powers. He doesn't want to be on the wrong end of those powers. (Plus the wands look pretty sharp.)

"Hey, you shouldn't be tossing those around! You're close to customers here!"

That's what Joel tries to say. But in his confusion, all he can think of is the word "toss". So when he says "you're

close to customers", here's what comes out:

"*Estás* close to customers!"

As a quick recap of what we have so far, remember the stressed syllables "toy" (for Joel), "stah" (for the lizard), and "toss" (for Tar).

Estoy aquí. = "I am here."

Está aquí. = "He/she/it is here."

Estás aquí. = "You are here."

The lizard has had enough of this nonsense. He smells something interesting among the store merchandise. He tries to sneak away, but he can't get anywhere, because the pandas are still standing on his tail.

This confuses him. He keeps scrambling with his four feet, but he's not getting anywhere. And he doesn't know why, because he can't see the pandas on his tail thanks to his sunglasses and the dimness of the room.

Joel sees the lizard struggling, and he tries to explain the situation to him.

"The pandas *están* on your tail."

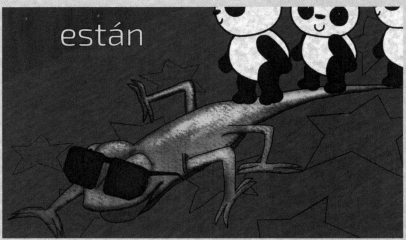

Tar hears this.

"Are you guys standing on something?"

She remembers that she spent the entire afternoon creating some cut-out pictures of paper stars. She was hoping to decorate the room with them (as if it wasn't decorated enough) by hanging these paper stars from the ceiling.

But she left the paper stars on the floor.

"How dare you come in here and just *stamp* on my stars like that!"

Joel looks down on the ground. Sure enough, the star cut-outs are beneath their feet. The lizard has severely wrinkled them.

"Yes," admits Joel, in a voice of sarcastic indifference, "We are indeed 'stamping' on your paper stars."

To re-state this fact, he says more simply, "*Estamos* on your paper stars."

As always, make sure that this scene is very clear in your mind. Mentally place each of these five new words in its location.

estoy = "I am"

está = "he/she/it is"

estás = "you are"

están = "they are"

estamos = "we are"

You might be thinking that today's story was pretty long. Why did we need such an elaborate story to teach just five words?

In future lessons, the stories will be getting gradually shorter, and the list of new words per lesson will grow continually longer. Until then, make sure you form the habit of truly internalizing the scenes described. When you think of the entrance of Estar, you should remember all the five words, associated with each of the characters.

The Red Tense

The pandas are responsible people. They climb off of the lizard's tail and help Tar pick up the paper stars.

But Joel and the lizard get out of there as quickly as they can. They head straight to the aisles of merchandise.

As we go through the rest of this lesson, we'll use the areas of the Estar shop very much like we used the Ser shop. The present tense is in the entrance (hint: we just covered that), the past tense is behind the counter, and other tenses and moods are outside.

But wait a second. Joel and the lizard are going to the merchandise aisles. What does that mean?

You might remember that in Ser's shop, Joel and his friends never bought anything. After they walked into the store, they went straight to the checkout counter.

However, in Estar, they go to a place we didn't see in Ser's store. In fact, there's an entire tense that we skipped when we learned Ser. We didn't go to the merchandise area at all.

This is because this new tense in the shopping aisles isn't used very much in Ser. But it's used pretty often with Estar, so let's introduce it here.

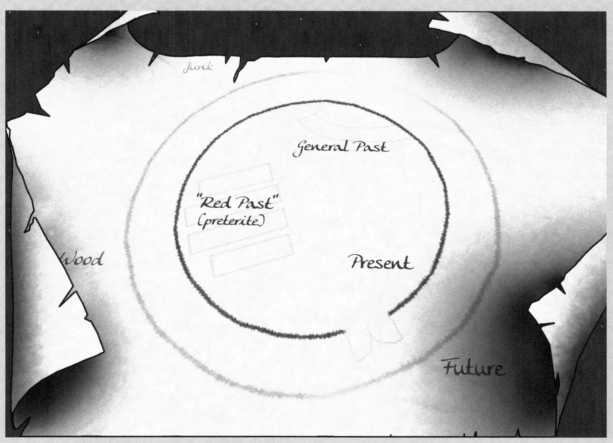

Basically, the merchandise area is a past tense. But it's a special kind of past tense, different from the past tense behind the counter.

What we learn behind the counter is the general past tense (called the "imperfect" past, if you're a nerd). It's the most common type of past tense for both Ser and Estar, the tense that you'll use all the time. But there's also something called the "preterite" past tense, which is also very common in Estar.

As a quick mnemonic: The stressed syllable of "Preterite" is "red" (it's pronounced pRED-er-it). In Yol, the shelves in stores are usually red, regardless of the color of the rest of the store.

In fact, as a teaser, we're going to learn the preterite (merchandise) forms of Ser in a future lesson. But not yet.

More to the point: Why does Spanish have two different past tenses?

The different forms of the past can help clarify certain situations. To illustrate this, let's abuse the lizard.

Suppose the lizard walks toward the shelves, blinded by his sunglasses, and hits his face against the corner of a shelf.

At this point, if the pandas look at the lizard's face, they're going to see a big red mark and wonder what happened.

If they go to Joel's house the next day, sit down with a cup of tea, and ask Joel what happened, he has two ways of saying that the lizard experienced pain:

(1) "The lizard <u>was hurting</u>." This makes it sound like nothing happened at the store; the lizard was already in a state of pain when they entered the store. That's not quite true.

(2) "The lizard <u>got hurt</u>." Ah-ha. This indicates an *event*, something that happened while they were shopping. Compare this to the previous option, and you'll see that this is a more accurate description of what happened.

But there's a problem. Joel never uses the word "got". (The reason for this was explained in Lesson 1: He doesn't like to talk about greed and the idea of "getting" things.)

Spanish simply doesn't use words the same way that English does. Spanish speakers don't say that someone "was hurting" or that someone "got hurt".

Instead, here are the two ways of saying this:

(1) "The lizard was hurt" in the general imperfect tense. This indicates that it was the case all along.

(2) "The lizard was hurt" in the preterite tense. This indicates an event.

So there you go. The general imperfect tense (behind the counter) means that something was going on in general. But the preterite tense, the "red" tense, indicates an event. Something changed at a particular moment.

To remember this, think of the red shelves and the red mark on the lizard's face.

Okay, grammar lesson = done, and lizard abuse = done.

Let's learn a couple of preterite forms of Estar.

The Cauldron of the Stew of Transformation

The lizard is wearing sunglasses and can't see much. But he follows his nose. There's an amazing smell that he can't resist.

Joel tags along to see where the lizard is going, and then he too is struck by the aroma. Something smells like beef stew.

An enormous cauldron is responsible for the smell. But it's in the shadows, so it's very hard to see. Joel tries to lean in and sniff the substance, and in doing so, he loses control and falls in. When he comes out, his face is covered with the beef stew.

Meanwhile, the lizard crawls along the

edge of the cauldron, but he slips and gets one of his feet covered in the stew.

Joel looks at the lizard and feels his own face with his antennae. His thoughts start to run wild with worry. This won't be good for his reputation. What would people think if they saw him?

They'd probably call him names, like "stew face".

Meanwhile, the lizard's situation isn't so bad, because "stew foot" sounds much less insulting than "stew face".

Joel desperately begins rubbing the stew off of his face, using various items from the shelves. This causes loud noises, which reach the attention of Tar.

"What's going on over there?" she yells from the front of the store.

Joel tries to tell her, "I was in the stew for a moment". But since he's obsessed with the fear of being called "stew

face", it comes out like this:

"*Estuve* in the stew for one moment."

The stress of that word is "stew", and you can see that the end of the word sounds kind of like "stew face".

Tar approaches them, just to see if they're OK and to make sure that the cauldron didn't turn them into something weird like snakes or humans (a terrifying thought; I'd hate to see Joel as a human).

When she sees that the lizard has something on his foot, she asks if he's OK too.

"Yes," says Joel, "he *estuvo* in the stew too, but just for a moment."

So our words are *estuve* for Joel ("I was") and *estuvo* for the lizard ("he/she/it was"). Both words have "stew" as the stressed syllable, but Joel's sounds more like "stew face" and the lizard's sounds more like "stew foot".

These words can be used to indicate that someone was at a place, emphasizing the "event" of being there.

A good example is "I was here yesterday." If you say "*estuve aquí* yesterday", it sounds like you arrived yesterday. It was a special event. But if you use the general past tense instead, it sounds like you were already there all along.

Speaking of the general past tense, let's go behind the counter.

Stab Pandas

Joel and the lizard pick up a couple of magic wands and then go to the check-out area, where they're reunited with the pandas. But Tar is nowhere to be seen. They look around and call out, impatient to get out of there.

Finally, Tar presents herself. With an evil-looking grin on her face, she slowly stands up from behind the counter, holding three wands behind her back. The wands look very sharp.

This looks terribly suspicious. Joel wonders why she was crouched behind the counter, and he's afraid she might be about to stab them.

"Why were you hiding there?" Joel asks. But since he's preoccupied with

estabas

the thought of being stabbed, his words come out a little differently:

"Why *estabas* back there hiding?"

Joel is thinking she might "stab us", so he uses the word *estabas*, which means "you were" in the general past tense.

Notice one thing: The word *estabas* has an S at the end. Remember in Ser's store that the word *eras* has an S on the end, and it means "you were". Basically, as a general rule, when you're talking to someone, you use the S at the end of the word.

But what if we take the S off of the word? Then we end up with *estaba*, which refers to Joel or the lizard. It still has the stress on "stab", but it's a

simpler version of the word.

Tar seems to be at a loss for words, so Joel grows confident. He pulls out his own magic wand, holds up the toy star he brought with him, and stabs the toy violently.

"See?" he says. "I was safe. What did you think you were doing? You couldn't touch me!"

To say "I was safe," Joel says "*Estaba*

estaba

safe." He's awkwardly trying to demonstrate his ability to defend himself from wand stabbings.

Joel also points out that the lizard has a magic wand. "He *estaba* safe, too."

So *estabas aquí* means "you were here", and *estaba aquí* can mean "I was here" or "he/she/it was here".

But what about the pandas? Were they safe?

Still breathing heavily with anger and valor, Joel looks over at the pandas. His three stuffed friends stare stupidly back at him, empty-handed and defenseless.

Tar could stab the pandas if she wanted. Joel continues staring at them. What would it look like if they were stabbed? Would their stuffing spill

out all over the magic shop, and then would it blow around in the wind, maybe even getting mixed into the beef stew?

Suddenly Joel bursts out in loud, uncontrollable laughter.

Even in the face of danger, Joel is readily amused by the pandas, and he's always susceptible to a good laugh at someone else's expense.

At this point, Tar finally finds her voice and asks a question to the group: "What's the bee laughing at?"

Joel tries to answer between bouts of laughter. What he tries to say is "The pandas were vulnerable to stabbing," or something along those lines.

But all he can think of is "stab pandas!", and this makes him laugh harder.

Instead of "The pandas were vulnerable," he says "The pandas *estaban* vulnerable."

The word *estaban* means "were", or "they were", and it seems to be a mixture of "stab" and the first half of the word "panda".

This is another general rule about verbs. The pandas tend to have the letter N at the end of the verb. If you associate N with the paNdas, that can help you remember *estaban*.

Of course, we also have a pattern for the whole group: The "-mos" suffix. You'll remember that from *somos*, *éramos*, and *estamos*. Let's use that now in a new word.

When Joel is done laughing, he turns back to Tar. He and the lizard both point their wands at her, demonstrat-

ing that she is outnumbered.

"I know why you didn't stab the pandas, Tar. You couldn't ever overpower us. We have the *most* stabbing power! We could stab the most."

This is a bit strange to say, but Joel puts some emphasis on the word "most". The word for "we were" is *estábamos*.

Note that all of these words have the main stress on the syllable "stab":

estaba: "I was"

estaba: "he/she/it was"

estabas: "you were"

estaban: "they were"

estábamos: "we were"

For example, *estábamos aquí* means "we were here", and *estaban aquí* means "they were here".

Before moving on, I recommend that you ensure you can remember the words labeled on all of these characters. Can you say "he was here" (using the lizard)? How about "you were here" (using Tar)?

For now, don't worry too much about the preterite forms that we learned earlier (*estuve* and *estuvo*). You'll see examples of those in the part of the lesson where we focus on phrases.

Also, don't worry about the safety of Joel and the pandas! Tar wasn't wanting to stab them, even though that's what Joel's twisted mind assumed.

The real reason she was holding the wands behind her back was because she wanted to surprise the pandas with gifts. The pandas helped her pick up her paper stars from the floor (while Joel and the lizard were sniffing her stew), and she intended these free wands as the pandas' reward.

But now Tar is worried that Joel might spread bad rumors about her. She doesn't want to be known as the local magic nut who tries to stab customers.

So to get on Joel's good side, she lets him and the lizard get their wands for free. All five friends walk out of the store without paying for their wands.

Magic Rays and Magic "Rah"s

Now Joel is in a very good mood.

Mission accomplished: He got one of these infamous magic wands for free!

On the way out the front door of Estar, Joel wonders what he should do with his wand. What's its potential? What are its powers? As he ponders this, he points the wand at a star-shaped decoration on the front of Estar.

Suddenly, a ray of bright light shoots from Joel's wand and hits the decoration.

This is very exciting to Joel. He's never been able to create spontaneous rays of light before.

He announces to the group, "I don't know what you guys are doing, but I'll be at home practicing with my wand and its rays of light."

But when he says "I'll be at home", Joel is thinking of the ray of light, and he ends up saying "*estaré* at home."

This word is pronounced with a stress on "ray", as in a magic ray of light. "Es-ta-RE."

Joel looks over at the lizard, who is staring down at its own wand with a look of curiosity. Is the lizard ambitious? Will it aspire to create majestic rays of light, like Joel is doing?

The lizard points its wand at the store. But instead of producing a bright ray of light, the wand simply produces a pathetic noise: "Rah!"

Joel rolls his eyes. "I'll be at home practicing, but the lizard will probably just be right here, making "rah" noises with his wand."

The word is *estará*. It has a stress on "rah", and it means "he will be", "she will be", or "it will be".

Remember to store both of these words here in front of the store. Here are some simple sentence examples:

Estaré aquí. (Joel) "I will be here."

Estará aquí. (the lizard) "He/she/it will be here."

You might have noticed that the word *estará* is very similar to *será*. We've simply put the letter "a" (with an accent) at the end of the infinitive *estar*, creating a "rah!" sound.

Well that's very observant of you! Keep watching closely, because as we learn more verbs, you'll notice that this is a pattern that's consistent. Every "it/he/she" verb in the future tense has a stress on"rá" at the end.

In other words, the lizard always says "rah!" in front of the verb shops.

The lizard continues to stare down at its wand, fascinated at its powers. But Joel and the pandas have had enough of this. While the lizard is distracted, they sneak around to the back of the store. There's one last thing that they have to see.

174

The Night Sky

As Joel and the pandas round the hat-shaped store and reach the back yard, it turns out that the rumor is correct: This astronomy-themed shop has a beautiful outdoor telescope.

Joel is struck by the beauty of this scene. It's so quiet, so peaceful, and so stunningly brilliant, that even before he approaches the telescope to explore the planets, he pauses to let it sink in.

Slowly Joel flies up to the telescope, with the pandas filing silently behind him, as performing a religious ceremony. This environment is so different from the distressing interior of the store that it seems like an entirely different world. And of course, the lizard with his noisy wand that says "Rah!" is fortunately on the opposite side of the building.

Before looking through the telescope, Joel looks carefully around to make

sure nothing disturbs his peace. Thankfully, the lizard and Tar are still nowhere to be seen.

Just before looking through the telescope, Joel closes his eyes and sincerely wishes, "I hope that the lizard would just stay in the front of the store."

Then, when he puts his eye to the telescope, the breathtaking wonders of the planets and stars strikes a chord in his hard bee heart. His new wish: "I wish I could stay here forever!"

Notice that he keeps using the word "stay". Here are a couple of ways to interpret his wishes:

"I hope that the lizard *esté* in front of the store." (I hope that the lizard *is* in front of the store.)

"I hope that I *esté* here forever. (I hope that I *be* here forever.)

The word *esté* is the subjunctive form of Estar (stressed syllable: "stay").

For example, take this sentence:

"I hope *que esté aquí*."

Depending on context, this can mean "I hope that I am here" or "I hope that he/she/it is here."

Joel's focus is shattered by a loud, all-too-familiar voice.

"Oh, you found the telescope! Isn't it amazing? Check out the distance settings; you can even see Planet Earth from here! Hey, your head is really small. Do you close one eye or are you able to look at the planets with both eyes? Does that even work?"

Joel's fury rises. He spins around to see Tar, who has just come out the back door of the shop.

With no control of his anger, Joel yells rudely, "I want you to be somewhere else!"

But Joel's exclamation comes out more like "I want that you be somewhere else."

And to say "you be", he uses the word *estés*. It's just like *esté*, but with an S at the end: "I want *que estés* somewhere else!"

176

As another example of *estés*, to say "I hope that you're here", Joel would say "I hope *que estés aquí*."

So we have the words *esté* and *estés*, just like we had *sea* and *seas* in Ser.

Now, you might be connecting the dots on something: Since *estés* ("you be") is just *esté* with an S at the end, shouldn't it be easy to change it to the "they" (panda) form, or the "we" form, just by putting an N or a "mos" at the end?

You would be right. So "I hope that they're here" is "I hope *que estén aquí*." And "I want us to be here" is "I want *que estemos aquí*."

But for now, since *esté* and *estés* are more common by far, we'll just practice perfecting those forms in our sentence examples. It should be easy to expand from there.

The most important thing to remember in the back yard is the stressed syllable "stay". That's going to be the stressed sound in all of Estar's subjunctive forms.

Where a Lizard Would Be

Joel is in a bad mood. Tar has ruined the sublime experience of the telescope, so he tells the pandas it's time to leave.

As they walk back around the side of Estar's shop toward the front, Joel wonders where the lizard is now. He wants to get home as soon as possible, but he doesn't hear any "rah!" sounds in the front of the store.

Then Joel remembers that the lizard has been overly exposed to light this evening. The lizard really can't stand much bright light, so it's probably fled to the darkest place it could find.

Joel ponders this for a moment. Where would that dark place be? Then it occurs to him: The mountain of Ría is the darkest place in Yol.

"We're going to Ría!" says Joel.

Just then, Joel hears a "rah!" sound. The lizard is not at Ría after all; it stuck around the whole time. It turns out that the sunglasses were so dark that the lizard wasn't able to see well enough to go anywhere at all.

Joel is surprised, and the pandas begin to think that Joel's idea was ridiculous. Why would the lizard go all the way to the mountain of Ría?

But Joel defends himself: "Maybe I was wrong, but still, if the lizard had gone to a dark place, he would be in Ría."

But to say "he would be in Ría", Joel says "*estaría* en Ría."

You can probably see the connection between this verb and *sería* from Lesson 2. The word *estaría* simply adds the word "would" to Estar, just as *sería* adds the word "would" to Ser. So *estaría bien* means "it would be fine", and *estaría aquí* might mean "she would be here".

I have to point out that in Spanish, there is no individual word for the English modifier "would". A lot of Spanish students make the mistake of translating *sería* or *estaría* as "would", creating strange sentences. For example, they might want to say "I would go", and they end up making a mistake like "*Yo estaría* go."

In reality, *estaría* means "would be". Each Spanish verb has its own version of "would". Just as a hint, the word for "would go" is *iría*, though we won't officially learn that for a while.

At this point, everything that we've learned in this lesson refers to a specific person. As some examples, *estoy* means "I am", *estában* means "they were", *estará* means "he/she/it will", and *estés* means something like "you be". Meanwhile, *estaría* can mean "I would be", "he would be", "she would be", or "it would be".

All of these words take place on the ground. Each one can change based on

the person that it refers to. So *estará* (it will be) can change to *estaré* (I will be), and *está* (he is) can change to *están* (they are).

Similarly, *estaría* (he/she/it would be) can change to *estarías* (you would be), *estarían* (they would be), or *estaríamos* (we would be).

But we won't worry about those forms for now. Just remember the stressed syllable "Ría", and the word *estaría* is the only conjugation we need for now.

An Unattended Party

Joel is very bored of the Estar shop at this point. Maybe you are too.

It may seem like there are just too many forms of the verb. So far, every single scene has several different possible words, because the word changes slightly based on the person.

But we've now learned all the conjugated forms of Estar that we need. There are still a couple of unconjugated forms to learn, but these are very easy because they don't change forms at all.

For example, there's the word *estar* itself, which is the infinitive of the word (the name of the store). There's only one version of that; it doesn't change based on whom it refers to.

Before Joel goes home, he wants to see what kind of damage his wand has done to the front of Estar's shop. He hopes that maybe he burned a hole in the store front.

But no, the wand doesn't seem to have done any damage. Joel is disappointed. He turns to leave, but then he remembers that before leaving a store, he likes to ring the bell.

Joel is surprised to see that Estar doesn't seem to have a bell! Remember that when we learned Ser, we had *siendo*, which was represented by a bell on the corner of the shop.

Well, Estar is round, so it doesn't have any corners. Tar has no place to hang a good-bye bell. (This is because that form of Estar isn't used very often.)

As Joel looks around, puzzled by the fact that there is no bell, he realizes that there are some curious noises coming from the roof of the store.

"Testing…1, 2, 3…" *screech*

"Oh! I'm too close to the speaker! Or maybe I bought the wrong equipment? Sorry, that's probably my fault…"

Someone is testing a microphone on the roof of Estar. Joel flies up to investigate. (Besides, it's a habit: He usually can't resist checking out a store's roof, as you'll see in future lessons.)

To Joel's dismay, Tar is the one behind the microphone, and she sees him as soon as he shows his face.

It seems that this flat, round roof is where Tar tries to host late-night parties. She has a microphone, but no audience at all. Joel is the only other person present.

Tar is excited to see Joel. Honestly, she would probably be excited to see anyone; nobody ever comes to her parties, except by accident. But whenever someone shows up, she tries to play up the guest as much as possible.

Pointing the microphone at Joel, she rambles bubblingly, "I know you! You've been in my store, I think! That makes you one of my favorite people. You've been in my store, right?"

Joel admits, "Yes, I have been in your store…"

"You're a STUD!"

This is the only compliment that Tar knows.

estado

"Why do you think I'm a stud?"

"Because you have *estado* in my store!"

She thinks very highly of her customers, and so she uses this compliment on people who have been in her store. For her, this word "been" is *estado*. She stresses the "stad" part of the word, which sounds a little bit like "stud".

The word *estado* means "been", kind of like *sido* from Ser's roof. But *estado*, of course, refers to things like location, not what you are, because it's part of Estar rather than Ser.

For example, "I have been here" is "I have *estado aquí*."

But it applies to anyone: "We have been here" is "We have *estado aquí.*" "You have been here" is "You have *estado aquí*," and "They have been here" is "They have *estado aquí.*" The word *estado* never changes forms.

Recap of Estar

As always, our next step will be to learn phrases that use today's vocabulary in context.

First, make sure that you've truly internalized the layout of the Estar shop. Make sure you can close your eyes and walk around the Estar shop, visualizing the words that appear in each scene. Sit down and draw your own map of the store from memory to make sure it's all solid.

If any of the images are not clear in your mind, go back to that part of the lesson. Try to enhance the images in your imagination until they're really vivid.

Maybe you're forgetting *estuve* because the stew on Joel's face isn't smelly enough, or perhaps you can't remember *están* because in your

imagination, the pandas don't always appear on the lizard's tail. Imagine what it would be like to be a stuffed panda standing on a lizard's skinny tail, trying to stand up among the dizzying bright lights. Do anything you can to trigger the memory of the word "stand".

Once you can consistently remember the words from every scene, you're ready to move on to the next part of the lesson and learn some phrases.

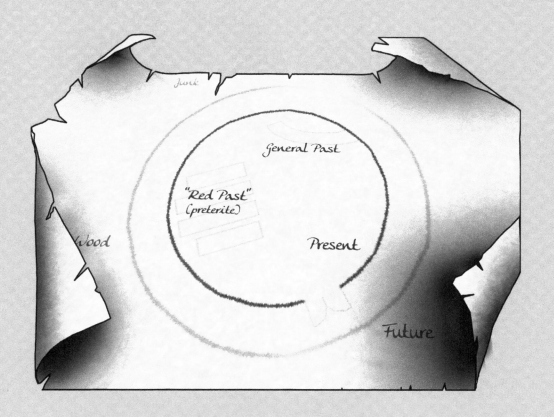

Lesson 4 Application:
Idioms

JUST LIKE WE'VE done before, we're going to learn a bunch of sentences. Most of these will probably make sense to you. However, there are several phrases that don't really make sense, and these phrases are called "idioms".

Before we get into those, let's work on some normal phrases below, modifying them for practice as we've done in previous lessons.

Estar Conjugations

Learn the sentences that are highlighted in blue. Some of them are now entirely in Spanish.

I am here.	*Estoy aquí.*
We are here.	*Estamos aquí.*
She will be here.	*Estará aquí.*
They were here.	*Estaban aquí.*
They are here.	*Están aquí.*
You were here.	*Estabas aquí.*

How is Isabella?	¿How *está* Isabella?
How are the kids?	¿How *están* the kids?
How was Matías?	¿How *estaba* Matías?
How were your friends?	¿How *estában* your friends?
How would by brother be?	¿How *estaría mi* brother?

Remember that preterites, such as *estuve* and *estuvo*, tend to indicate a one-time event.

I got really lonely.	*Estuve muy* lonely.
My brother got really sick.	*Mi* brother *estuvo muy* sick.

In Lesson 2, we learned the word *siendo* on Ser's bell. This word is normally preceded by a conjugation of Estar, which ends up being the part of the sentence that indicates who it is that's doing the action. Meanwhile, *siendo* doesn't change.

For example, *"estás siendo* a baby" means "you're being a baby". If I change the Estar conjugation from *estás* to *estoy*, then suddenly I'm the one that's being a baby.

You're being mean.	*Estás siendo* mean.
I'm being mean.	*Estoy siendo* mean.
They were being mean.	*Estaban siendo* mean.

Subjunctive Estar

I want her to be fine.	I want *que* she *esté bien.*
I hope that Matías is fine.	I hope *que* Matías *esté bien.*
I recommend that you be here.	I recommend *que* you *estés aquí.*

Remember the *para que (subjunctive)* construction that we learned in Lesson 3? It's coming back to bite us in the next examples. If you're not comfortable switching out words and customizing customizing this sentence, just focus on learning the sentence highlighted in blue.

I did it in order that you should be here.	*Lo* I did *para que estés aquí.*
He did it in order that I should be here.	*Lo* he did *para que yo esté aquí.*
They did it in order that Santiago be well.	*Lo* they did *para que Santiago esté bien.*

Unconjugated forms

I love being here.	I love *estar aquí.*
I want to be here.	I want *estar aquí.*
You need to be at home.	You need *estar en* home.

Isabella has not been well.	*Isabella no* has *estado bien.*
Matías has not been here.	*Matías no* has *estado aquí.*
We all have been well.	We all have *estado bien.*

Idioms

Sometimes Joel puts words together, and suddenly they don't seem to mean what they mean. For some reason, combining two or three words can suddenly creates a new meaning that doesn't really have anything to do with the original words.

This happens in English as well. Just look at those two words I just used: <u>"as well"</u>.

We would translate that phrase as"also". But the individual words don't have anything to do with "also": The word <u>"as"</u> means "like", "how", or "while". The word <u>"well"</u> means "fine" or "excellently". But somehow, when you put them together, you get a different meaning:"also". It seems illogical, but it's how our bizarre language works.

Spanish has its own idioms. A great example is ***"Ya está."***

Based on the individual words, this seems to translate as"now it is". But actually, ***"Ya está"*** is used to mean something reassuring or forward-looking: "It's OK" or "It's done."

Let's create a sample scenario. Suppose you spill hot sauce all over the table and ask your waiter for an extra napkin, but he's crazy busy and forgets to bring it. You can't wait any longer, so you go ahead and get the napkin yourself. He comes back, realizes his mistake, and apologizes: "Oh, did I forget to get you extra napkins? I'm so sorry!"

You respond politely: "It's OK, I got it. It's done."

Everything that you said in that response is summed up in the phrase ***"ya está"***. It's kind of like saying, "It's all said and done. There's no need to worry about it at this point."

This phrase is used twice in our dialogue between Matías and Santiago, which we'll look at again soon. They use it to indicate that the past is in the past and it's time to focus on the future.

Another idiomatic phrase is ***"no está"***. This is not terribly strange, but it's very different from English. ***"No está"*** literally means that someone "isn't". But it's used to mean that someone "isn't around" or "isn't here". (This kind of makes sense since the verb Estar, by default, tends to refer to location.)

This is used several times in the dialogue that we're studying between Matías and Santiago. Some people are on summer vacation, and others are just disappearing for no reason.

Yes, Sebastián, he isn't around anymore.	***Sí, Sebastián,*** he ***ya no está.***
No, Sofia, she isn't around anymore.	***No***, Sofia, she ***ya no está.***
Yes, Matías, he isn't around anymore.	***Sí***, Matías, he ***ya no está.***

Just one more idiomatic phrase. You've been taught that *en* means "at". Well, let's throw a wrench in the works. When talking about time, Joel usually uses *a* instead of *en*. Joel likes clocks, and it gives him pleasure to say "ahh!" when thinking about moments on the clock. To say "at four o'clock", Joel says "*a* four o'clock".

Now let's make it even more complicated. In old, formal English, someone might use the following statement: "I'll be happy upon arriving at home." In that case, the word "upon" was used to indicate the time that an action takes place: The action of "arriving".

Joel likes this formal mode of talking, but instead of "upon", he prefers to use his "ahhh!" voice. In Lesson 3, we learned that *al* means "to the". But since *a* can refer to time, *al* can be used to refer to the time something happens, such as "upon being at home" (*al* being at home) or "when standing in the rain" (*al* standing in the rain). In these cases, *al* is always followed by the infinitive.

I'll be happy upon being at home.	*Estaré* happy *al estar en* home.
I'll be delighted upon being a teacher.	*Estaré* delighted *al ser* a teacher.
I was upset upon being sick.	*Estuve* upset *al estar* sick.

That last one basically means "I was upset upon getting sick". As you can see, if you translate word by word, you get something very different from the meaning: "I was upset to the to be sick." The better you can get to know these genuine Spanish sentences and idioms, the less you'll have to worry about the frustration of word-by-word translation.

Are You In Your Comfort Zone?

Be honest with yourself: Do you have a strong grasp of what's been taught in this lesson? Even if you think you're understanding a lot of these words and idioms, you need to make sure you've actually mastered them before moving on. Do you think you could use *"ya está"* or *"al estar aquí"* properly in a conversation?

The best way to test yourself is with a native Spanish speaker who will give you honest feedback. Nothing can replace real conversation.

But even if you don't have someone like that, the next best thing is to use the practice materials at SpanishIn1Month.com. Make sure you've truly mastered Lesson 4, and test yourself to make sure you're pronouncing everything correctly. Every word and phrase in this book has been recorded by native speakers for you to listen to, all for free.

Of course, that includes a recording of our conversation between Matías and Santiago.

- Hello, I'm Matías. Who is this?

- Hi Matías, it's me, Santiago.

- Santiago, all this time, ¿right?

- Yes I know! ¿How are you?

- Fine thanks, and you? ¿How is Isabella?

- Not so well, you know, she left her house.

- What! This isn't good at all.

- No, this time she doesn't have a place to be. You have to do her a favor, on my behalf.

- Yes, I want to be with her now. What can I do for Isabella or for you?

- You're very nice! I have her things at my house, as it should be, but...

- ¿Can I do something?

- I think so, it's a big deal.

- ¿But, why did she leave?

- She left, that's all... right, so, now we're going to do something when Valentina isn't around.

- ¿Valentina? But... why? If those two are like one, as you know, a...

- I know that they were, but now they aren't.

She left, **eso es todo**... right, so, now we're going to do something when **no** Valentina is around.

¿Valentina? **Pero...** ¿**por qué**? **Si** those two **son como** one, as you know, **una**...

I know **que lo eran, pero ya no lo son.**

- Valentina is that way, and with her everything's like that, that's Valentina... And Sofía? She can...

- No, not Sofía, she isn't around.

- I am here, you are there... we're all here, the time is now.

Valentina **es** that way, **y con** her **todo es** like that, that **es** Valentina... ¿**Y** Sofía? She can...

No, Sofía **no**, she **no está**.

Yo am **aquí**, you **estás aquí**... all of us **estamos aquí**, **el** time **es** now.

- Maybe so, us both, with her. This time I don't know what to do.

- She can be at my house all the time. I can do you that favor, because I only want her to be well, and you to be well.

It might be **que sí**, us both, **con** her. **Esta** time **no** I know **qué** to do.

She can **estar en mi** house **todo el** time. **Te** I can do that favor, because I only want **que** she **esté bien y que** you **estés bien**.

189

- That which was, is not anymore... now, everything's this way!

- Give it time. She's around, and her things at your house, at least it's something. And that gentleman?

- ¿Sebastián?

- I don't know, that man that was around with her at the house.

- Ah, yes, Sebastián, he isn't around anymore, and because of this she can't be at Mr. Sebastián's house.

- ¿He isn't? ¿What do you mean he isn't around? ¿Really? That can't be, but if the house was his!

- He left from the house, that's the truth. This has been this way for a while now. Now I know that she's doing badly.

- All right, well then, Isabella has been unwell for a while. Now we have to do something for her, I want to do something for her, both of us.

- Yes, I want... I'm leaving now, I'll go with Isabella.

- All right, I also will go to your house, I want to be with her.

LESSON 5

Gamify

If you don't love language learning, you're going to give up.

It's not enough to want to be fluent in Spanish. To succeed, you have to love the learning process itself. You have to look forward to studying and practicing. You have to find a way to enjoy every moment.

Let's learn how hard work can be a game, how adults can learn languages faster than children, and how you can put positive energy into every challenge that comes your way.

Lesson 5 Theory:
Gamify

Calvin: "Hey, wait a minute! It's summer! I'm on vacation! I don't want to *learn* anything!"

Hobbes: "If nobody makes you do it, it counts as fun."

IF YOU'VE made it past Lesson 4, congratulations! You're beyond the point where most students go down in flames.

After working with hundreds of coaching students one-on-one, I have a steadily growing roster of successful students who stuck to the process. They now speak good conversational Spanish, and many are fluent.

But sadly, I have a longer list of ex-students who all quit before they reached their goals. Each one has their own reason for giving up:

- "I just can't find the time anymore."

- "It's harder than I thought it would be."

- "I get really distracted and can no longer focus on this."

- "It doesn't seem to be worth all the trouble."

All these excuses demonstrate one thing that these students have in common:

They lost their love for the process.

Before you go any further, I want to get one thing clear: No excuse is valid, period. If you really want to learn Spanish, you can do it. But if you give up, it's because you don't love learning enough. Your attention has drifted to other places.

Don't complain that you have no time, that you're not smart enough, that you have no empty space left in your mind. These problems are all imaginary, and serious Spanish learners have overcome them and many more.

For anyone who is starting to get frustrated or lose their passion for learning Spanish, here's the reality: The surest way to meet your goal is to regain a child-like obsession with it.

Speaking of "child-like obsession", here's one of the most common (and least valid) excuses that I hear:

"I think I'm just too old."

If you're tempted to use your age as an excuse, I have news for you.

Children are NOT better than adults at learning second languages. Controlled studies throughout the decades have demonstrated this fact.

Just a few examples:

Asher and Price, 1967: Three groups of students were tested on how well they could learn German: elementary (4-11), junior high (12-14), and college (18-25). The conclusion: "Both the junior high and college groups are superior to the elementary age group."

Olsen and Samuels, 1973: Adolescents and children were given short lessons in German pronunciation. The adolescents performed better than the children.

Fathman, 1975: Non-English-speaking children, ages ranging from 6-15, were tested on their ability to learn grammatical structures of the English language.

The older children scored higher.

Ekstrand, 1976: Immigrants of many ages were tested on their learning of Swedish within a short period of time. The older students performed better than the younger students in all areas tested.

Snow and Hoefnagel-Höhle, 1978: Three groups were working on learning Dutch naturalistically: children, adolescents, and adults. Over ten months, the adults and adolescents performed better than the children.

Ferman and Karni, 2010: Three groups of students were tested on their ability to learn the morphology of a new language: 8-year-olds, 12-year-olds, and young adults. The adults performed best in general, and the 8-year-olds performed worst in all evaluations.

Yet the myth persists.

Admittedly, it seems reasonable on the surface.

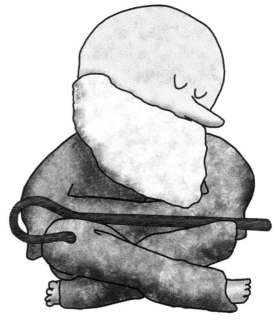

In real life, children DO seem to learn languages faster than adults. In fact, they seem to learn everything faster than adults!

Perhaps the studies mentioned are irrelevant to reality. Sure, adults may perform better in "controlled" circumstances, but real life isn't controlled like that. In day-to-day living, adults behave very differently from children.

Children have an easier time learning languages because their lifestyles are extremely different. Adults have countless obligations and pressures every day. But kids have a fun time finding a new challenge and sticking to it, day in and day out.

Let's think about the process of learning to ride a bicycle. Imagine that there are two people who are late to the game of learning to ride a bicycle: a 10-year-old child and her 30-year-old dad. The daughter is much more likely to end up learning. The dad is too busy with other things. But the kid REALLY wants to learn. All of her friends are riding bikes, and she feels left out. She's going to stay focused on that one thing, hour after hour every single day, until she's ready to fly around the neighborhood on two wheels like all the cool kids.

With language learning, the same thing happens: Adults and kids both say that they "want" to learn, but the child is more likely to have the focus and determination to stick through.

Still, some adults have maintained their passion and tenacity, using a principle that applies to any learner of any age:

Gamification.

Be Young and Be Reckless

Have you ever witnessed an 8-year-old playing a video game for 4 hours straight?

Pat Flynn, author of the WSJ best-seller "Will it Fly?", reports that during a long period of time in his life, he spent an average of 12 hours per day playing "World of Warcraft". One time he stayed up for 48 hours straight because of the addiction.

When a child finds a new obsession, whether it be a

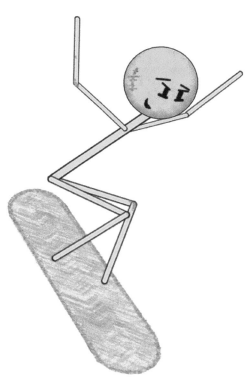

Lego set or a snowboard, you know that he'll spend every waking hour of every day on it if he can. His whole world will revolve around it. Your mind will be blown when you see how quickly he masters its nuances.

Children might even forget about eating and drinking for hours on end to engage in a stimulating, focused pursuit; they achieve complete flow. Maybe they're driven to reach more World of Warcraft milestones than their friends, or maybe they're dreaming of some day snowboarding down a slope in the Alps at 65 miles per hour. Either way, nothing else matters. The drive to accomplishment gives them a high that's more than worth the hunger, thirst, sleep deprivation, and injuries.

But here's the thing: This ability to obsess on one thing is not restricted to kids. Pat Flynn was in college during his World of Warcraft binging phase. He remains child-like in the best way possible, because throughout the years, he has retained this critical skill:

Relentless focus on something exciting.

Too many adults have lost this. Whether it's video games or new languages, we've been conditioned to have a short attention span outside of urgent work projects. External pressures cause us subliminally to question the way we use our time and our attention. It's uncomfortable to spend four hours trying to understand a ten-page children's book in Spanish. In the back of our minds, we feel like we're losing precious time.

In other words, many adults have lost their youthful persistence. We trade it for stress-based stimuli. If a project isn't urgent and pressing, it subconsciously doesn't feel worthwhile to spend time on it.

The solution: Don't just focus on learning. Focus on **loving** learning.

Notice the moments that you get bored. Identify

the parts of the learning process that frustrate you. Then turn them around by making them into a fun challenge.

- Have you gotten tired of memorizing verb conjugations? Instead of studying lists, imagine yourself walking around a "verb shop" made of funny scenes, identifying conjugations as you look around.

- Does pronunciation frustrate you? Pretend you're a bee from another planet, or maybe a bird

in a comic strip. Be an actor, and get into a separate personality while you practice. Have fun judging that person instead of yourself.

- Are you frustrated with how much vocabulary there is to learn? Instead of memorizing long lists of words, keep focusing on the essential vocabulary that you've already learned. Treat those words as solid landmarks in your mind. Then learn new words between those landmarks, as if coloring in the details or connecting the dots.

In Lesson 5, we have more vocabulary to learn than ever. But most of that vocabulary will be in scenes you already know, such as the amusement park and the plaza.

Reawaken your childlike wonder, and let's explore more of Joel's world than we've ever seen before.

Don't breeze over anything. You now have a solid foundation to build on, with essential vocabulary organized in your memory. But this method will collapse if you don't continue learning your vocabulary the same way, playing by the same rules, storing words in Joel's world even if you think you can remember them without the mnemonics.

But once again, this all comes down to one principle. Don't rush it, don't leave any pieces out, and don't get frustrated. Focus on the here and now, and enjoy each step. Love the game.

Lesson 5 Vocabulary:

Joel's House
(Home to Adjectives and Nouns)

IN THIS LESSON, as we learn more words than we've ever learned in a single lesson before, use a playful mindset.

Vocabulary is a game of discovery: We previously learned a few words here and there, but now we're finding the hidden treasures between them.

Try to beat each level, one at a time, by remembering what we previously learned and also mastering every new word in each scene.

Games with Pandas

Joel brings the pandas to the amusement park today. He's in a good mood, in a mischievous sort of way. He hopes to have fun by seeing the pandas get dizzy on one of the rides.

First of all, Joel goes to the binoculars to try to pick a ride. There are two rides in the park that go around in circles: The carousel and the ferris wheel. Both of these rides are round, so they're shaped like the letter O.

Looking back and forth between the two rides quickly, Joel asks himself, "Carousel, or ferris wheel?"

Instead of saying "or", Joel uses a new word: *o*: "Carousel *o* ferris wheel?"

The word *o* means "or", and you might use it when choosing between two O-shaped rides.

To represent this word, notice that one of the power lines has a tire on it instead of shoes. Between some of the

rides, the power lines make a Y shape for the word "and". But here, we have an O shape for the word "or". These two words, *y* and *o*, are very simple conjunctions, and they're used in similar ways.

There's one more word that's used this way. Joel looks further to the right, and the long power line between the ferris wheel and the water slide gives him an idea. Once in a while, the most adventurous guests in the park climb up the water slide, walk along the power line, and then hang from the power line by their knees. It would be

very interesting to see the pandas do that!

Joel asks the pandas, "Would you like to try hanging by your knees? It's lots of fun."

The pandas look down at their legs. "We can't," they say sadly. "We don't have any knees."

Joel investigates. Sure enough, these toy pandas can't bend their legs at all.

"None of you have knees?" Joel asks, looking at them one by one. "Not even one of you?"

Eventually, he gives up. "Nope. Neither this panda, nor this one, nor this one has any knees. Bummer."

It sounds like he says "neither" and "nor" a lot, but actually the word he uses is *ni*. This word serves as both "neither" and "nor". (It's pronounced like the word "knee".)

"*Ni* this panda *ni* this one *ni* this one."

Even though modern English doesn't use the words "neither" and "nor" very much, Spanish uses *ni* all the time.

To represent the word *ni*, let's once again use the power lines. In this case, there are knee guards hanging from the wire that runs from the ferris wheel to the water slide. Apparently, the last person to hang from this line had an unfortunate accident.

The words *y*, *o*, and *ni* are very similar in their uses. Remember that they're

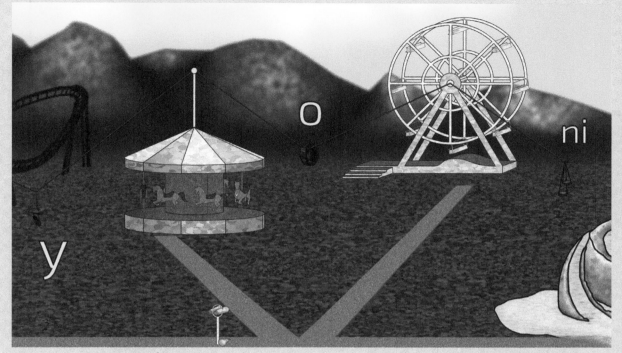

all conjunctions, so they can be used between entire phrases. But these tiny conjunctions are particularly special: They're often used between items in a list.

Meanwhile, we have two more conjunctions before we go to the rides themselves.

First of all, Joel continues to be indecisive of which ride to put the pandas on. Then a new thought occurs to him: "Maybe I can get them dizzy without putting them on a ride! I just have to convince them to spin around in circles."

He knows exactly how to do this. Pulling out his magic wand, Joel tells one of the pandas, "Here's how we'll decide which ride to take. You hold this magic wand and start turning around in circles. We'll go to the ride

it's pointing at when it lights up."

This selection method is like spinning a bottle or rolling dice. The idea is that they'll know which ride to take when the wand lights up. To say "when", Joel uses the word *cuando*: The'll know which ride to take *cuando* the wand lights up. (*Cuando* has the stressed syllable "wand".)

Joel's trick works. The panda spins around in circles, and when the magic wand lights up, it's pointing at the ferris wheel. However, the panda is so dizzy that it staggers around and falls over.

Between bouts of laughter, Joel remarks, "The wand lit up *cuando* it pointed at the ferris wheel! That's where we're going next."

Joel's laughter is rudely interrupted when he's knocked over by a pig, which proceeds to run into the binoculars.

In his fear and fury, Joel screams, "Why is there a pig in the amusement park?"

A strange, inebriated-sounding voice shouts back: "Because we have to sell pork in our concessions!"

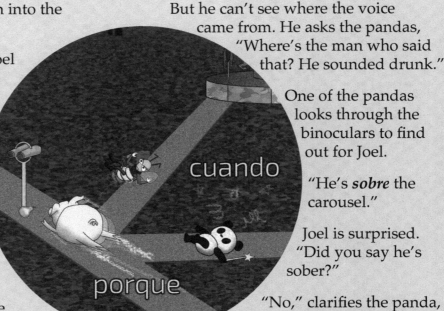

But to say this, the voice says "*Porque* we have to sell pork."

The word *porque* means "because". Note that the stressed syllable sounds like "pork".

Joel hates mammals, and he is furious that someone would try to justify their presence in an amusement park.

But he can't see where the voice came from. He asks the pandas, "Where's the man who said that? He sounded drunk."

One of the pandas looks through the binoculars to find out for Joel.

"He's *sobre* the carousel."

Joel is surprised. "Did you say he's sober?"

"No," clarifies the panda, "He's drunk. But he's *sobre* the carousel."

The word *sobre* means "on top of" or "over". The intoxicated man is on top of the carousel.

Some English speakers confuse the word *sobre* with the word *en*. Remember that *en* means "at", but it can also mean "in" or "on" in certain contexts. If you want to say that something is "on" something, you'll use *en* only if it's the normal way of being on something. Meanwhile, *sobre* clearly means "on top of", even in an unusual way.

As an example, if you're sitting "on" a chair, that's *en*, because that's the normal way to be at the chair (*en* the chair). If you're "on" a stage, that also is *en*,

because that's the normal way to be at the stage (*en* the stage).

But if you're on top of a house, or on top of a carousel, you probably won't use *en*; you're more likely to use *sobre*.

Now Joel is excited to ride the ferris wheel. He can't wait to see the pandas go around in circles and get dizzy again.

However, there's a complication. When Joel arrives at the ferris wheel, the operator tells him, "You can't get on the ferris wheel with those wings. I'm afraid you'll have to remove them." They point at a basket, where another insect's wings have been stashed.

Joel is shocked. "I can't take my wings off! I could NEVER be seen without my wings!"

His excuse is that he could never be "seen" without his wings. His word for "without" is *sin*, pronounced like "seen": "I could never be seen *sin* my wings."

Joel asks the operator, "Can I please ride with my wings on?" The operator refuses, but Joel asks again. When he asks, a big question mark falls out of Joel's mouth onto the ground.

This sometimes happens when Joel talks; his words turn into physical objects. This intimidates the ride operator a bit, but then Joel asks again. And again. Meanwhile, the question marks keep falling on the ground. He keeps asking for so long that the operator finally lets him get on. Joel walks up the staircase created by his question marks.

The pandas ask him, "How did you get the operator to change his mind?"

Very happy with himself, Joel explains, "I just asked! That's how I get everything I want! I just kept asking <u>until</u> success."

To say "until success", Joel says "*hasta* success." The word *hasta* roughly means "until", and the stressed syllable sounds kind of like the word "asked". Remember that like all other prepositions, it should be followed by a noun; for example "*hasta* that day" or "*hasta* next year".

Before proceeding to the countryside, look back through the pictures in this lesson and make sure you've internalized all the words. We have a lot more vocabulary to learn in this lesson, and you need to have *o*, *ni*, *cuando*, *porque*, *sobre*, *sin*, and *hasta* solidly in their places before moving on.

Remember: It's a game! Pull out a piece of paper and see if you can draw all of your conjunctions and prepositions from memory.

Once you've truly conquered the amusement park, you'll be ready for the army of challenges that the countryside will bring.

Games with Sheep

In Lesson 1, we learned that Joel likes to call himself *yo* when he's at the sheep pastures. This happens when he's the subject of the sentence; for example, sometimes he says "*yo soy* a bee."

Now we're going to learn what he calls other people in similar situations.

Today, Joel brings the pandas with him when he meets the shepherd. He wants to find a way to get tea from this shepherd, and he thinks the pandas will be able to help him. He's come with a plan.

But Joel's plan is to use a very strange excuse: He tells the shepherd, "The pandas and I all have oats stuck in our noses."

As you can see, Joel is holding a barrel of oats. He hopes that he can convince the shepherd to have compassion on him and the pandas. "We can't get these oats out of our noses, and it's very uncomfortable. If we have hot tea, the steam will soften the oats, and they'll slide back out of our noses. So can we please have that steaming hot tea?"

Here Joel is talking about both himself and the pandas, so the word he'll need is "we". For Joel, this word is *nosotros*. The stressed syllable sounds like "oat".

The shepherd tells Joel, "I'm sorry, but the tea isn't hot right now; it's actually cold. And I can't really heat it up at the moment, because both of my hands are full."

Joel gets a bit upset. He really wants

hot tea, but the shepherd has the pot in one hand and the staff in the other hand, so he can't really do much. Joel tells the shepherd, "Maybe you can't do it because you're holding two things, but I can do it!"

To say "you", Joel calls the shepherd *tú*, thinking about the fact that he's holding two things. Remember that Joel used the word *tu* in the woods because he had two staffs. Actually, believe it or not, *tú* is the shepherd's real name!

Notice that this version of the word has an accent mark, which means it's stronger than the version in the woods: *tu* means "your", but *tú* means "you".

Meanwhile, the sheep are continuing to do interesting things. The drunk male sheep is trying to dance, but it's not going very well. The shepherd laughs and says, "Look, *él* is trying to dance!"

Él is the name of the male sheep that drinks ale. Previously, we learned that *el* means "the", as in "the sheep". But this word has an accent mark over the E: *él*.

The word means "he". So when the shepherd says "*él* is trying to dance", he means "he is trying to dance".

But what about the word "she"? Let's look over at the female sheep. She also is dancing, but she's actually pretty good at it. So the shepherd says, "Heya! She's dancing too!"

To say "she", the shepherd uses the word *ella*. Don't be confused by the two letter Ls in that sentence; *ella* is pronounced "EY-a". In Spanish, when two Ls are together, they make a "Y" sound. (Don't ask me why, but I'm guessing that it has something to do with the fact that Joel always used to say "yeyo" instead of "yellow" when he was a larva.)

The point is that *ella* sounds a lot like "heya", and it means "she".

Before we move on, let's look at all of our new words together. We'll also include the word *yo* because it's grammatically similar.

These words are <u>subject pronouns</u>, which means they're used to indicate who is doing something. They're like the English words "he", "you", "she", "I", and "we".

The sentence "I am here" might be *yo estoy aquí*. If you change that to "he is here", it's *él está aquí*. It's similar with *ella está aquí*, *tú estás aquí*, and *nosotros estamos aquí*.

Of course, these subject pronouns aren't used all the time, because they're generally optional; in fact, Joel usually leaves them out of the sentence. For example, instead of *nosotros estamos aquí*, he's more likely simply to say *estamos aquí*, because *estamos* already implies "we are".

Still, these subject pronouns are used in order to be very specific or emphatic. We'll see examples later.

For now, just make sure that you can remember them all.

Also, while we're here, see if you can remember how to use all of our articles (words for "the" and "a"), which are painted on the fences. We don't have any new articles to learn today, but it's good to review them quickly, especially because it's important to distinguish them from the subject pronouns around them. The subject pronouns that we learned today (*él*, *ella*, etc.) are used like nouns: "*Él está aquí*" or "*nosotros estamos aquí*". But articles are used <u>before</u> nouns, as in "*un* man *está aquí*" or "*las* girls *están aquí.*

Noses (object pronouns)

The shepherd tells Joel, "Let's go sit down, and then I'll be able to get some tea ready for you." So they all go up to the hill where the tree is. He's about to pull out his hymnal, but Joel has no time for this.

"Come on, *tú*, you need to help!" says Joel.

"Whom do I need to help?" asks the shepherd.

"You need to help US and our noses!" yells Joel. But instead of "us", he uses the word *nos*, because he's thinking about their noses.

So *nos* is a direct object, just like *lo*, *la*, *me*, and *te*. For example, "you found us" would be "*nos* you found", just like "you found him" is "*lo* you found."

The shepherd doesn't like Joel's demanding attitude. "You need to learn to be patient," says the shepherd. "Let's take a walk."

Naturally, this doesn't make Joel any less frantic to get the tea. As they arrive at the crossroads, Joel asks the shepherd, "OK, we've been patient for two minutes. Will you give the tea <u>to us</u> now?"

Once again, Joel uses the word *nos*: "*Nos* will you give the tea?"

So *nos* means "us" as a direct object, but it also means "to us" here at the crossroads scene.

The shepherd looks carefully at Joel. "I don't believe that you actually have oats in your noses," he says frankly.

Joel is speechless. How dare the shepherd accuse him of lying!

But the shepherd keeps walking, and Joel and the pandas follow him to the reflexive stream. There, the shepherd says, "Look in the water at your reflections."

Staring back at them, Joel and the pandas see themselves, but with

enormous, pink, human-like noses.

"No oats!" says the shepherd. "So you don't get any tea."

The shepherd turns to walk back to the sheep pastures. "After him!" yells Joel. "Get the tea from him!"

But the pandas have already run in a different direction. They were freaked out by the appearance of strange noses on their faces. Joel looks around for a second and decides to go home alone.

More Eggs and Cards

When Joel arrives at the lake, he sees that there are now three cards floating on the water. The one in the middle is called *eso*, which means "that (thing, whatever it is)".

But now that he knows what these other two cards are, he calls them "that card" and "that card". He calls the one on the left "*esa* card" and the one on the right "*ese* card".

The word *eso* is a general "that", not referring to a noun of a particular gender. But if you're going to say "that (noun)", as in "that (card)" or "that (guy)", you'll use *esa* and *ese* before the noun, depending on the gender. For example, "*esa* (panda)" or "*ese* (lizard)".

Closer up, we have *esto*, which just means "this (thing, whatever it is)." But now, in addition to *esta* egg on the left, Joel also picks up *este* egg on the right.

Remember that *eso* and *esto* are neuter, which means they don't refer to actual nouns. But if you say "this" or "that" before a noun, like "this cup" or "that house", you need to match the gender with a feminine word (*esa* or *esta*) or a masculine word (*ese* or *este*).

Close your eyes and hold up two fists in front of you. Imagine you're holding two eggs, with one extra egg sitting in your lap. There's also a lake in the distance. What do you call the eggs in your two hands? How about the egg in your lap? What are the names of the three cards in the distance?

If you can remember all six words from this scene, you're ready to move on to the most mysterious scene in the countryside.

The Voices of the Swamp

In Lesson 1 we learned *qué* in the swamp when the shepherd fell in and found his wife's robe. *Qué* basically means "what", and it's generally used in questions. When Joel comes back today, he sees the cloak floating in the mire, and he wonders, "What is that?"

But then he also notices a hand floating in the water. It seems to be clutching a fistful of money. Of course, this greatly interests Joel! "Who is that?" he wonders, looking at all the Yen in the pale hand. But when he says "who", he actually says *¿quién?*

The word *quién* is like *qué* because it's used in questions. But this one means "who?", and it's pronounced "kYEN".

Joel says out loud, "I wonder if I can claim that money." He's hoping nobody will stop him from just taking it for himself, since the hand doesn't seem to need it for anything.

As soon as he says this, he thinks he sees a bunch of people nodding "yes" on the left side of the swamp. Yay! Someone agrees with him! This is enough for Joel: He flies down to the hand and takes the Yen away from it.

Looking back at the shore, Joel says, "Yay! The money's mine! Aren't you going to cheer now?"

But when he looks at his audience, he realizes that there's nobody there. The "people" that he thought were nodding are actually just some tall

nadie

"Yes," says the gravelly voice. Joel can't see anyone, but the sound is coming from the direction of the branch lying at the edge of the swamp. "I have all your Yen."

Joel is distressed. "Somebody has all my Yen, and I don't even know who it is."

The word for "somebody" is *alguien*. The stressed syllable is "all", but it also has "yen" at the end: "ALg-yen".

Make sure not to confuse *quién* with *alguien*. The word *quién* is in the deep part of the swamp right next to *qué*, and it's used in questions: "Who?" But *alguien* is used in statements when you're talking about "someone": "*Alguien* has all the Yen."

Joel is determined to get the money

green plants blowing in the wind.

This is disappointing. Joel's ego doesn't get to be stroked by an audience. He was hoping everyone would "nod" and say "yay", but there's nobody there.

Joel's word for "nobody" is *nadie*. This has the stressed syllable "nod", but it also has something that sounds like "yay" at the end. Nobody nodded and said "yay".

But Joel's disappointment isn't over. He suddenly realizes that there's nothing in his hand. The money has all disappeared!

"What?" shouts Joel. "Not a single piece of money is left? Now I have nothing?!" Joel's word for "nothing" is *nada*, as in "<u>not a</u> single piece of money".

A deep, croaky voice responds, "I have all your Yen now."

Joel is shocked. "ALL my Yen?"

alguien

nada

back. He flies close to the branch to see if he can find the source of this strange voice. But then, some toxic-looking bubbles of green algae start heaving in the swamp.

"RUN!" shouts the voice, and suddenly, a bunch of tiny stick men jump off of the branch, running in all directions. Each one is holding a Yen bill in his hand.

This frightens Joel. These stick figures were bold enough to steal his money, but now they're running away because there's something even scarier? What is this bubbly algae? It must be something very strange.

Joel's word for "something" is *algo*. It made them "all go" away, which is how you pronounce the word. And the spelling looks kind of like the English word "algae". One way or another, it's

"something" mysterious.

When the bubbling stops, there's one stick that stayed behind.

Joel is very impressed. What a courageous stick man, who, when everyone else ran away, bravely <u>stayed</u>!

"Who are you?" asks Joel. "Who is this brave stick man who <u>stayed</u> when everyone else ran away?"

But instead of simply saying "Who are you?", Joel says out of respect, "Who is *usted*?"

The word *usted* is a strange word for English speakers. It basically means "you", but it's used out of respect. And when you use verbs with it, you don't use the "you" conjugations; instead, you use "he/she/it" forms (what we call "lizard verbs").

So instead of saying "Who are you?", which sounds too rude and direct, what Joel is asking is something more like "Who is this?" or "*¿Quién es usted?*"

The words *algo*, *alguien*, and *usted* are located at the dead branch sitting next to the swamp. All three of these words are roughly interchangeable in

214

a sentence.

For example, you could say "something is here:" *"Algo está aquí."* You can also say "someone is here": *"Alguien está aquí."* To say "you are here", in a respectful tone, you would say *"Usted está aquí."*

Before moving on, we have just two more words in the swamp. You might have noticed that we placed *nada* and *nadie* on the left side of the swamp, where there's nothing and nobody. What's the opposite of each of these words?

Well, the right side of the swamp is where all the toads hang out. We already saw toads in Joel's bedroom, where we learned *todo* to mean "all", as in *"todo* the floor".

The toads can also be used as pronouns to mean "everything" or "everybody", which is why they're also here at the swamp.

In the mire of the swamp itself, we have *todo*, which can mean "everything". As you can see, that's directly across from *nada* ("nothing"),

because these words are opposites.

On the shore, we have a bunch of toads representing *todos*, meaning "everybody". That's the opposite of the shore on the left, where we have *nadie* ("nobody"). For example, to say "Everybody is here," Joel would say *"Todos están aquí."*

Look carefully at the illustration with all of our words in the swamp.

We went crazy with this scene today.

Remember that the whole point of this entire swamp game is to get one thing straight: You need to know where all the words in the swamp are.

Close your eyes, picture the swamp scene, and sweep from left to right: How do you say "nobody"? "nothing"? "somebody"? "something"? "you" (respectfully)? "everything"? "everybody"? In the deepest, darkest part of the swamp, how do you ask "what" and "who"?

Once you've owned the entire swamp, you're ready for one last scene in the countryside.

Joel's Parched Imagination

As Joel goes through the woods to go home, he becomes extremely thirsty. He didn't get any tea from the shepherd, and he forgot to take a drink at the lake.

He's so exhausted that he's forced to stop for a moment and rest. Sitting at the top of a tree, Joel begins to hallucinate.

The first thing that he thinks is, "That shepherd's tea is intended for me."

But the picture he imagines makes the shepherd's face into a pot of tea. The tea is dripping onto the word *mí*, which is sitting on a bed of oats. To the right and left, the *ella* sheep and the *él* sheep are dancing around with hula hoops and glasses of ale.

Joel is startled awake from his dream when he nearly falls out of the tree. What does it all mean?

These words are used at the end of a phrase, after a *preposition* (words at the amusement park rides). For example, to say "for me", Joel says *para mí*. This works for all the words in this scene:

> The tea is *para mí*. (for me)
>
> The tea is *para ti*. (for you)
>
> The tea is *para ella*. (for her)
>
> The tea is *para él*. (for him)
>
> The tea is *para nosotros*. (for us)

We'll see more examples of these words later, but for now, make sure you can remember each one in this scene. You'll notice that some of them look exactly the same as the words we learned in the sheep pastures, though *mí* and *ti* are very different from *yo*

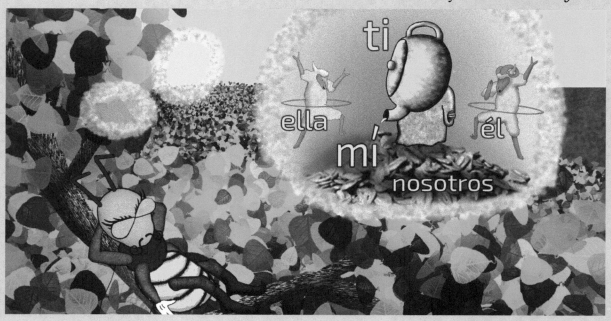

and *tú*. Keep the two scenes separate in your mind, and make sure all five words in this scene are very distinctly stored here.

Joel finally comes down from the tree and heads off to the marketplace. Before continuing, make sure you have your arms around the incredible number of pronouns we learned today. We've learn nearly all the pronouns that exist in Spanish, so once you've mastered these, you're close to a very high level of understanding of the language.

Games in the Plaza

Don't be intimidated by the fact that we have 17 new words to learn in the marketplace today.

Think of it as a game of connect-the-dots. We've already learned some words throughout the plaza. Quickly review these words, and think of them as landmarks. We're just going to fill in some of the blank space around each one.

First of all, when Joel arrives, he runs into the monument in the middle of the plaza. He's still dehydrated and a bit hungry, and in these situations he's always a bit clumsy. Joel's head gets stuck in a hole at the edge of the statue.

Confused, he looks around from this new position. When he sees the statue, he says "Hello!" But to say this, he says *hola*. The stressed syllable of this word sounds like "hole", but with a silent H: "OL-a."

He also sees a patch of grass, and in his state of confusion, he thinks that it might be food. Perhaps it's a steak made of grass-fed beef! Joel is very thankful to the statue: "Thank you! This is the grassiest grass-fed beef I've ever received!"

To say "thank you", Joel says *gracias*, which sounds a lot like "grassiest".

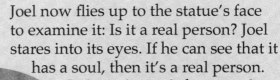

But the nearby butcher yells back to Joel, "That's not real beef! You have to buy from a real butcher, not a statue." Then it occurs to Joel that this patch of grass is not meat; in fact, it's not food at all. Disappointed, Joel says, "*Oh*."

The words *hola*, *gracias*, and *oh* are all interjections. They're often used all by themselves, not in a sentence. We're keeping these right here in front of the statue.

Joel now flies up to the statue's face to examine it: Is it a real person? Joel stares into its eyes. If he can see that it has a soul, then it's a real person. Only real people have souls.

One of the statue's eyes is open, and the other is closed. Joel stares into the open eye and says, "Only a real person has a soul." But the word he uses is *sólo*: "*Sólo* a real person has a soul."

Notice that the statue's eye looks like the letter O with an accent over it. This helps to represent the word *sólo*, which means "only".

The other eye, however, is closed, and the eyebrow makes it look like a question mark. Joel remembers the question marks that he created at the ferris wheel, and he's surprised: "Did I create enough question marks to go everywhere, even the statues face?" But when he says "even the statue's face", he says "*hasta* the statue's face."

Hasta means "even" in this sense. For example, to say "That's so easy, even I can do it," Joel would say "That's so easy, *hasta yo* can do it."

After staring at the statue's eyes for a while, Joel finally concludes that it doesn't have a soul. However, he thinks it

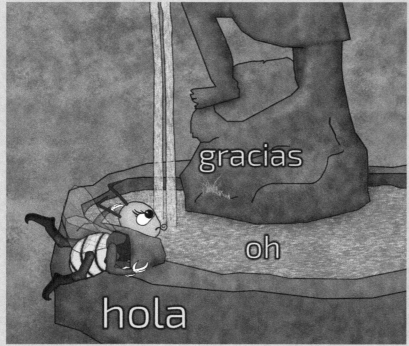

needs a name anyway. "I'm going to call it Tom," he says.

"Wow, Tom!" he tells the statue when he sees something in its ear. "You have money in your ear!" Sure enough, there's a rolled up Yen in the ear of "Tom".

"Let's see if there's Yen in the other ear also," says Joel. He looks in the left ear. Yep, there's a bill of Yen there as well!

"Cool, there's Yen in this ear too!" says Joel. To say this, he uses the word *también*, which means "also" (or "too" or "as well", all of which mean the same thing in English). This word has the stressed syllable of "yen", but there's also a slight emphasis on "tom": "tom-be-YEN."

These three words on the statue's face are used roughly the same way, as we'll see when we study sentence examples.

Tanned Butcher

Now that Joel's confirmed that the statue is not a living soul, and now that he has gotten a little free money from it, he goes over to the steak stand. Remember the landmark that we've already learned here: *muy*.

However, Joel doesn't buy anything at the butcher's stand today, because he sees something freaky happen.

The butcher prepares to talk to Joel about his steak, when suddenly a cloud moves away from the sun and the butcher is struck by the sunlight. Immediately, the previously pale butcher gets a total tan, a tan so dark that he's almost as red as the meat he sells.

Joel finds this very peculiar. How can the butcher tan so quickly? And why is he as red as the meat?

To say "so quickly", Joel says "*tan* quickly." The word *tan* means "so" in this sense. As you can see, it's exchangeable with *muy*: Something can be *tan* red (so red) or it can be *muy* red (very red).

Joel doesn't want to mess with this guy, so he goes over to the baker's stand.

Aunties Before Uncles

Here he sees something strange. A bunch of people are in line, wanting to buy bread. But as always, the baker doesn't want to sell it to them. Today the baker has come up with a new tactic: He's trying to confuse everyone with some strange, arbitrary rules for how to wait in line.

As you can see, he has painted some instructions on the front of his stand that insist that the ladies go first. But instead of saying "ladies first", the baker shouts over and over again, "Aunties before uncles!"

Then, every time either a man or a woman approaches, he asks, "Are you an auntie?" If she says "no", he responds, "Well, I

can't sell bread to you. I need to serve the aunties <u>first</u>."

The word here is *antes*. This word basically means "beforehand" or "first", and it's used in a variety of ways to indicate that something happens before something else. For now, just remember that the baker insists on serving the aunties *antes*.

Of course, in reality, he doesn't want to sell bread at all. To verify this, Joel cuts to the front of the line, insisting that he's an "auntie".

When Joel approaches, he's surprised by the rope that stretches all the way around the edge of the stand. Remember that previously, the stand slammed closed on the tip of the baker's knife. Joel asks, "How is it that this rope didn't break?"

The baker, happy to talk about something other than bread, says, "Oh yes, it's the finest hemp rope in

the world. It's always there; it never breaks."

Joel is impressed and says, "How long have you had this same hemp rope around your stand?"

The vendor says, "Always." But to say this, he uses the word *siempre*.

This word has a stressed syllable that sounds like "hemp" without the H. Notice that the hemp rope stretches all the way around the edges of the stand, which means that it represents all time, or "always". Meanwhile, the knife that we used to learn the word *ya* in Lesson 3 is small, sticking out of the middle of the stand. The word *ya* only takes up a small moment of time in the present. Compare *siempre* to *ya*, and you can see how this is illustrated.

If *siempre* surrounds the whole stand ("always") and *ya* takes up a small moment in time in the middle ("already" or "anymore"), where would we put the word for "never"?

This word won't be on the stand at all. The baker is hiding something behind the stand, and he never gets it out, as you're about to see.

Joel asks, "Do you have any new, freshly baked bread?"

The baker says, "Yes, of course! It's behind the stand here. But I only sell it at noon, so you'll have to come back then."

Joel doubts that the baker is serious, but he tells him, "OK, I'll order two loaves of new bread. Here, take ten yen. I'll be back at noon to pick it up."

Then Joel flies around for a few minutes. He comes back at exactly 12pm.

"OK, it's noon," he says. "Where's the new bread that I ordered?"

"You're too late," says the baker. "It's a few seconds after noon. So it's not available."

Joel concludes that when the baker says "noon", what he really means is "never". Joel's word for "never" is *nunca*, which has the stressed syllable "noon".

Now Joel is really angry. He tells the baker, "I want what I ordered, and I want it NOW!"

As he says this, he slams his fist down on the biggest loaf of bread in the center of the stand. "I want my order *ahora!*"

The word *ahora*, which sounds vaguely like the word "order", means "now". Remember that the H is silent, so the word is actually pronounced "a-OR-a".

Just then, there's a strange ringing sound, like a high-pitched buzz. One of the ears of grain sitting on the stand is ringing.

The baker tells everyone, "OK, that means it's 5:00, closing time! I'll see you all tomorrow!"

Joel is baffled. "What do you mean 5:00? It was just now noon."

"No," says the baker, "You see these ears of grain? Their ringtones are always correct. This particular ringtone means it's 5pm. And if the tone says it's 5:00, then it's 5:00."

To say this, the baker actually says, "If the tone says it's 5:00, *entonces* it's 5:00."

The word *entonces* basically means "then", and the stressed syllable sounds like "tone". These wheat ears lying around the stand are a gimmick that the baker uses to convince people he needs to close up shop.

Before we move on to the next stand, make sure you can remember all the words from the baker's stand. *Ya* and *ahora* are in the middle, because they represent the present moment. *Entonces* is all around them, because "then" can happen at pretty much any time. *Siempre* is around the edges, because it represents all time. *Nunca* is behind the stand, because it represents no time. And then, of course, if you look at the line of people, we have the aunties first, or *antes*.

Dawn-Day Melons

When Joel arrives at the fruit stand, he's frightened to see a spider.

"Ay!" he shouts. "There's a spider on your fruit there!"

The fruit merchant says, "Where is it?"

Joel responds, *"Ahí!"*

The word *ahí* roughly means "there", and it's pronounced "ah-EE". As you can see in the picture, it's on the basket of fruit, but closer to the fruit stand owner.

"Your fruit is spider-infested," says Joel. "I could report you for this."

The fruit merchant doesn't like that idea at all. He quickly tries to distract Joel.

"Um… hey, look at the beautiful sunrise! It's dawn!"

But it's early afternoon. Why is the fruit merchant saying it's dawn?

Joel looks back and forth. "I don't see the sunrise anywhere. Where am I supposed to look?"

The fruit merchant improvises: "What I meant is, look at that melon hanging there. It looks like a sunrise. It's a dawn-day melon!"

Once again, Joel is confused. There are two slices of melon hanging up, and they both look like pictures of the sunrise. "Where do you want me to look?" asks Joel.

But the question sounds like this: *"¿Dónde?"*

The word *dónde* means "where?" in questions. The two "dawn-day" melons hanging on the fruit stand represent Joel's confusion as he asks, "Where?" *"¿Dónde?"*

Based on the way that we've arranged these words, you can answer the question at the top with either of the questions at the bottom. If someone asks, *"¿Dónde?"*, you can answer with either "here" or "there": *aquí* or *ahí*.

223

Monkey See, Monkey Comb

Joel is annoyed at the crazy fruit merchant with his spiders and "dawn-day" melons, so he goes over to the vegetable stand.

Once again, he's struck by the farmer's interesting hairdo. He asks the farmer, "How do you comb your hair that way?"

To ask this question, Joel uses the word *cómo*: "*¿Cómo* do you comb your hair that way?"

This word is very similar to one of our words from Lesson 3, *como*, which means "as". But in this case, it has an accent mark. The word *cómo* is used in questions, and it means "how?"

As a joke, the farmer answers: "*Muy bien!*"

He's proud of the way that he combs his hair; when Joel asks "How do you comb it?", the farmer answers "Very well!"

"Yes," says Joel, "I can see that. But how exactly do you do it?"

"Like this, <u>as you see</u>!" says the farmer. He picks up a comb and once again combs the top of a carrot. "Just comb it *así!* As you

see, like this!"

The word *así*, which sounds like "as see", means "like this" or "like that".

Notice the way that these words are arranged at the vegetable stand. If someone asks the question, "*¿Cómo* do you do it?", you can answer with any of these words:

- *Así.* (Like this.)

- *Bien.* (Well.)

- *Como* I do it. (As I do it.)

Practice with yourself a little bit, asking and answering questions like *¿Cómo?* and *¿Dónde?*

Also walk around the entire plaza for a while, making sure you can remember all of the words. Once you're ready, follow Joel back to his house.

224

Joel's Messy Yard

Before Joel goes inside, he decides to take a trip around the outside of the house.

The first thing he encounters, of course, is his mossy car, where we keep the word *más* (more).

There's a similar word kept here as well. Inside Joel's blue car, he keeps a special hoard of tea bags. Just like the car, these tea bags sit on his driveway completely unused; they're just there to comfort Joel and give him a sense of security.

When Joel compares himself with other people, he likes to talk about his hoard of tea: "My hoard is better than anyone else's hoard!"

Joel's word for "better" is *mejor*, which sounds a lot like "my hoard".

If we go over to the other side of Joel's garage, we can see that he has a second car.

This is the car that Joel actually drives once in a while. But he doesn't like it very much. He thinks the color is wrong; it's pale yellow, like a giant oat. While his blue car in front is special, Joel just calls this his "other" car. And his word for "other" is *otro*, with the stressed syllable "oat".

Something important to know about *otro* is that, like many adjectives, it actually changes slightly based on the noun that it's modifying. You can see that it ends with the letter O. But it will actually change to *otra* when it's used with a feminine noun. For example, to say "another woman", you would say "*otra* woman."

Next we come to an area in Joel's yard that he's not very familiar with: The back yard. Joel really doesn't like this area at all, because he thinks that too many animals visit this area. Remember that he's afraid of all mammals. In particular, there was one night

225

when he got lost in this part of his yard, and it was very frightening for him.

This is the part of the yard designated for numbers. For most practical purposes, it's most important to learn two numbers: The numbers for 1 and 2.

Now the thing about the number 1 is that it's actually based on the article *un*, which we learned at the sheep pastures in the country. When you put it before a noun, it's *un* or *una*. But when it's by itself, "one", you put an "O" at the end, *uno*. Joel sometimes refers to himself as "number one", so we'll just stick the number 1 on Joel here as he's in this place he doesn't like.

Today, Joel realizes that he's in this scary area when he sees two female

deer lying down. There are two deer here, and they have really long necks that are curved like the number 2. These deer are <u>does</u>, so whenever Joel sees the number 2, he remembers these deer, and he thinks "does", or *dos*. So for the number 2, think about the long curved necks of these does, and remember that that 2 is *dos*.

Next, Joel comes to the front yard. This is where we store words that describe people.

Let's begin with Joel's description of himself: Joel would describe himself as a "winner". He's such an egotist that he thinks he's the standard of all that is good. He has even painted a giant trophy on the front of his house to indicate how great he is, and when he looks at it, he thinks to himself, "I win!"

The word *bueno*, when pronounced by a native Spanish speaker, has something that sounds like "win" as the stressed part of the word. *Bueno* means "good" or "nice" when used to describe a person.

Also note that *bueno* changes to *buena* when it describes a feminine noun, such as a female

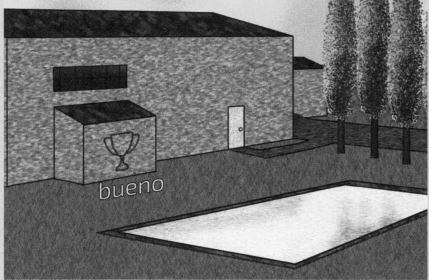

person or a noun that we'll store on the left side of the rooms where nouns are located.

Speaking of which, let's start storing those nouns. It's time to take a quick look around inside Joel's house.

Flying Tour of Joel's House

As we learn nouns in this lesson, note that we're only learning a few landmarks throughout the house. The game right now is to remember each individual word and the name of the room that it's in. Later, in Lesson 7, we'll connect all these dots so that you can walk around the house in your imagination.

The first room we'll visit is Joel's living room. Joel has a private theater, where very tiny creatures put on shows to entertain him. Joel's favorite show is about a rich man and a poor man. The rich man, on the far right, lives in a palace, while the poor man lives on his mule.

Joel loves this play, because the rich man laughs at the poor man constantly. The poor man has trouble sleeping at night, because his "home" is very noisy: The mule brays during the night, making it hard to sleep. Joel calls the man an *hombre*, which sounds like "home bray" (with a silent H), because his <u>home brays</u> all the time.

Meanwhile, he calls the rich man *señor*. The reason is a little strange:

227

Joel associates rich men like this with "olden times", or "days of yore". He likes using quaint, formal language with people he respects, so "yor" is the stressed syllable of his word for "mister" or "gentleman".

Also note that one of the actors on the stage is a card that says *uno*. This card is one of the characters in the play, and it represents the fact that the word *uno* can mean "a person" in Spanish, just like in English sometimes we say "one" when we are referring to a hypothetical person. You'll see examples of this soon.

Next we come to Joel's kitchen.

Joel often hires a professional to cook food for him. But he actually never pays the guy. For some reason this cook is happy to serve Joel without any pay. Anytime Joel wants this man to make a meal for him he asks the man to do it "as a favor"; he asks the man to do it *por favor*.

The word *favor* literally means "favor". Note that it's not pronounced like the English word "favor". Our English word has a stress on the first syllable, but the Spanish word has the stress at the end: fa-VOR.

The reason this such a common word is because of the idiom *por favor*, which is how Joel says "please". Meanwhile, for each favor that the chef does for Joel, he puts another tally mark on the countertop. These tally marks represent the favors that the chef has done Joel.

On the left side of the island in the middle of the kitchen are some of Joel's magic coasters. These are special hand-crafted coasters, but Joel doesn't just set his coffee or his tea on these coasters. He uses them for other things. They're extremely special and technologically advanced. In fact, they are made so that when Joel snaps his wings together, kind of like snapping his fingers, the coasters momentarily

turn into whatever he wants them to be. The coasters can be absolutely anything. Joel can snap his wings and they turn into teacups, although they'll go back into being coasters after a little while.

Joel calls these coasters his *cosas*. The word *cosa* simply means "thing" and it is probably the handiest noun in the Spanish language. You can use it to mean almost anything you want it to mean.

When you use this word, note that these coasters are on the left side of the kitchen. That's because the word "thing" is feminine. So you would apply feminine articles and adjectives: *la cosa* (the thing), *una cosa* (a thing), *otra cosa* (another thing).

In Joel's refrigerator, he keeps a pair of wings that his dad gave him. There's a backstory to this.

When Joel was a child, he and his father were out for a walk, when Joel stumbled across a pair of insect wings lying on the ground. "Whose wings were these?" wondered the young Joel.

His dad told him, jokingly, "Oh no, my wings! I lost my wings! …Oh look, I grew another pair."

Of course, those weren't Joel's dad's wings. But for some reason, Joel thought his dad was telling the truth. And he was so impressed that he took the wings home and decided to preserve them for the rest of his life. "These are the wings my dad lost! But he grew another pair really fast!"

Even as an adult, Joel often tells people the story of his dad's wings. But other people don't believe that it's true. In reality, his dad could never grow wings back so quickly. But Joel denies that his dad would ever tell a lie. "Everything my dad says is truth," he insists.

Joel's word for truth is *verdad.* The stressed syllable is "dad". Whenever Joel wants to insist that something is true, he takes an oath on his father's wings: "It's as true as if my dad said it. It's *la verdad.*"

Let's go upstairs. In Joel's ballroom, we have several nouns related to time. In fact, there are two nouns that mean "time". Let's start with those.

There's a large, ancient temple on the right side of Joel's ballroom. This temple is not very conveniently placed because it's hard to dance around it, but Joel doesn't mind. This old temple has been here for a long time. In fact, Joel has no idea how old this thing is; it's probably older than the house itself. But all Joel knows is that it's been here an extremely long time. To say "a long time", we would say that it's been here for a lot of *tiempo*, which sounds like a mispronunciation of the word "temple". Notice that this word has the same stressed syllable as the word *siempre*, "emp". *Tiempo* means "time", as in "the passing of time".

But on the left side of the ballroom, there's another large item that gets in the way of the dancers: A giant vase. This is extremely different from the temple; it's very fragile, and in fact it breaks every time Joel has a party. So he has to go out and buy a new vase every single time he has a party. And in each case, he hopes that the vase doesn't break "this time". To say "this time" he says *esta vez*. "I hope that the vase doesn't break *esta vez*."

So we have *el tiempo* on the right side, which is time: The stuff that goes by. But have *la vez* on the left side, which is a one-time occurrence, the "time" that something happens. *Una vez* refers to a single instance or event.

On the left side of the ballroom are some enormous windows. Joel's parties always take place at night, but Joel isn't particularly fond of the dark. During his parties, Joel does not like to be chased, especially toward the dark windows, because he likes to pretend that it's daytime and he would rather not be reminded that it's dark outside. So for his parties Joel has a "no chase" policy. No chasing anybody towards the window, especially Joel. The word for "night" is *noche*.

Joel tries to spend more time on the right side of the ballroom, where he has painted the letter D over and over to look like the sun. For him, daytime is all about the letter D (as in "day"). His word for "day" is *día*.

Note that *día* is on the right side; it's a masculine noun, even though it may appear feminine since it ends with an "a". But it's 100% masculine. For example, to say "another day", we would say *otro día*.

Now look at the ceiling. There are onions hanging down on the right side, instead of chandeliers. Joel buys a new onion every year for his biggest annual party. Joel is very eccentric this way, and for some reason he likes to have a giant party with a new onion each year. So on the right side of the room you can see three onions so far. And each of these onions represents a different year that he had a party. The word *año*, which sounds kind of like "onion", means "year".

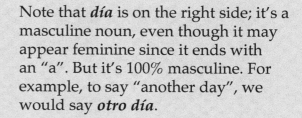

Next let's go to Joel's library, where one of the most prominent features is a bookshelf shaped like a house.

Joel thinks about money whenever he looks at this bookcase, for three reasons. First of all, he paid a lot of money to have this bookcase custom made. Second, it reminds him of his house itself, which cost a fortune. Third, he uses this shelf to store his books that actually

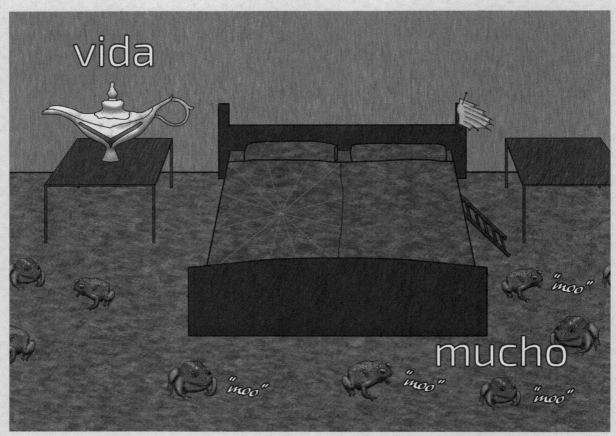

cost him money. (He normally steals or "borrows" books, but he actually paid for these books.)

Because Joel thinks about money and cost, his word for "house" or "home" is *casa*. We'll continue to use Joel's library to store nouns related to location, but for now, just keep in mind that the *casa*, or "home", is on the left side of the library.

While we're upstairs, let's go to Joel's bedroom. Remember that we learned the word *todo* here as a noun for "all" or "everything". All of his floor was covered with toads. Joel's bedroom is where we remember parts of something or amounts of something.

All of the toads are an inconvenience, but some are worse than others: Many of the toads "moo" during the night, like cows (or fresh steaks).

This makes it very difficult for Joel to sleep sometimes. He's haunted most of the night by some of the toads, who say, "Moo, Joel! Moo!"

The word for "many" or "much" is *mucho*. The stressed syllable is "moo". (Remember that this isn't all of the toads, but it's a lot of them.)

On a nightstand to the left of Joel's bed is a lantern. Joel believes in magic, and he thinks that if he sleeps with a magic lantern next to his bed, it will give him a longer life.

Joel calls this lantern his "V lantern", because it's shaped like a letter V. His word for "life" is *vida*, which he thinks is a magical-sounding word.

You've now learned all of the most common nouns in Spanish. You might wonder why some of these nouns, such as "truth" (*verdad*) and "life" (*vida*), are so common in Spanish (they aren't as frequently used in English). But the reason will become clear as we study idioms in the next section.

Lesson 5 Application:
More Idioms

AS YOU WORK ON phrases today, treat each section as a game with two levels. To pass "Level 1", you have to be able to say the highlighted Spanish sentences from memory, and you know what you're saying. To pass "Level 2", you need to gain proficiency in modifying those original sentences by switching out equivalent words (as we've done with some examples that aren't highlighted).

Conjunctions

The phrase *o sea* is an interesting idiom. It basically means "I mean…" or "In other words…" In fact, you can use it to rephrase what you're saying without explicitly admitting that it was a mistake.

It's my friend's… I mean, my brother's.	*Es de mi* friend… *o sea, de mi* brother.

Our weird uncle the subjunctive mood is coming back to haunt us with the word *cuando*. For some reason, when speaking about a future event, Joel always uses a subjunctive after *cuando,* as if to say "when that <u>be</u> the case…" So "When she's here" changes to "When <u>she be</u> here" (*cuando <u>esté</u> aquí*).

However, if you change this sentence and replace *cuando* with almost any other conjunction, the mood changes back to the normal verb mood. You can practice switching out other conjunctions with *cuando*.

We're going to do something when Valentina's not around.	We're going to do *algo cuando no esté* Valentina.
We're going to do something but Valentina's not around.	We're going to do *algo pero no está* Valentina.
I'm going to do something when Valentina's not around.	I'm going to do *algo cuando no esté* Valentina.
I'm going to do something and Valentina's not around.	I'm going to do *algo y no está* Valentina.

Now for an idiom that makes no sense at all. The phrase *"de vez en cuando"* sounds like complete nonsense when it's translated to English ("of time at when"?), but it's used to mean "once in a while". Use it a few times to get the hang of it.

It was only once in a while.	*Era sólo de vez en cuando.*
I was here once in a while.	*Estaba aquí de vez en cuando.*

Now let's use the word "ni". We already know that it means "nor"/"neither". But it also is used in a weird little idiom for "as soon as": *ni bien*. Once again, this idiom doesn't make sense when translated, but just get used to it…

As soon as that happens, I'll tell him.	*Ni bien eso* happens, *le* I'll tell.
As soon as I do it, I'll tell you.	*Ni bien lo* I do, *te* I'll tell.

Neither he nor she was around that time.	*Ni él ni ella estaban esa vez.*
Neither I nor you was around that time.	*Ni yo ni tú estábamos esa vez.*

Prepositions

We have two idioms to learn with today's prepositions.

First of all, in order to say "especially", Joel generally just uses simple vocabulary and says "above all". So to say "especially", use the phrase *sobre todo*.

Especially with this type of things.	*Sobre todo con este* type *de cosas.*
Especially at the house.	*Sobre todo en la casa.*

Often, *hasta* is used when we say "until" something, for example "until yesterday". Since it's a preposition, it gets a noun after it:

So I was with Ignacio until that day.	*Entonces estaba con Ignacio hasta ese día.*
So I was with him until that night.	*Entonces estaba con él hasta esa noche.*
So we were with her until that year.	*Entonces estábamos con ella hasta ese año.*

In each of the cases above, the word *hasta* was followed by some sort of noun. However, what if you changed "until today" to "until you're here"?

In that case, we suddenly have the equivalent of an entire sentence after the *hasta*: "You're here." For this to work, we have to use the idiom *hasta que*….

Remember that phrases starting with *que* are often exchangeable with nouns. That's what's happening here. You could say *hasta ese día*, in which case *hasta* is followed by a noun. Or you could say *hasta que estaba aquí,* in which case *"hasta que"* is followed by an entire sentence.

But here's where it gets even more complicated: The phrase *hasta que* is a lot like the word *cuando.* If it refers to the future, the phrase after *que* has to be subjunctive. For example, "Until you be here."

If all that is too complicated, no worries. You can review this later. For now, just make sure to learn the next highlighted sentence by heart.

| I'll be with José until you be here. | *Estaré con José hasta que estés aquí.* |
| She'll be with him until I'm there. | *Estará con él hasta que yo esté ahí.* |

Subject Pronouns

When are subject pronouns used? You might be wondering why we should ever use words like *él, ella, tú,* and *nosotros* in a sentence if the subject is already implied by the verb. For example, *"estás aquí"* means "you are here". Why would we ever have to say *"tú estás aquí"*?

Nerdy answer: It's generally when you're either emphasizing the subject, when you want to be extra clear, or when you're using a conjunction.

Practical answer: Start learning some real Spanish examples, imitate them, and begin customizing them. You'll end up using these words correctly if you imitate what native speakers say.

In the next phrase, we'll be using subject pronouns (from the sheep pasture). Our example uses the word *o,* which can mean both "either" and "or". It's basically always followed by subject pronouns rather than any other pronoun.

Someone, either he or she.	*Alguien, o él o ella.*
Someone, either you or I.	*Alguien, o tú o yo.*
Someone, either you or we.	*Alguien, o usted o nosotros.*

Nos (and other direct objects)

She always understands us.	*Siempre nos* she understands.
She always sees us.	*Siempre nos* she sees.
She always understands him.	*Siempre lo* she understands.
I always understand her.	*Siempre la* I understand.

Swamp Pronouns

Another idiom to learn: To say "not at all", Joel actually says *para nada* (literally "for nothing").

It's not like that at all.	*No es así para nada.*
We aren't like that at all.	*No somos así para nada.*
They aren't here at all.	*No están aquí para nada.*

Remember that the pronoun *usted* means "you", but it indicates respect or formality. When you use a verb with *usted*, you use the lizard conjugation (such as *está*), not the normal "you" conjugation with an S at the end (such as *estás*). This is simply something to get used to with practice.

¿Who is this?	*¿Quién es usted?*
How are you?	*¿Cómo está usted?*

It also affects the "he/she" version of pronouns, such as *su* instead of *tu*. Joel is a rude bee and points directly at the shepherd with words like *tu*, but a polite bee would point to the side instead and use *su* (unless they were already on really friendly terms).

Does anyone else in your(formal) family know about this?	*¿Alguien más en su* family know *sobre esto?*

In this next example, you'll see an example of a double negative: "It's not nothing." In Joelspeak, double negatives are necessary; *"es nada"* or *"no es algo"* simply doesn't work. It has to be *"no es nada"*.

It's nothing.	*No es nada.*
It was nobody.	*No era nadie.*

Possessives

We've learned *mi* as "my", *tu* as "your", and *su* as "his/her/their". These words are used with singular nouns, such as *mi casa* and *su cosa*.

But when there's more than one item and the noun is plural, such as *cosas*, then you have to put an S at the end of the possessive pronoun.

I have her things at my house.	*Yo* have *sus cosas en mi casa.*
I have your things at my house.	*Yo* have *tus cosas en mi casa.*

Prepositionals

Prepositional pronouns generally happen at the end of a phrase; they're always preceded by a preposition (from the amusement park rides). Play the potato head game with this sentence, switching out either the preposition or the prepositional pronoun.

The hardest thing for me is not to worry.	*Lo más* difficult *para mí es no* to worry.
The hardest thing without her is not to worry.	*Lo más* difficult *sin ella es no* to worry.
The hardest thing with him is not to worry.	*Lo más* difficult *con él es no* to worry.

Time Adverbs

We learned that *antes* means "beforehand". However, the most common use is in the idiom *antes de*, which means "before". Of course, since that has the preposition *de* at the end, it will be followed by a noun. For example, to say "before tomorrow", you would say "*antes de* tomorrow". "Before tonight" is "*antes de esta noche*".

| We're going before tonight. | We're going *antes de esta noche.* |

The idiom *nunca está de más* does not translate directly, but it very roughly means "it's very helpful" or "it's a big deal". Since this idiom is a complete sentence, don't worry about modifying it; just learn the phrase as it is.

| It's a big deal. | *Nunca está de más.* |

Joel's illogical use of double negatives rears its head in this next example. Instead of "better than ever" or "more than ever", Joel literally says "better than <u>never</u>" or "worse than <u>never</u>".

| I was better than ever! | *¡Estuve mejor que nunca!* |
| I have more than ever. | I have *más que nunca.* |

| She always knows it all. | *Ella siempre lo* knows *todo.* |
| I never have it all. | *Yo nunca lo* have *todo.* |

The phrase *para entonces* means "by that time".

By that time she will have left.	*Para entonces* she will have left.
By that time he will be here.	*Para entonces estará aquí.*
By that time he'll have a house.	*Para entonces* he'll have *una casa.*

Other Adverbs

Oh, adverbs… why are you so complicated?

We have eight new idioms to learn with our adverbs. But it's worth the trouble.

First of all, *"Qué tal"* doesn't seem to mean anything if you try to translate it. But it's often used before a noun to ask how something is or was. This is especially used in greetings, because you're asking someone to describe how things are going for them.

Hi! How was your day?	*¡Hola! ¿Qué tal tu día?*
Oh! How is the house?	*¡Oh! ¿Qué tal la casa?*
Thanks! How was the evening?	*¡Gracias! ¿Qué tal la noche?*

The idiom *dónde estar* is actually used as a noun, and it indicates "a place to be" or "a place to stay". Here's an example that the bird Santiago uses in our dialogue:

This time she doesn't have a place to be.	*Esta vez no* she has *dónde estar.*

The phrase *sí o sí* means "yes or yes", and it indicates that something is definitely sure. It's pretty much equivalent to the English phrase "either way".

Whatever it is, it's something good either way.	*Sea lo que sea, es algo bueno sí o sí.*
Whatever it is, it's something bad either way.	*Sea lo que sea, es algo* bad *sí o sí.*

The word *que* gets combined with other words an awful lot (in case you haven't figured that out yet). One example is the phrase *así que*, which is used as a filler phrase, like "so…" in English.

I'm reading, so I can't.	*Estoy* reading, *así que no* I can.

Another example is *cómo que*, which is used at the beginning of a sentence that someone screams in disbelief, such as "What do you mean I can't dance?!" and "What do you mean he's not here?!"

What do you mean he's not here?!	*¿Cómo que no está?*
What do you mean you're not OK?!	*¿Cómo que no estás bien?*
What do you mean the house isn't good?!	*¿Cómo que la casa no es buena?*

The word *por* is pretty common in idioms as well. We've learned that it generally means "by", sometimes in the sense that something is "near" something else. So *por aquí* means "near here" or "around here".

But the idiom *por ahí* is very frequently used to mean "around" in a vague sense. For example, "Where is he?" "Oh, he's around…" (*"Oh, está por ahí…"*)

She's around.	*Ella está por ahí.*
I'm around.	*Yo estoy por ahí.*
We're around.	*Nosotros estamos por ahí.*

The word *por* is also used before *dónde* in a very specific situation: When you're asking someone "how far" they've gotten. You are likely to use this idiom if you find your friend reading your favorite book: "How far are you?"

Awesome! How far are you?	*¡Qué bueno! ¿Por dónde estás?*
How strange! How far are they?	*¡Qué strange! ¿Por dónde están?*

Before we get out of the marketplace, we have one more idiom, and that's related to the English word "as". Remember that the butcher turned "almost as red as the steak". When we say something is "as red as" something, or "as good as" something, or "as lonely as" someone, it doesn't translate directly into Spanish. Joel always says "<u>so</u> good <u>as</u> something" (*tan bueno <u>como</u> algo*) or "<u>so</u> lonely <u>as</u> someone" (*tan lonely <u>como</u> alguien*).

Right now he's as lonely as she.	*Ahora está tan lonely como ella.*
It's always as nice as the house.	*Siempre es tan bueno como la casa.*
He's never as nice as we.	*Nunca es tan bueno como nosotros.*
Now she's as well as he.	*Ya ella está tan bien como él.*

Here we have a few words from the statue, including *sólo*, *hasta*, *también*, *no*, and *sí*. These words are generally exchangeable.

Yes, everything, even the house.	*Sí, todo, hasta la casa.*
Yes, everyone, even he.	*Sí, todos, hasta él.*
Yes, I, also she.	*Sí, yo, también ella.*
No, nothing, only one thing.	*No, nada, sólo una cosa.*

I only want that she be well.	*Sólo I want que ella esté bien.*
I also want that she be well.	*También I want que ella esté bien.*
I do want that she be well.	*Sí I want que ella esté bien.*
I don't want that she be well.	*No I want que ella esté bien.*
I even want that she be well.	*Hasta I want que ella esté bien.*

Adjectives

Remember the phrase *lo más* for "the best"? Joel often says that when he's really impressed by something in general. The phrase *lo mejor* can be used in a similar way, but usually when it refers to a specific situation. Not when something is "the best of the best", but when it's the best of the available options. For example, "the best thing about that house" or "the best part of my day".

It would be the best part of my day!	*¡Sería lo mejor de mi día!*
It was the best part of my day!	*¡Era lo mejor de mi día!*
It's the best thing about the house.	*Es lo mejor de la casa.*
It's the best thing about this city.	*Es lo mejor de esta city.*

Joel likes to avoid using the word "both". Instead, he says "the two". For example, to say "they're both doing fine", he sometimes says "they are the two doing fine." We translate *los dos* as "both".

They're both doing well. How are you?	*Están los dos muy bien. ¿Cómo estás tú?*
We were both very well. How is he?	*Estábamos los dos muy bien. ¿Cómo está él?*
They were both here. Where was she?	*Estaban los dos aquí. ¿Dónde estaba ella?*
We're both doctors. What do you do?	*Somos los dos doctors. ¿Qué do you do?*
They're both very nice. How is he?	*Son las dos muy buenas. ¿Cómo es él?*

Nouns

We have just two more tricky words to learn, our two words for time: *tiempo* and *vez*.

It's very common to say that "it's time to do something". For example, "time to be at home". The phrase is *"tiempo de* (infinitive)". That literally translates to *"time of* (infinitive)", which is something to get used to.

It was time to be at home.	*Era tiempo de estar en casa.*
It's time to be in Argentina.	*Es tiempo de estar en Argentina.*
It's time to be nice.	*Es tiempo de ser buena.*

The phrase *tiempo al tiempo* is often used by itself to mean "give it time" (be patient, wait for things to get better).

Let's give it time...	*Tiempo al tiempo...*

Now for our last complicated word, *vez*. One use, *otra vez*, is used to say "another time". That's the normal way to say "again" in Spanish.

He was nice again.	*Era bueno otra vez.*
I was well again.	*Estuve bien otra vez.*
I'm home again.	*Estoy en casa otra vez.*
She is with him again.	*Ella está con él otra vez.*
I want that thing again.	I want *esa cosa otra vez.*

The idiom *a la vez* means "to the time/instance", but it's translated to mean "at the same time". Since *vez* is used to mean that something happens at a particular moment in time, if you make more than one thing happen *a la vez*, those things are happening at that same moment in time.

All those things at once?	*¿Todas esas cosas a la vez?*
Both at once?	*¿Los dos a la vez?*
All the food at once?	*¿Toda la* food *a la vez?*
All of that at once?	*¿Todo eso a la vez?*

Similarly, *de una vez por todas* means either "for once" or "once and for all". It's as if to say that this one "time" (*vez*) is good enough to cover the rest of the times.

He did it once and for all.	*Lo* he did *de una vez por todas.*
I've fixed it once and for all.	*Lo* I've fixed *de una vez por todas.*
I've defeated him once and for all.	*Lo* I've defeated *de una vez por todas.*

When Joel says that he wants one thing ***instead of*** something else, he actually says he wants it *en vez de* the other thing. It's like saying "in place of", but it's "in *vez* of", literally "in instance of". It's like he's replacing one instance or event with another. So imagine that he is in the ballroom, switching out the broken vase for a new one. He wants the new one instead of the broken one; he wants a good vase *en vez de* a bad one.

Instead of that, he has something else.	*En vez de eso,* he has *algo más.*
Instead of his work, he's doing something else.	*En vez de su* work, he's doing *algo más.*
Instead of my food, she's making something else.	*En vez de mi* food, she's making *algo más.*

In Joel's house, we learned only the most common nouns in Spanish. You might be wondering why the word *verdad* came up. "Truth" isn't a very frequently used word in English, so why is it so common in Spanish?

It's because *verdad* is used in idioms that replace English words. For example, in English, we use the word "actually…" all the time. But in Spanish, the equivalent is an idiom: "in truth" (*en verdad*).

Actually, I'm not sure.	***En verdad, no estoy* sure.**
Actually, she's at home.	***En verdad, ella está en casa.***

Another one is *de verdad*, which means "really" or "truly". This is often used in situations of disbelief: "Really?" **"*¿De verdad?*"**. It may seem strange and arbitrary that *en verdad* is used to mean "actually" and *de verdad* is used to mean "really", but practice interchanging them for the different meanings and you'll get used to it.

Really?	***¿De verdad?***
Are they really here?	***¿De verdad están aquí?***
Is it really your house?	***¿De verdad es tu casa?***
Are you really a doctor?	***¿De verdad eres* a doctor?**
Is she really at home?	***¿De verdad está en casa?***

Until tonight!	***¡Hasta esta noche!***
Until that day!	***¡Hasta ese día!***
Until the party!	***¡Hasta la* party!**
Until that year!	***¡Hasta ese* year!**

Dialogue

I presented you with an insane number of idioms today. If you can master these, you've learned almost 50% of the Spanish language.

Meanwhile, our dialogue between Santiago and Matías will look almost like preschool Spanish by comparison.

- Hello, I'm Matías. Who is this?

- Hi Matías, it's me, Santiago.

- Santiago, all this time, ¿right?

- Yes I know! ¿How are you?

- Fine thanks, and you? ¿How is Isabella?

- Not so well, you know, she left her house.

- What! This isn't good at all.

- No, this time she doesn't have a place to be. You have to do her a favor, on my behalf.

- Yes, I want to be with her now. What can I do for Isabella or for you?

- You're very nice! I have her things at my house, as it should be, but...

- ¿Can I do something?

- I think so, it's a big deal.

- ¿But, why did she leave?

- She left, that's all… right, so, now we're going to do something when Valentina isn't around.

- ¿Valentina? But… why? If those two are like one, as you know, a…

- I know that they were, but now they aren't.

- Valentina is that way, and with her everything's like that, that's Valentina… And Sofía? She can…

- No, not Sofía, she isn't around.

- I am here, you are there… we're all here, the time is now.

- Maybe so, us both, with her. This time I don't know what to do.

- She can be at my house all the time. I can do you that favor, because I only want her to be well, and you to be well.

- That which was, is not anymore... now, everything's this way!

- Give it time. She's around, and her things at your house, at least it's something. And that gentleman?

- ¿Sebastián?

- I don't know, that man that was around with her at the house.

- Ah, yes, Sebastián, he isn't around anymore, and because of this she can't be at Mr. Sebastián's house.

- ¿He isn't? ¿What do you mean he isn't around? ¿Really? That can't be, but if the house was his!

248

- He left from the house, that's the truth. This has been this way for a while now. Now I know that she's doing badly.

- All right, well then, Isabella has been unwell for a while. Now we have to do something for her, I want to do something for her, both of us.

- Yes, I want... I'm leaving now, I'll go with Isabella.

- All right, I also will go to your house, I want to be with her.

LESSON 6

Learn Grammar First

We've learned almost enough words to bring us to 50% comprehension of the Spanish language.

But before we can boast of that ability, we have to perfect our skills in Spanish phrasing. Sophisticated thoughts and complex tenses can be understood and expressed only with a thorough foundation of Spanish grammar.

Let's wrap up this volume by learning all the sentence structures that we need in order to be fluent in Spanish.

Lesson 6 Theory:

Learn Grammar First

"The most contrarian thing of all is not to oppose the crowd but to think for yourself."

- Peter Thiel

ALL WORDS are not created equal, whether in Spanish or in any other language.

We've spent most of our time in this book learning vocabulary, but as I've emphasized, that's only useful if you can effectively piece phrases together. Fortunately, our selection of words has been strategically planned to make this easy for you.

In any real Spanish conversation, some words will be repeated a lot. Check out the word cloud infographic on the next page. More than half of the words spoken in a Spanish conversation will be these words, which

are shown in proportion to how often they're used. As you'll see, some are MUCH bigger than others. (I've left off any words that would be too small to read.)

You may be familiar with Pareto's principle, also known as the "80-20 rule", which states that generally, some items in a collection provide some sort of extremely disproportionate results.

- 80% of the world's wealth is owned by 20% of people.

- 80% of sales come from 20% of clients.

- 80% of angry inquiries are made by 20% of customers.

We can apply this rule to language, because there's a very handy benefit: When we choose vocabulary to learn, we can cheat the system by learning the small percentage of words that make an enormous percentage of the language.

Look at the infographic again. The words *que*, *de*, and *no* by themselves account for 9.5% of all words used in Spanish!

But wait a second. If you listen to a conversation, you're going to notice something strange: These most commonly used words are not very easy to hear. They seem to blend into the background, between other words; they're hardly even emphasized.

This leads us to an interesting paradox: **The most important words in a language tend to be emphasized the least.**

That's because these are the words that hold the language together. In the graphic, I've shown these words as big and bold. But in real life, they seem to fall between the cracks.

However, it's essential to remember: It's the mortar between the bricks that holds a house together.

Once you've finished Lesson 6, you will have learned enough vocabulary to account for 50% of the Spanish language.

But more importantly, you will have learned enough Spanish to construct nearly any sentence.

To be fair, you'll still be missing some vocabulary that you'll need in order to have meaningful conversations. But you'll be fully ready to learn that vocabulary and actually use it like native speakers do.

In other words, when you're ready to close the cover of this first volume, you'll truly know Spanish. Not all the words, but how the language works. After that, new vocabulary will integrate into your Spanish sentences seamlessly.

But the only way to get there is to perfect our grammar.

Some of you are screaming right now: "But wait. Shouldn't we be rebelling against academic priorities? Isn't grammar just a pointless exercise that kids have to learn in school?"

I'm afraid that argument doesn't hold up. We can't just automatically choose to be 100% opposite everyone else.

The goal is not just to be "different" from other language learners. It's to get things right. Maybe studying lists of conjugations isn't efficient or effective, but grammar is important.

Let's keep the objective in mind: We want to be able to converse effectively. And in our experiments, we've found that the students who end up having the best conversational skills are the ones whose grammar is the strongest.

Fortunately, you've already learned an immense amount of grammar, perhaps without even realizing it.

Remember the potato head game we played in Lesson 2? Essentially, our "grammar lessons" are nothing other than that. If you're learning your phrases and vocabulary properly, you've come a long way in speaking with perfect Spanish grammar.

The best grammar isn't the type taught in school. Instead, it should be completely practical and hands-on, with real sentence examples that you'll use yourself.

For Lesson 6, here are some of the complex sentences you're going to need. Learn them in English first, and we'll convert them to Spanish over the course of this lesson.

"I have to leave."

"I was going to be there."

"I had been here."

These sentences are grammatically pretty strange. In particular, the word "have" (and its variants, such as "had") are complex. But if you learn how to say these sentences in Spanish, they'll take you a long way. Let's dive in and learn how they all work in Joel's voice.

Lesson 6 Vocabulary:

Verbs
(Ir, Tener, and Haber)

IN LESSON 5, we learned more vocabulary than we'd ever learned before.

Now, in Lesson 6, we're going to set a new record: We'll learn three new verbs.

That's a lot. In the past, we spent an entire lesson on one verb shop at a time. Ser had its own lesson, and so did Estar.

But today, we'll be learning Ir, Tener, and Haber, including all their essential conjugations. We'll also learn some things about Ser that we haven't covered yet.

Speaking of Ser, let's look at a map of Yol that shows where Ser is, as well as the new shops we're learning.

Notice that Ser is very close to Joel's house. In fact, it's the first building that Joel goes past every day when he leaves his yard.

The very next building that he goes by is across the street from Ser. That's our first lesson for today.

The Ir Doctor

Ir is an ear doctor. We'll spend a lot of time at his "shop", because this is one of the most multi-purpose verbs in the Spanish language.

The strange Ir building looks like a giant ear on its side. The doctor

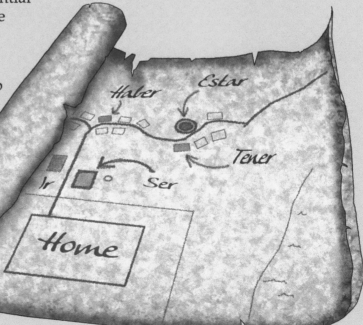

that a cotton swab walking stick is probably normal when making a journey through an ear canal.

Joel waves his walking stick and says, "I'm going on a voyage!" But to say this, he says "*Voy* on a voyage." The word *voy* means "I go" (or "I am going").

is extremely eccentric, and he went overboard on his building design. It's not just the exterior that looks like the ear; the inside is designed to be like an inner ear.

Although it's easy to enter the front of the building, it's difficult to get to the doctor's office. He designed a long, dark tunnel, shaped like an ear canal, leading from the entrance to the office itself.

Perhaps this is why Joel uses the word *ir* as his word for "to go". He never comes to the ear doctor to check his hearing. Instead, he treats it as a challenge: Can he go all the way from the entrance to the office?

When Joel arrives, he's prepared for the "voyage", as he calls it. He carries a cotton swab, which will serve as a walking stick, because he wants to make the journey on foot instead of flying. He assumes

The pandas, meanwhile, are not experienced travelers, so they arrive in a toy van. Their little toy legs won't take them very far, but perhaps these toy wheels will.

To describe this situation, Joel says "They're going in a van" by saying "*Van* in a van." (*Van* means "they are going".)

The lizard, unlike the pandas, is very accustomed to voyages through caves. That's its natural habitat, so it's very experienced going long distances in dark tunnels. Joel isn't worried about the lizard, because it goes very far in such circumstances all the time.

To say "It goes very far", Joel says "*Va* very far."

But Joel is a little confused that there's nobody here to receive them. He calls down the long, dark hallway: "Hey, some guests have arrived! Where are you?"

Ir (the doctor) shouts back, "Oh! OK, I'm in my office but I'll be there in a couple of seconds." Then, surprisingly, Ir does show up in just a couple of seconds.

Joel is shocked. Supposedly the tunnel is a couple of kilometers long, so this doctor must be a very fast runner!

"You go very fast!" he tells the doctor. But to say this, he says "*Vas* very fast."

So we have *voy* for "I go", *va* for "he/she/it goes", *van* for "they go", and *vas* for "you go".

If you simply remember *voy* and *va*, you should be able to remember all the rest of them simply based on our patterns. The letter S means we're talking to "you", and the letter N, of course, represents the pandas ("they go").

Thinking logically, what do you think is the word for "we go"?

It's *vamos*.

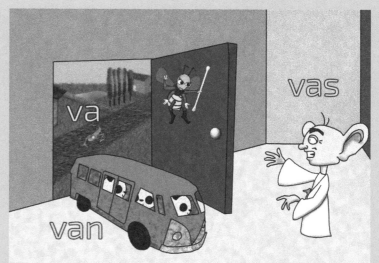

So hopefully the pattern is very familiar to you by now. Joel's word, *voy*, is a bit different from everyone else's (go figure, he rarely follows rules), but the others are predictable:

- *va*

- *vas*

- *van*

- *vamos*

The word *vamos* is one of Joel's favorite words. He likes bossing people around, especially his friends. The word *vamos* doesn't just mean "we're going"; he uses it to mean "let's go". Joel enjoys dragging his friends wherever he wants to go: "*Vamos!* We're going! *Vamos!* Let's go!"

Speaking of *vamos*, Joel is impatient to start the journey.

Holding his cotton swab in his hand, Joel flies down to the ground in order to start his walking "voyage". But then suddenly everything goes dark and blurry for a moment…

Joel Goes Himself

Before we move on to the next place in Ir's shop, we need to embarrass Joel a little bit.

Joel opens his eyes and glances down at the floor. He's shocked to see his own reflection looking back up at him.

Where did this puddle on the floor come from?

When he sees that everyone is looking at him, he doesn't know what to do. Did he just "go himself"? How humiliating!

Joel hates being shamed in front of other people in public. So he shouts out: "I'm leaving!"

But to say this, he actually ends up saying *"Me voy."* ("I'm going myself.")

When Joel shouts this, his words echo slowly. Something weird is going on.

He looks around, confused, and then notices that the lizard has a puddle under itself, too. Joel asks, "Is he leaving?" by saying *"¿se va?"*

Suddenly Joel wonders if he's dreaming. But that's not exactly what's happening.

Actually, he's accidentally fallen into an alternate reality, where everyone uses the *reflexive* versions of Ir. That means that we have to use the *reflexive pronouns* (which we learned in the countryside at the stream, in Lesson 5).

So instead of saying *voy*, Joel says *me voy*, and so on:

- me voy

- se va

- te vas

- se van

- nos vamos

In this alternate reality, Ir doesn't mean "to go", it means "to leave".

The word *voy* normally means "I go" (or "I'm going"). But when it's used reflexively, as in *me voy*, it takes on an alternate meaning: "I leave" (or "I'm leaving").

Why does Ir's meaning change from "go" to "leave"?

This is actually something that happens a lot with Spanish verbs. They have alternate realities. The normal verb means one thing, but the reflexive version, with *me/se/te/nos*, means something completely different.

So when Joel "goes", he says *voy*. But when he "goes himself", that's *me voy*, and it's translated to mean "I'm leaving". (Perhaps "leaving" is what you would expect to do if you were to "go yourself" in public.)

We'll get more practice with this in section 6c when we work on phrases. For now, let's get Joel and his friends out of here and back into the normal world.

Joel looks around at his friends and suggests, "Are we leaving?" *"Nos vamos?"*

They all jump through the puddle, and once again they find themselves back

in the "real" Ir building.

Just to make sure everything is back to normal, Joel uses his words one more time. Sure enough, when he talks about "going", he's using the positive-sounding terms ("to go") instead of the negative-sounding reflexive terms ("to leave"):

voy: "I go"

va: "it goes"

vas: "you go"

van: "they go"

vamos: "we go"

By the way, you're in luck if you're accustomed to the verb patterns (N for "they", S for "you", and -mos for "we"). Maybe this lesson started slow, but for most of this chapter, we'll be moving fast, because the verbs tend to follow those patterns. That will help us learn today's three verbs very quickly.

However, the next place that Joel's friends go, unfortunately, doesn't fit the normal patterns. It's a strange, rule-breaking area that has a mysterious connection to Ser:

Ir's Forbidden Closet.

The F. Closet

"Wait a second," you might say, "Where did this closet come from? Ser and Estar didn't have a closet."

Sure, but Ir works a bit differently from the other stores. Remember, it's not exactly a "store"; it's a doctor's office, so there's no merchandise. Instead of red shelves of stuff to buy, Ir has a red closet where he keeps doctor-ish stuff.

Also, remember that in Ser and Estar, we focused on the general, "imperfect" past tense, behind the counter. For lots of verbs, the imperfect tense is going to serve you well.

But for Ir, the more common past tense is the preterite tense, in the closet.

The preterite tense is more common because "to go" is an action verb. Normally, "to be" (as in Ser and Estar) isn't a one-time action, it's just something that happened in the general past. For example, "he was a kid". That's not an action; that's just how things were.

But "to go" is an action. For example, "He went home." That's a one-time event, so you use the preterite tense.

For now, just remember that you'll generally use the "behind-the-counter" tense for Ser and Estar, but for Ir, you're going to use the preterite (closet) tense.

Joel is impatient to be led down the dark hallway. The doctor, Ir, is supposed to take them. But instead, Ir says something about gloves and runs into the closet.

This makes Joel angry. He watches as the doctor plays with his gloves, counting the fingers, stretching the latex, and generally wasting time.

Joel angrily tells the doctor, "We want to go down the hall, but you went into the closet to waste time."

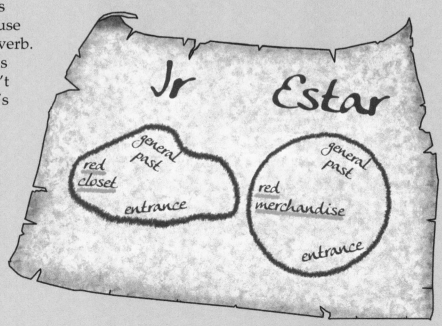

awkwardly.

Joel says, "They went to the closet too, to try to wear those gloves."

Thinking about the word "wear", Joel produces the word *fueron*, which means "they went".

All of a sudden, a loud, unexpected noise shakes the whole building. There's a loud "Bahhhh!" sound, like a sheep, and the Ir shop seems to turn sideways, throwing Joel into the closet.

Joel screams, "Whee!" at this unexpected occurrence. He doesn't know what's going on, but it seems to be exciting and enjoyable, which is an improvement over his formerly bored state of mind.

When Joel lands in the closet, he observes, "Hmm. I went into the closet too."

Thinking about the word "waste", Joel creates the word *fuiste*, which means "you went".

Then Joel sees the lizard in the closet, standing on a scale and weighing itself. Joel says, "He went to the closet too."

Thinking about the word "weigh", Joel creates the word *fue*, which means "he/she/it went".

So for example, *"fuiste a la casa"* means "you went to the house", and *"fue a la casa"* means "he/she/it went to the house".

To his dismay, Joel sees the pandas enter the closet as well. They try on the latex gloves, which, of course, don't fit their hands very well. Stuffed pandas don't have fingers, so the ends of the gloves dangle down

To say this, thinking of the exclamation "whee!", he says *fui*, which means "I went."

Looking around, it occurs to him that everyone has now gone into the closet. To say "we went", he uses the word *fuimos*, which is simply *fui* with "-mos" at the end.

Make sure you can remember all of these new words when you think of Ir's closet:

fui: (Joel) "I went"

fue: (lizard) "he went"

fuiste: (doctor) "you went"

fueron: (pandas) "they went"

fuimos: "we went"

I'll be the first to admit that these words are very complicated. Don't blame me; I didn't make them up (Joel did). My recommendation is that you mainly focus on remembering the stressed syllable of each word: "whee" (*fui*), "weigh" (*fue*), "waste" (*fuiste*), "wear" (*fueron*), and "whee" (*fuimos*). Remember those English words along with the characters (like "weigh" for the lizard), and you'll have a strong anchor that will help you remember the rest of the word.

Now, although Joel enjoyed being thrown into the closet, the Ir doctor doesn't seem so amused. He looks timidly toward the dark hall, which is

where the loud sound came from. "Oh no, not again!"

Joel doesn't know why the doctor is scared. "Come on guys, let's go on our voyage."

Joel's friends hesitate. If the Ir doctor isn't willing to go, they would rather stay behind.

"If you don't go down the hall with me, I'll go by myself."

Joel picks up his "walking stick" and marches away, toward the dark hall.

The "Eeh!" "Baa!" Sheep

As Joel disappears into the darkness, Joel's friends wait anxiously for a few minutes.

A terrified scream breaks the silence: "EEEEHH!" Joel comes flying back, with a petrified look on his face.

Meanwhile, a loud "Bahhhh!" sound thunders behind him.

After gathering his breath, Joel explains the horrifying situation. He was going down the dark hall when suddenly an enormous sheep appeared, visible by the light of a torch it

was holding. The sheep tried to stomp on Joel, and he barely got away.

When Joel starts his story, he tries to say, "I was going down the dark hall…"

But all he can think of are the loud shouts: "Eeeh!" and "Baahh!"

So he says, "*Iba* down the dark hall…"

The word *iba* means "I was going". This is the imperfect past tense. It's like *estaba* for Estar or *era* for Ser; this word indicates a general situation in the past, not a particular event.

Normally with Ir, you'll use the F words (from the red closet). But there are some situations in which you'll use *iba*, especially when something was generally happening in the past, rather than emphasizing a certain action.

That's how Joel used *iba*. First, he set the stage using the imperfect tense (*iba*), before describing the actions that happened on that stage: The sheep trying to stomp on him.

A real-life example might be, "He was going down the street, and he got sick." The first verb sets the setting: *"Iba* down the street." But the second verb is an action: *"Estuvo* sick."

In that case, the Ir verb is setting the scene, but the Estar verb is the action. Normally it's the other way around; for example, "He was at home, and he went to the store." That would be, *"Estaba en casa, y fue a* the store."

Meanwhile, don't worry about it for now. Just focus on remembering the F words in the closet and *iba* at the dark hall.

When Joel describes his story, the Ir doctor is horrified. "It's my old enemy, the sheep. Oh no, he's brought a torch!" The doctor goes into a panic.

Joel looks around at his friends and tells them, "OK, we're leaving! *Nos vamos.*"

Will Go, Would Go

As they exit the store, Joel is still holding his cotton swab. The pandas look at it, and they wonder if Joel plans to go hiking.

Joel says no, he's too worn out from the encounter with the sheep. "I'll go home," he tell them.

But before he does, he has a sudden urge to pull out his magic wand and shoot a ray of light at the front of the Ir shop, exactly as he did at Estar.

To say "I will go home", Joel says *"Iré a casa."*

The stressed syllable of this word is "ray". It's just like the word *estaré*, which means "I will be". The future tense, as always, is simply the infinitive with an extra stressed E at the end, creating the accented "ré".

vaya

Meanwhile, the lizard says "rah". His word is *irá*, meaning "he/she/it will go". Once again, this fits the pattern of *será* and *estará*, which should be very familiar by now.

"Fiyah!"

The pandas start sniffing the air. A very strange smoky smell has invaded the scene. To investigate, all of Joel's friends walk around to Ir's back yard.

Sure enough, the strangely-shaped back of the Ir building is on fire. The pink, waxy material that composes the shop is simultaneously melting and burning, giving off a very uncomfortable odor.

Evidently, the giant sheep that Joel found in the tunnel has set the whole building on fire.

When you think of Ir's back yard, the important word is *vaya*, which sounds kind of like "fire". This is Ir's subjunctive form.

Joel hopes he never goes to Ir again: "I hope *que yo no vaya* to the Ir doctor again."

He also hopes that the pandas don't do it: "I hope *que* the pandas *no vayan* to the Ir doctor again."

And of course, the second person is *vayas*. Joel shouts in the direction of the Ir doctor, "I hope that you leave Yol!"

"Que te vayas de Yol!"

Fuera

Warning: Out of the fire shall emerge another grammatical concept we haven't seen yet.

Joel wants to leave Ir before things get worse, but the lizard has disappeared.

"Where did the lizard go?" Joel asks the pandas. "I hope he didn't go in the fire. He's very sensitive to heat."

The pandas reassure Joel, "He's in the storm shelter, finding something to wear."

One of the regulations in Yol is that every business has to have an outdoor storm shelter, and those storm shelters need to have emergency equipment such as fire-proof clothing.

So the pandas tell Joel, "We told the lizard to go down there. He needs to wear something to protect himself."

Remember the word "wear". The word we're learning is *fuera*, which is another subjunctive... but in the past.

"We told him *que fuera* to the storm shelter to find clothes."

So *fuera* means "he go", but referring to past situations.

If you want an example, Joel might say to the pandas, "Tell the lizard that he should go home." That would be "Tell the lizard *que vaya a casa.*" That's a normal subjunctive, in the present tense.

But if it's a past event, the pandas might tell Joel, "We told him that he should go home." That's "We told him *que fuera a casa.*"

You might wonder whether this really happens very often. Are you actually going to need the past tense subjunctive in conversation? Well, yes... because this word is also used in several other ways, as we'll see later in the lesson.

For now, just remember that *fuera* is another type of subjunctive mood, and it's located underground behind Ir's shop.

fuera

"Get Lost. Find a Vet."

Doctor Ir suddenly emerges from the burning building. He's covered with melting wax, and he seems out of his mind.

When Ir sees the pandas and the lizard, he shouts to Joel, "Why did you bring these animals to an ear doctor? What they need is a vet!"

Joel doesn't know how to respond. The doctor continues:

"Get out of here and find a vet!"

To say "Go away," the doctor says *"Vete."*

The word *vete* means "leave". It's an example of an order, and it's not very polite, although it is commonly used in informal situations (between parents and children, for example).

Before Joel can respond to this rudeness, the Ir doctor kicks Joel onto a moving sidewalk on the side of his store, shouting, *"Vete* and find a vet!"

Joel can't take this kind of treatment anymore. He shouts to his friends, "Let's get out of here!"

To say "Let's leave," Joel uses the word *vámonos*.

You'll notice that *vámonos* is a lot like *vamos*, which means "let's go". The difference is that it's strangely merged with the word *nos*, which changes the meaning from "let's go" to "let's leave".

Incidentally, some people think that *vámonos* means "let's go", but it doesn't. It means "let's leave".

The reason is a little bit complicated. For now, just remember these two words: *vete* ("leave") and *vámonos* ("let's leave"). They're orders that have to do with leaving a place, and we think of them on this moving sidewalk.

ido

Gone from Ir

As Joel leaves, he looks back to see what has become of Ir. He's surprised to see the doctor standing on the roof of the store, eating some of the melted wax from the burning building.

Joel calls back, "Why are you eating that nasty stuff?"

All the doctor says is, "It's not nasty. It's delicious! Want to try some?"

Joel concludes that the doctor is psychotic. Joel turns quickly to leave, shaking his head at the strange Ir doctor that eats wax on his burning building's roof.

The word on Ir's roof is ***ido***. (The stressed syllable sounds like "eat".) ***Ido*** is the participle meaning "gone", as in "you have gone", "she has gone", "we have gone", and so on.

Joel might use this word to say, "I have gone to the Ir doctor once."

"I have ***ido*** to the Ir doctor once."

This "voyage" wasn't nearly as much of an adventure as Joel wanted to have, so he decides to go down the road to a local toy store. Joel loves toys, and there may be a way to get some money out of the owner.

But first, he has to wait for the lizard to catch up. The lizard is still underground in the storm shelter, uncovering a secret that connects Ir and Ser.

270

Ser's Forbidden Closet

Ser is a very dishonest, secretive person. Although she has trouble hiding the fact that she is very short (that secret was spoiled in Lesson 2), she does have some skeletons in her closet that very few people know about.

We've seen that the lizard went underground when the Ir shop was on fire. The pandas told it to put on fireproof clothing. But the lizard discovered something very interesting.

Basically: Ir and Ser are more closely related than you might think.

As the lizard climbed into the storm shelter, it spotted an opening at the other end. After climbing through that tunnel, he emerged in Ser's back yard.

Evidently, Ser and Ir share a storm shelter. What does this mean?

It means that Ser and Ir have the same past tense subjunctive: *fuera*.

When in the world are you going to use a past tense subjunctive of Ser? Well, there's a very special role for this common word. To demonstrate, let's look at an English sentence you may have used yourself:

"If I <u>were</u> taller, I would be a basketball player."

I have a question for you. What does "I were" mean in that sentence?

Seriously. Who says "I were"? Shouldn't it be "I was"? But wait, it shouldn't even be in the past tense at all, should it?

But in reality, this is correct. The phrase "If I were…" is used to indicate <u>something that we know isn't true.</u> When you say "If I <u>were</u> taller…" or "If I <u>were</u> president…", you're talking hypothetically about something you know isn't true.

271

This is how *fuera* is most often used. Here's a real Spanish example:

If he were a man, he'd be there:

Si fuera un hombre, estaría ahí.

Now, this isn't all that the lizard discovers before re-joining Joel.

Ser's back door has been left open. The lizard sneaks in the store to take a look around, and he discovered a strange-looking door near the merchandise.

When he opens it, he finds himself in Ir's closet again!

This secret portal between Ser and Ir indicates that these two verbs have the same preterite tense. *fui, fue, fuiste, fueron*, and *fuimos* can indicate the past tense of either Ir or Ser.

As I mentioned in Lesson 2, you'll rarely use the preterite form of Ser. Normally, you'll just use the words behind the counter: *era, eras, eran*, and *éramos*. So the words that start with F are normally going to be used with Ir.

But this is something to be aware of. For example, if you were to read the following sentence, you might find it confusing:

Eso fue sólo una vez.

It looks like "That <u>went</u> only one time", but what it means is "That <u>was</u> only one time."

So Ser shares a lot of F conjugations with Ir. Unfortunately, the lizard is unable to share this with Joel, because the lizard can't talk. But at least you're in on the secret.

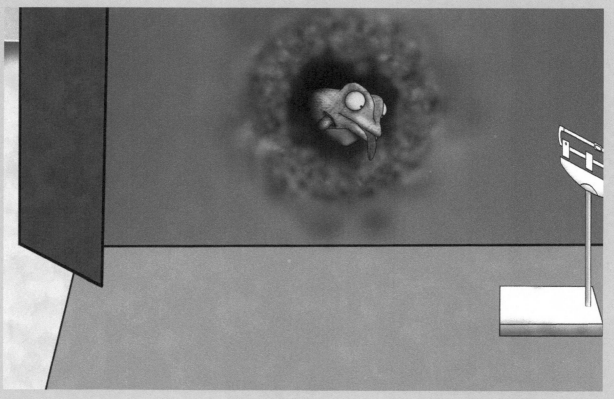

Tener: Everyone Has to Have Toys

After the lizard catches up with Joel, they all head down the street to the toy shop.

This shop is called "Tener". The owner, Ner, lovingly calls his store "Nerland". It's like "neverland", but named after Ner, because he thinks highly of himself.

But he's a good-hearted guy: Funny, eccentric, and extremely generous, to the point of being a terrible businessman. His philosophy is that everyone has to have anything they want. If you want a toy, you have to have it!

Remember this phrase, "have to have". This uses the word "have" twice, because there are multiple versions of the verb "to have":

- "I have a toy" is possession. You're holding it in your hand, so you "have" it.

- "I have to work" is obligation. It's something you "have" to do.

The verb Tener means both of these things. When Ner says "You <u>have to have</u> a toy," he uses the verb Tener twice.

When Joel first enters the toy shop, he is overcome with joy at the idea of free toys. He grabs the first thing he sees, an ugly-looking doll, and tries to dance with it. He pretends to tango with the doll.

Joel's word here is *tengo*, which means "I have". Ner tells Joel, "You have to have that doll! Do you want to buy it?"

tienes

tiene

tienen

tengo

Joel examines the doll. It's actually pretty cheap and not worth spending money on. So Joel lies to Ner: "I don't have any money. The lizard and the pandas have all of my yen."

Then Joel kicks the lizard and whispers, "Come on, play along!"

Fortunately, the lizard finds a bunch of toy money on the floor. It scoops up several toy yen into its hands and also wraps some around the pandas hands. (That's the only way the pandas can hold the money since they don't have fingers).

The word *tienen* means "they have" and the word *tiene* means "he/she/it has". These words have a stress that sounds like "yen".

Ner is happy to accept toy money, if it makes his customers happy. Joel sees that Ner has a lot of toy money in his pockets. This is a little bit of a disappointment, because Joel was privately hoping to steal some real money.

To say, "You have lots of fake money," Joel says, *"Tienes* lots of fake money." Once again, the stressed syllable is "yen".

274

Joel asks Ner, "How much do these toys actually cost?"

Ner responds, "You can name your own price! Whatever you want. What price would you name?"

Joel is excited by this. "Did you hear that guys? We have whatever we want! We just have to name a really low price."

The word here is *tenemos* for "we have". The stress is on "name", as in "name your own price".

This was a quick story, but that's all the present-tense verbs for Tener. Just remember the key syllables "yen", "name", and "tango", and you'll remember the words:

> *tengo* (Joel): "I have"
>
> *tiene* (lizard): "he/she/it has"
>
> *tienen* (pandas): "they have"
>
> *tienes* (Ner): "you have"
>
> *tenemos* (we): "we have"

"Yen" applies to the lizard, the pandas, and Ner. Joel says *tengo* to say "I have", and to say "we have", the word is longer than the others because it has "mos" at the end, so it has its own stressed syllable, "name": *tenemos*.

Say each of these words a few times, thinking of the scene. Then you'll be ready to move on. We'll cover the rest of Tener very quickly.

The Two-Faced Doll

Joel and the lizard go to Tener's red shelves of merchandise. This is where the *preterite* past tense is stored, just like the merchandise area in Estar (or the equivalent closet area in Ir).

As you might have suspected, Ner doesn't run a very strong business. He loses money every day, and so the toys that he buys for his shelves are always getting cheaper and uglier.

The first thing that Joel and the lizard find is a giant, malformed toy. It's a doll that was put together so carelessly that it was accidentally given two heads, and all of its bodily features are falling apart.

Joel tries to pick up the doll, but when he realizes that it has two faces, he chooses to leave it where it is.

275

The word is *tuve*. Think "two face", because this is a two-faced doll. This means "I had" in the preterite tense. This is used in very particular situations, usually when "having" something is a sudden event. For example, "I was going to leave, but then *I had* more work to do." That might be "I was going to leave, but then *tuve* more work to do."

Meanwhile, on the floor, the lizard examines the doll's two feet. It tries to move the doll.

Suddenly there's a shattering noise, and the doll's knees explode into tiny pieces. Apparently the doll's knees were very fragile, constructed from a glass-like material.

Joel shakes his head at the lizard, rolls his eyes, and yells, "The lizard had an accident again!"

To say this, Joel uses a word that sounds like "two foot": "The lizard *tuvo* an accident!"

The word *tuvo* means "he/she/it had".

But Tener isn't like Ir, where the preterite tense is more common than the imperfect tense. There are some common cases, like "I had an accident" (*tuve* an accident) or "she had a baby" (*tuvo* a baby). Normally, "having" something is an ongoing thing, not a one-time event.

So for now, we don't need to learn more than a couple of preterite conjugations. Just remember Joel at the doll's face and the lizard at the doll's feet. The stressed syllable for both words is "two", but for Joel it's *tuve* ("I had") and for the lizard it's *tuvo* ("he/she/it had").

tenía

The Bee's Knees

Joel and the lizard go to the counter to tell Ner about the broken doll. The shards of plastic seem pretty dangerous, and maybe Ner shouldn't keep such hazards in his shop.

What Joel and the lizard don't know is that those shards of plastic got stuck in their own knees.

When they go to the counter to complain loudly, Ner sees the plastic in their knees. He tries to quiet them down, and he calls them behind the counter.

"Hey guys, I hate to embarrass you, so I'll tell you quietly: You had something stuck to your knees. I didn't want anyone to see that. That's kind of embarrassing."

Ner gratuitously dusts off their knees, saying, "You don't have to have plastic in your knees! Let's clean you up."

The important syllable is "knee", and these are the words:

tenía (I had, he/she/it had)

tenían (they had)

tenías (you had)

teníamos (we had)

That's quite a few words, but the beautiful thing is that they all have the same stressed syllable! Just remember "knee", and then change the ending slightly for each person. The patterns are all normal: "S" for the second person, "N" for the pandas, and "mos" for "we had".

This is the normal past tense. When Joel says "I had something in my knee", he says "*tenía* something in my knee." To say "we had something", he says "*teníamos* something."

We'll continue to move faster and faster through these scenes. By now, you should be used to the conjugation patterns so that just by remembering the syllable "knee", you can remember *tenía, tenías, tenían,* and *teníamos* for the normal past tense of Tener.

Draw

After they're done shopping for toys, Joel and his friends step outside the store. The lizard lies on the ground and uses some broken crayons to draw a picture of Tener's store. Meanwhile, Joel pulls out his magic wand and shoots a beam of magical light at the decorations on the front of the store.

The lizard shouts, "Rah!" and adds Joel to his broken-crayon masterpiece.

Remember that we always store future-tense verbs in the front of a verb shop. The lizard's word is *tendrá*: "he/she/it will have". Meanwhile, Joel's word is *tendré*: "I will have".

As usual, you can modify the lizard's word to refer to other people: *tendrás* is "you will have", and *tendrán* is "they will have".

Toy Junk

Joel wasn't very satisfied with the toys that Tener had to sell. He decides to go behind the store to see if there's anything worth salvaging from Tener's pile in the back.

The first thing he sees is a doll, which he pulls out of the mud and tries to dance with. But when he realizes how muddy and ugly it is, Joel yells "Ah!" and drops it.

The word is *tenga*, which is kind of like *tengo* but with "ah" at the end because it was interrupted by Joel's yell.

As you can see, the pile of junk back here is even cheaper and uglier than the store's merchandise. *Tenga* is Tener's subjunctive. For example, to say "I hope that he has something" is "I hope *que tenga algo*." (This word applies to both Joel, "I", and the lizard, "he/she/it".)

Ten Yen

Suddenly Ner comes around the corner. He's shocked to see Joel rummaging through the junk pile in the back yard.

"I didn't know you were so poor!" he says. It's unthinkable to him that anyone would be destitute enough to dig through a junk pile.

Joel, of course, isn't poor at all, but he's interested to hear what Ner might say next.

"You need money. You HAVE to have everything you need!" says Ner. "Here, I can give you some money. Have ten yen!"

Ner pulls out all the money in his pockets and tries to give it to Joel. The word for "have", as an imperative, is *ten*. For example, "Have two more!" would be *"Ten dos más."*

Unfortunately, all ten Yen bills blow out of Ner's hand and are crumpled by the moving sidewalk. Joel flies after them to catch the bills.

tenido

ten

Everything You Need

After Joel gathers the bills and his friends, they all walk off toward the sunset to go home.

Ner stands on his roof and shouts after them, "Thank you for coming! Come back any time you have to have something! Remember that you have <u>had</u> everything you need!"

To say "you have <u>had</u> everything", Ner says "you have *tenido* everything". Since this word is the version on the roof, it's the equivalent of *sido*, *estado*, and *ido*, which we learned with previous verbs on their roofs.

We'll talk a little bit more about these verbs next. First, make sure you can remember all the forms of Ir and Tener that you learned in this lesson.

50%: The Other Have

As you've seen, the words *sido*, *estado*, *ido*, and *tenido* all happened on the roofs of the verb shops. They're used in these past-tense situations:

She has *sido* a teacher.

She has *estado* here.

She has *ido* there.

She has *tenido* something.

Those words can apply to anyone. If we change "she has" to "we have", we get this:

We have *sido* a teachers.

We have *estado* here.

We have *ido* there.

We have *tenido* something.

In each case, we didn't have to change these words (*sido*, *estado*, etc.); they remained the same. But we did change what happened *before* those verbs.

I'm afraid that the phrases "she has…" and "we have…" are NOT examples of Tener.

Remember that Ner always uses the phrase "have to have." Tener is used for obligation ("we have to do it") or possession ("we have a house").

Look carefully at the sentences that I've listed above. When I say "We have been teachers", I'm not expressing obligation or possession. I'm just indicating something that happened in the past. So the word for "we have", in this case, is not a form of Tener.

There's a special verb that's used for this exact purpose: Putting put things in the past. It's used before words like *sido* and *estado*, just like the phrases "she has *sido*…" and "we have *estado*…" We're about to learn that verb.

Once we've learned it, we'll have learned 50% of the Spanish language.

Sip Part of the Roof (how to use participles)

Any word that takes place on the roof of a store is called a <u>participle</u>. Place stresses on the syllables "part" and "sip" (PART-a-**sip**-ol).

When we say "participle", we think about a big, black, blind bear.

This old bear walks around Joel's neighborhood, looking for water. He only seems to be able to find water on the roofs of other people's shops. Any time it rains, he goes around from shop to shop, sipping "part" of the water that accumulated on each roof.

Not only is he blind, but he's mostly deaf. His social skills are in the gutter, he mumbles clumsily, and he's very bigoted: He doesn't like you if you don't have skin.

His own shop, "Haber" (pronounced like "a bear"), is a skin shop. He sells the skins of snakes, lizards, foxes, minks, and so on. Most of these skins were harvested from his own deceased friends after they grew old and expired.

Somehow the bear himself lives on, occasionally making a few new friends here and there, but only with creatures who have skins. As you might imagine, he and Joel won't get along very well when they meet.

Meanwhile, the bear has a special relationship with the roofs of all the store's shops: Every participle uses Haber before it.

Haber means "to have", in the sense of putting something in the past. Here are some good examples:

To have been here: ***Haber estado aquí.***

To have gone there: ***Haber ido ahí.***

To have been something: ***Haber sido algo.***

To have had something: ***Haber tenido algo.***

As you can see, we're always putting *haber* right before a word that's on the roof. You've been waiting for this for a long time, ever since Lesson 2: Now you finally get to learn how to use words like ***sido*** and ***estado*** in a sentence!

Remember that these participles never change, no matter who is doing the action. However, the word that comes before them does change. That's why we need to learn a few different forms of Haber.

Joel and his friends wander into Haber today on their way home from the toy shop. When they walk in, Joel realizes that this place is vaguely familiar; it turns out that he's been here before (you'll hear about that incident soon).

As soon as it occurs to Joel that he's been here before, he remembers that he doesn't like Haber. He shouts to his friends, "Oh wait, we've been here before. I don't like this place. Let's leave."

But before he can go, the bear says, "What's that? You don't like this place, eh?"

Joel freezes. He doesn't know how to respond.

Fortunately, the bear suddenly notices the lizard. "Ahh!" he says. "I like lizards."

Then he looks back up at Joel and says, "Eh?" again.

This continues for a while. The bear keeps looking back and forth between Joel and the lizard, alternately saying "Eh?" and "Ahh!"

Joel's word is *he*, which is pronounced like "eh". And the lizard's word is *ha*, pronounced like "ah". These words mean "I have" and "he/she/it has", when used before a participle. Let's look at a few examples:

I have been here: ***He estado aquí.***

It has been here: ***Ha estado aquí.***

She has been here: ***Ha estado aquí.***

These words are pretty much only used when they're followed by a participle.

As you might guess, the word for the pandas is *han* ("they have…") and the word for the bear is *has* ("you have…"). Those two words are based on the lizard's word, *ha*. Meanwhile, the word for all of them together is *hemos* ("we have…"), based on Joel's word *he*.

Here are a few more examples you can play with:

They have been here: ***Han estado aquí.***

You have been here: ***Has estado aquí.***

We have been here: ***Hemos estado aquí.***

Make sure not to get these words confused with Tener. Words like *tengo* and *tiene* are used when you have something, or when you have to do something. Haber is used grammatically, preceding a participle to put something in the past.

We'll learn just two more conjugations of Haber before Joel can go home.

The bear wanders back to the counter, muttering to himself, "A bee! There was a bee in my store today! And he had been here before, too… for shame, for shame."

He starts fishing around under the counter for something, muttering "A bee!" over and over. Joel is afraid that he might be looking for a flyswatter.

The word behind the counter is *había*, with the stressed syllable "bee". It means "I had", "he had", "she had", or "it had".

But wait a minute. Doesn't Haber already put words in the past? How can this verb have a past tense? This may seem technical, but *había* is used to put things in the <u>past of the past</u>.

Compare the two English sentences "I <u>have</u> been here" with "I <u>had</u> been here", and you'll see that although both of them happen in the past, one of them indicates something even further back.

Here are some examples of *había*:

I had been here: ***Había estado aquí.***

He had been here: ***Había estado aquí.***

By saying that I *had* been here, I'm not just indicating something that happened in the simple past; it's something that happened even further in the past.

Joel and his friends turn and get out of there as quickly as they can. As they leave, the lizard says "Rah!" as always. The future tense of Haber is *habrá*.

This is used to indicate the <u>past of the future</u>.

He will have been here: ***Habrá estado aquí.***

We'll explore these complex tenses some more when we study phrases. First, let's go back in time and talk about Joel's first visit to Haber.

283

hay

había

Haber: Existence

One night several months ago, Joel and his friends were out late. They were hungry and tired, and they decided to go to one of their local restaurants. But this was before they had magic wands to light their way. In the darkness of the night, they accidentally stumbled into Haber.

Joel realized something was wrong as soon as he entered and heard a voice muttering, "What's that? There are four things in my store… What are they doing here?"

Terrified, Joel heard the creature coming closer and closer. "What are these things?" asked the bear. But its attitude suddenly changed when it stumbled over the lizard and felt its scaly skin. "Ahh! Four things… and a lizard, it seems."

The bear likes lizards because lizards have skins. But this mostly-blind bear had to ask to confirm: "Is there really a lizard in my store?"

Joel blurted out, "Aye! Aye, there's a lizard in your store."

"Cool," said the bear, "I like lizards."

The word *hay* sounds like the English word "I" or "aye", and it means "there is". It's like saying that something exists in a particular place.

This is an extremely unique word in Spanish. *Hay* can be used before any type of noun, without changing forms. Here are some examples:

There is a lizard in the store: *Hay* a lizard in the store.

There are three pandas in the store: *Hay* three pandas in the store.

There is a person in the house: *Hay* a person in the house.

There are three cars on the driveway: *Hay* three cars on the driveway.

For some reason, this word, *hay*, is considered a form of Haber, even though it has nothing to do with the versions of the word that we learned earlier. There are two completely different meanings for this verb, almost as if it's two entirely different verb shops: Haber during the day (to use with participles) and Haber during the night (to indicate existence).

Hay has a past tense as well. It's a word we've already learned: *Había*. Imagine yourself exploring Haber at night, unable to see anything. You discover a lizard in the entrance of the store and a bee behind the counter.

There is a lizard here: *Hay* a lizard here.

There was a bee here: *Había* a bee here.

As you can see, *había* has two meanings, both of which are somewhat complicated. First, you can use it to put something in the <u>past of the past</u>, as previously described. And now you can also use it to indicate that "there was" something somewhere.

The best way to practice these words is to work with sentence examples, as we'll do in the last part of this lesson.

Reviewing 5 Verbs

Many students are discouraged by lesson 6 because of the sheer number of verb forms to memorize.

Remember that the entire purpose of using Yol for our vocabulary is that we need to have everything laid out clearly and in order. If the words just all feel jumbled around in your head, here is the exact three-part exercise you need to focus on right now.

(1) Choose one verb (either Ser, Estar, Tener, Haber, or Ir).

(2) Look through the pictures of the shop, making sure to absorb the images in your head and associate those images with the words.

(3) Close the book and try to walk through this entire verb building in your head, scene by scene, naming all the words as you go. Some students choose to draw out the map themselves on paper as they do this exercise.

After you've done that, of course, you'll want to practice using those verbs in sentences. But this initial exercise is important for making sure the foundations are set with all the words stored where they belong.

Take your time and don't get frustrated. Focus on solidifying your palace one verb "shop" at a time.

Lesson 6 Application:

Verbal Phrase Structures

T HE PRESENT TENSE of Spanish verbs aren't 100% equivalent with English. This is something that I've hinted at before, but it's important to emphasize now: Words such as *voy* and *vamos* are used very broadly. For example, *voy* can be translated as either "I go" or "I am going". *Va* can mean "he goes" or "he is going".

The implications of this extend beyond the present moment. With Spanish action verbs, you can sometimes use the present to indicate that something is going to happen in the future.

It's like English: If I tell you, "I'm going to the party tonight!", I'm technically referring to the future ("tonight") even though I'm using the present tense ("I'm going").

Keep that in mind while playing with modifications of this sentence:

I also am going to your house.	*Yo también voy a tu casa.*
She also is going to her house.	*Ella también va a su casa.*
We also are going to my house.	*Nosotros también vamos a mi casa.*
He and she also are going to his house.	*Él y ella también van a su casa.*

For things that happened in the past, we normally use the preterite tense (from the closet). To "go" somewhere is considered an action, a one-time event with a definite starting point.

Did you go to their house?	*¿Fuiste a su casa?*
Did we go to your house?	*¿Fuimos a tu casa?*
He went to my house.	*Fue a mi casa.*
I went to the house.	*Fui a la casa.*

There's an interesting idiom with Ir involving *por*. When these two words combine, it means indicates that someone "picks up" someone or something. For example, although *voy por él* sounds like "I'm going by him", it's used to mean "I'm picking him up."

I'm picking him up.	*Voy por él.*
They're picking us up.	*Van por nosotros.*
We're picking up some food.	*Vamos por some food.*

Ir, reflexive

When Ir is reflexive, the meaning changes from "go" to "leave". The literal phrase "I'm going myself" is translated as "I'm leaving".

OK, I'm leaving.	*Bueno, me voy.*
OK, they're leaving.	*Bueno, se van.*
Are you leaving?	*¿Te vas?*
Oh, we're leaving?	*Oh, ¿nos vamos?*

Finally, here's an example of the imperative.

Get out of here.	*Vete de aquí.*
Let's get out of here.	*Vámonos de aquí.*

The "Ir hack" for the future tense

Let's think back to the Ir shop with our present-tense verbs: *voy, va, vas, van,* and *vamos*. Believe it or not, just using these five words, you can put any verb into the future tense extremely easily. You simply use one of these words, plus the word *a*, plus the infinitive or basic form of the word that you want to put in the future.

So let's try this with Estar, for example. We learned *estaré* and *estará* in front of the shop as "I will be" or "he will be" in a certain place. But now, thanks to Ir, we can actually put Estar in the future tense for any person. We just use *"voy a…", "va a…", "vas a…", "van a…",* or *"vamos a…"* and then the infinitive of another verb (the name of another shop).

So instead of *estaré ahí* for "I will be there", I could say *voy a estar ahi*. That literally means *"I am going to be there"*.

Similarly, instead of saying "he <u>will</u> be there", *estará ahí*, I could say "<u>he is going</u> to be there", *va a estar ahí*. "You are going to be there" is *vas a estar ahí*. "They are going to be there" is *van a estar ahí*, and "we are going to be there" is *vamos a estar ahí*.

So in the end, we're really not conjugating Estar at all! We're just using the basic form, *estar*, but now it's in the future tense because we're using the "*Ir + a*" construction. This is actually quite standard and possibly even more common than the "normal" future tense that we've been learning in the front of each store.

I'm going to be there.	*Voy a estar ahí.*
Nacho and José are going to be there.	*Nacho y José van a estar ahí.*
She's going to have something.	*Ella va a tener algo.*
Are you going to go there?	*¿Vas a ir ahí?*

Now, just for fun, let's add more dimensions to this. Suppose I want to use a complex tense, like the <u>future of the past</u>, as if to say that something "was going to happen" (but then maybe didn't). We'll just keep doing what we're doing, but using Ir's past tense instead of its present tense.

For this purpose, we always use *iba*, the imperfect past tense. The reason that the imperfect past tense is used in these cases is because "going to be somewhere" or "going to do something" isn't an event; it's an ongoing thing. For example, "He was going to be a teacher" would be *"iba a ser* a teacher", and "I was going to have three houses" would be *"iba a tener* three houses". That's a statement about the ongoing past, not some momentous action. It indicates something that <u>was going to happen</u>.

So she was going to be there too.	*Así que ella iba a estar ahí también.*
So I was going to be there too.	*Así que yo iba a estar ahí también.*
So he was going to be here too.	*Así que él iba a estar aquí también.*

Tener

Here's the simple use of tener, which can be modified to any tense:

They have something.	*Tienen algo.*
They had something.	*Tenían algo.*
I have something.	*Tengo algo.*
I had a house.	*Tenía una casa.*

There's an idiom for "it has some of everything". In English, we normally say "it has a little bit of everything". In Spanish, you can say this with fewer words: *tiene de todo*, literally "It has of everything."

It's small but it has a little of everything.	*Es* small *pero tiene de todo.*

Next we're going to go into some idioms that are more complicated but extremely important.

When I say "I have a house", the "have" verb is followed directly by a noun, "a house": "*Tengo* a house." But as strange as this is, it's possible to remove the noun and replace it with a special two-word phrase that starts with *que*: "*Tengo que ir.*"

Word-for-word, this looks like "I have that to go". But we're creating a particular meaning here. When the word *que* is used after Tener, it indicates <u>obligation</u>. This is very similar to English; it's like "I have to do something". We're using a Tener conjugation, then *que*, then an infinitive.

So for example *tengo que ser* would be "I have to be". *Tengo que tener algo* means "I have to have something".

Essentially, when Tener is followed by a noun, you're talking about owning something. But when it's followed by *que* and then an infinitive, you're expressing obligation, or "having to do something".

I have to go to the house.	*Tengo que ir a la casa.*
She has to go to the house.	*Tiene que ir a la casa.*
The man has to go.	*El hombre tiene que ir.*
We have to have a house.	*Tenemos que tener una casa.*
I have to be at home.	*Tengo que estar en casa.*

Let's put this in the past. We do this in English as well; "I have to leave" is present tense, but "I had to leave" puts the same idea in the past. We'll do that here, and we'll use the preterite (action) tense of tener to indicate that it's an action I had to take at a particular moment:

I had to leave.	*Me tuve que ir.*
She had to leave.	*Se tuvo que ir.*
We had to leave.	*Nos tenemos que ir.*
They have to leave.	*Se tienen que ir.*

Haber with participles

As you know, here is the normal way to use Haber with a participle to put something in the past:

She hasn't been well.	*No ha estado bien.*
We haven't been well.	*No hemos estado bien.*
They have indeed been well.	*Sí han estado bien.*

When we use the past tense version of Haber, we put something in the <u>past of the past</u>.

I had been in Argentina.	*Había estado en Argentina.*
She had had a thing.	*Ella había tenido una cosa.*
He had been nice.	*Él había sido bueno.*

One more example. This is much rarer, but as mentioned earlier, you can actually also create the <u>past of the future</u>. Put Haber in the future and then something "will have happened" before that future event.

By that time she will have left.	*Para entonces se habrá ido.*
By that time he will have had a house.	*Para entonces habrá tenido una casa.*
By that time he will have been here.	*Para entonces habrá estado aquí.*

Haber for existence

Remember that **hay** is used to indicate the presence or existence of something in a location.

There's never anyone in the mornings.	*Nunca hay nadie por las mornings.*
There's always something here.	*Siempre hay algo aquí.*
There's someone at my house.	*Hay alguien en mi casa.*

Here's an example of the past tense, *había*.

There was someone in the house.	*Había alguien en la casa.*
There was a thing here.	*Había una cosa aquí.*
There's someone at the house.	*Hay alguien en la casa.*

Now let's do a little trick with *hay*. Looking at the examples above, you'll notice that in each case, *había* or *hay* is followed by a noun (a thing). But in Spanish, a noun can very often be replaced by a *que…* phrase, very much like what we've done in the *tener que* examples above.

So in these next examples, you'll see that we're using *"hay que* (infinitive)" much like we would use *"tengo que* (infinitive)". A literal sentence translation would be "there is to go", which doesn't make sense in English, but it expresses the idea that "there is a need to go". This implies obligation, like *tener que*, but without really specifying who has to do it.

There's a need to go.	*Hay que ir.*
There's a need to have a house.	*Hay que tener una casa.*
There's a need to be there.	*Hay que estar ahí.*
There's a need be nice.	*Hay que ser bueno.*
There's a need to have something else.	*Hay que tener algo más.*

Ser, the F forms

Remember that the preterite of Ser, like the preterite of any verb, tends to refer to an event. The most common situation where an event is the idea of being something is when you're describing what the event itself was. For example, "That was really good" or "That was only one time."

That was only one time.	*Eso fue sólo una vez.*
That was very good.	*Eso fue muy bueno.*
That was the first time.	*Esa fue la first vez.*
This was something else.	*Esto fue algo más.*
This was the last time.	*Esta fue la last vez.*

For *fuera*, remember that it's used in abstract, hypothetical situations to mean "he were", "she were", "it were", or "I were". Use this sentence as a model.

If she were nice, she wouldn't go there.	*Si ella fuera buena, no iría ahí.*
If he were a man, he'd be there.	*Si él fuera un hombre, estaría ahí.*
If he were nice, he would be here.	*Si fuera bueno, estaría aquí.*
If it were a house, it wouldn't be there.	*Si fuera una casa, no estaría ahí.*

Wrapping Up

We covered a ton of verb-related grammar in this lesson. But the good news is that if you master these concepts, you've just about mastered the way that Spanish works.

If things seem too abstract, don't worry. All that matters at this point is to learn the highlighted sentences by heart. Get to know them like your best friends. The grammar should come naturally from there.

Better yet, practice with some sentences that have been customized to you individually. Instead of practicing with an irrelevant concept, such as "If she were nice, she wouldn't go there," why not practice with sentences that are actually valuable to you, personally?

After Lesson 6, we require our coaching students to work with their coaches on custom sentences and dialogues to practice with. This way not only are you practicing all the essentials, as we've been doing from Lesson 1, but you're getting good practice with sentences and conversational contexts that are actually relevant to you.

Now that you've mastered most of Spanish grammar, you're almost ready to have real conversations entirely in Spanish. Start writing your own sentences to prepare. Show them to a native speaker to make sure you have them right, and then practice them so that you have an arsenal of phrases that you can use when you speak in Spanish.

Meanwhile, let's revisit our dialogue with the two birds. Your understanding of Spanish is becoming much more advanced than what is portrayed in this dialogue. In the second volume, we'll be working extensively with on several more complex conversations.

For now, I'd like you to spend most of your focus on the sentences already presented in this chapter. Master these, and you'll be able to master anything.

But just for fun, here's the dialogue between Matías and Santiago, now with some examples of Ir, Tener, and Haber presented in Spanish.

- Hello, I'm Matías. Who is this? - Hi Matías, it's me, Santiago.	
- Santiago, all this time, ¿right? - Yes I know! ¿How are you? - Fine thanks, and you? ¿How is Isabella?	
- Not so well, you know, she left her house. - What! This isn't good at all.	

- No, this time she doesn't have a place to be. You have to do her a favor, on my behalf.

- Yes, I want to be with her now. What can I do for Isabella or for you?

- You're very nice! I have her things at my house, as it should be, but…

- ¿Can I do something?

- I think so, it's a big deal.

- ¿But, why did she leave?

- She left, that's all... right, so, now we're going to do something when Valentina isn't around.

- ¿Valentina? But... why? If those two are like one, as you know, a...

- I know that they were, but now they aren't.

- Valentina is that way, and with her everything's like that, that's Valentina... And Sofía? She can...

- No, not Sofía, she isn't around.

- I am here, you are there... we're all here, the time is now.

- Maybe so, us both, with her. This time I don't know what to do.

- She can be at my house all the time. I can do you that favor, because I only want her to be well, and you to be well.

- That which was, is not anymore... now, everything's this way!

- Give it time. She's around, and her things at your house, at least it's something. And that gentleman?

- ¿Sebastián?

- I don't know, that man that was around with her at the house.

- Ah, yes, Sebastián, he isn't around anymore, and because of this she can't be at Mr. Sebastián's house.

- ¿He isn't? ¿What do you mean he isn't around? ¿Really? That can't be, but if the house was his!

- He left from the house, that's the truth. This has been this way for a while now. Now I know that she's doing badly.

Se fue de la casa, esa es la verdad. Esto ha estado así por un tiempo ya. Ya I know que no está muy bien.

- All right, well then, Isabella has been unwell for a while. Now we have to do something for her, I want to do something for her, both of us.

- Yes, I want... I'm leaving now, I'll go with Isabella.

Bueno, ya está, por un tiempo Isabella no ha estado bien. Ahora hay que do algo por ella, yo want to do algo por ella, los dos.

Sí, I want... me voy ahora, voy con Isabella.

- All right, I also will go to your house, I want to be with her.

Bueno, yo también voy a tu casa, I want estar con ella.

To get the second volume, or to access the free online course that accompanies this book, visit SpanishIn1Month.com.